The Inte Student's Guide to American Colleges

Pallas Snider

PALTA BOOKS

DEDICATION

This book is dedicated to all the students I've had the pleasure of working with over the past ten years.

Table of Contents

Introduction

If you've picked up this book, chances are, you or someone you know is planning on attending college in the United States. You've picked a great place to study with some of the most interesting and diverse educational opportunities in the world. This is a country with over 4,000 colleges and universities. We have over 17 million students enrolled in these schools including approximately 820,000 international students. Students are attracted to our universities because we have options in just about every field, and we attract some of the most eminent professors and researchers in the world.

Chances are that academics alone aren't the only reason you're looking at US schools. Part of the reason many students want to come here is because our universities are much more than places to learn. They are places to live, places to build close relationships with a diverse range of students from around the world, and places that will provide you with a network that may serve you for the rest of your life regardless of where you are from.

How This Book Can Help You

The purpose of this book is to help you figure out specifically which of the many college options available most appeal to you and will ultimately be the best fit for your interests and personality. By the end of this book, you will have a college list, a specific list of eight to twelve colleges that would be good matches for you.

This list will include schools that fit your size, location, educational, financial aid, and even climate requirements. We will consider a number of characteristics that matter in making your college experience what you want, and by the time you finish reading, you will know exactly where to apply.

I wrote this book primarily for international students who may not have had a chance to visit the colleges they are considering before applying. Having spent time working with many international students who wanted to study in this country, I realized that most of them had never set foot on a US college campus and didn't know where to begin with their search. The number of options was overwhelming, and they wanted a systematic way to narrow down their college options into a succinct list of good match schools.

This book is structured to do just that. Using the College Match Profile Method, we will review the most important factors to consider when choosing a school and help you assess each of them without ever setting foot on campus. You will then be able to take your list of preferences and compare them to a list of 176 colleges and universities throughout the country to find the best schools for you. Whether you want to study English, biology, music, computer science, engineering, theater, history, or just about anything else, this guide will lead you to schools that offer what you are looking for in terms of both academic offerings and the overall experience.

Keep in mind that the focus of this book is on how to find and apply to a school for your undergraduate studies. In this country, undergraduate studies typically consist of a 4-year program that earns you a bachelor's degree in a field of your choosing. Most students enter their undergraduate studies between the ages of 18 and 20 and graduate between the ages of 22 and 24. After the completion of a bachelor's degree, you may choose to apply to school again to pursue a program that would earn you a master's degree or a PhD (also known as "postgraduate degrees"). A few of the schools featured in this book offer dual-degree programs where you can earn your bachelor's degree and postgraduate degree at the same time, but the focus of the book is on how to find and apply to schools in order to earn a bachelor's degree.

If you have had a chance to visit some colleges already, that is great. You will still be able to use the College Match Profile Method we cover in this book to find additional schools to add to your list. Nobody has time to visit all of the colleges out there, so chances are, by identifying your College Match Profile, you will find other schools in this book that you may not have had a chance to see during your college tour.

And even if you live in the United States, most of the categories we discuss will be applicable to all students regardless of whether or not they are coming from overseas. You can follow the same method outlined in this book to help you narrow down your search.

So whether you have or haven't had a chance to visit colleges, or whether you are a US citizen or non-US citizen, when you finish this book, you should have a specific list of colleges you are interested in and understand how to apply, gain admission, and secure financial aid.

The Advantage of the American Liberal Arts College

Before we delve into finding the best college match for you, let's talk about college more broadly. Why are you interested in attending college? Many people, probably most, would say that the purpose of attending college is to gain a particular skill or set of skills that will prepare you to enter the workforce, and in some cases give you the credentials necessary to enter into a particular field.

Regardless of where you go to college within the United States or elsewhere, hopefully your education will give you skills that you will use for the rest of your life. All that said, I believe that the value of college, specifically many of the colleges within the United States, extends well beyond skill-based education. The United States educational system has a tradition of **liberal arts**, a philosophy of allowing students to take classes and pursue extracurricular interests in a wide variety of areas. Even at most of the more technical four-year colleges in this country, some academic exploration is encouraged.

At many colleges there is an emphasis on creating four years where students can discover their passions, meet lifelong friends, and figure out what matters most to them. The American college experience is designed to be more than just a time to prepare for one's career. Students are encouraged to develop both professionally and personally.

Our university tradition is founded on the idea that by exposing oneself to many different types of people, academic subjects, and activities, we become better workers and citizens. We come out of college understanding many perspectives, having learned how to apply our ideas creatively, and feeling comfortable using interdisciplinary approaches to solving problems.

This idea is at the foundation of the American liberal arts philosophy which is a part of the academic tradition at most of the colleges in this country and is one of the reasons many students from around the world are interested in coming to school here. Although some purely technical schools do exist, our most highly prestigious and respected universities have adopted some elements of the liberal arts tradition into their philosophies.

Students at liberal arts colleges still typically choose a **major**, a field of focus, such as philosophy, chemistry, civil engineering, geology, and so on, but students are encouraged to spend a substantial amount of their time taking courses in other fields outside of their major. Gaining a broad education gives students a multidisciplinary toolkit, which can be useful no matter what field you end up pursuing. With this model, not only will you gain skills that will help you succeed in any field you ultimately choose, but you will also find college a lot more fun.

The Focus of This Book

Because our most cherished institutions have adopted this liberal arts model, this book is focused on schools founded in the liberal arts tradition. Again, these are schools that offer majors in a wide variety of fields and that encourage students to broaden the scope of their studies beyond the field of their focus.

Thus, we will not spend a lot of time talking about the best school for you to attend if you want to be a doctor or if you want to be a lawyer or if you want to be a marine biologist. We will talk a bit about each school's strengths and weaknesses academically so you can find schools that excel in your academic field of interest. But the truth is, most of the schools in this book have strong enough overall reputations and a wide enough scope (many offer 50 or more majors) to be able to give you the education you need to go into any of these fields and succeed (though you still may need to earn a masters or PhD before you can start working).

Your primary focus now should be on finding schools that have environments you find conducive to learning; you want to make sure that they are the right size, in the right location, and have an academic philosophy that is compatible with your own. Find the schools that fit you for these reasons, and you will be able to best take advantage of the opportunities they offer you and get where you want to go in life.

Regardless of which of these schools you choose and what major you pick, you will find that the American university experience is exciting – many people consider it to be one of the most exciting times in their lives. I hope this book gets you excited about what lies ahead.

As you begin to consider college, you have so many choices ahead of you. The college you decide to attend will in many ways define the friends you have, the interests you develop, and the career you ultimately choose. You want to make sure that you make the right choice. There probably isn't just one right choice for you, but there are likely many schools that would bad matches. Having an idea of what you are looking for as you begin this journey is important.

Building a Personal College List

By reading this book, you have already figured out that maybe you want to embark on the adventure of going to college and that maybe going to an American college would be a good choice. Having 4,000 colleges to choose from means having 4,000 different campuses, 4,000 cultures, and 4,000 unique academic programs and philosophies. My job is to help you figure out first and foremost whether an American college is a good choice for you to begin with, and if it is, to help you narrow down your options from these 4,000 schools to eight to twelve schools which you are excited about and that you feel are good fits for your personality and interests.

By the end of this book, you should walk away with a specific list of eight to twelve colleges that will form your "college list," the list of schools to which you should apply. This list will take into account many factors that are critical to the decision-making process including size, location, academic philosophy, selectivity, financial aid, among other important components. You will also understand the fundamentals of the application process and how you can tailor your application to stand out in the competitive world of American college admissions. You will be able to enter the process of applying to and selecting a college confidently even if you are from the other side of the world.

About Me

I won't dwell too much on me, but before we delve too deep I figure I should at least introduce myself. I graduated from Harvard in 2010. Since then I've been a college counselor, speaker, and blogger. I live in Cambridge, MA (one of the best college towns in the world) halfway between Harvard and the Massachusetts Institute of Technology (MIT). I can drive to 150 colleges within an hour of my home, which is pretty awesome. I'm an American and grew up in the United States although my family moved around within the country quite a bit. Whenever I can, I love exploring different colleges throughout the United States, and sometimes I write about these experiences on my blog (www.thecollegematchmaker.com).

I love sharing the things I've learned about America's rich diversity of colleges with the students I work with who come from all over the country and the world.

I'll tell you in the next chapter a story about how I first discovered my love for exploring different colleges, but the point is that learning about colleges has been my passion well before I ever went to college. In high school (near Washington DC), I would visit colleges during all of my school breaks. I had a list of literally hundreds of schools I wanted to see, and I would plan trips to visit them every chance I could get. When I couldn't make it out to a school in person, I would scour the Internet reading pages on each school's website, finding blog posts, and reaching out to alumni with questions. I know that sounds a little crazy, but I did this not because I was obsessive but just because I was genuinely excited about the number of options that lay before me, and I couldn't wait to go to college. To this day, years after I made my own college choice, I still find visiting colleges to be fascinating. They are each their own little worlds filled with students discovering their passions, meeting some of their best friends in life, and having a great time. I can't think of another environment like it.

In any case, back to my story. After visiting so many colleges, my high school classmates started realizing I knew a lot about college options. Even back then, I was frequently asked to help them figure out their college list. And I developed a system. I asked them a series of questions, and by the end of our 45-minute conversation, I handed them a list of schools. It worked pretty well. The next year, they told their friends, who told their friends, who then told their friends. I have continued to have a number of people ask me to help them develop their college lists, and my College Match Profile Method has continued to evolve.

As far as my own college experience, I started at Harvard in the fall of 2006. I had a fantastic experience. I studied an interdisciplinary field called Social Studies (a mix of history, government, economics, and anthropology), gained a secondary concentration (minor) in Dramatic Arts, and earned a language citation in Spanish. I also had the opportunity to start my own business, win the on-campus business plan competition, participate in theater, travel internationally on several funded trips, spend a semester studying at a university in Chile, and most relevant to this book, worked in the admissions office.

Beginning my freshman year, I got a job in the admissions office, preparing applications to be read by the admissions officers. I did not get to make any admissions decisions myself, but I got to see thousands of applications come through. I read the essays, looked over the extracurricular lists, saw interview reports and recommendations, score reports, transcripts, and every document come through our office. I watched as the admissions officers held their committee meetings and at the end of admissions season, my office sent off the acceptance and rejection letters.

Eventually, I became a campus tour guide and helped lead information sessions for prospective students visiting the campus. I met students from around the country and the world on college tours, and it was fascinating to see their wide range of reactions to my school.

During this time, I did two stints abroad, one in South America and the other in Asia. The students I met on both of these trips were fascinated with the combination of my search method and my admissions experience. Many of them told me that they were interested in coming to study in the United States, but they didn't know how. Since I graduated in 2010, I have continued to work with both domestic and international students helping them identify schools that are good fits and helping them understand the complexities of the American admissions process. I also publish profiles of different schools and articles related to admissions and college search on my blog, www.thecollegematchmaker.com. With this book, I hope I can help you find colleges you will love and help you achieve your dreams.

How to Use This Book

Before we begin, I wanted to give you a couple of tips on how to navigate this book. First of all, this book was written with the intent that you would read it start to finish. I know you might be tempted to skip around, and if you choose to do so, I've included section headings so you can navigate your way. However, if you have the time, the whole book would make a lot more sense if you read it beginning to end.

Throughout the book, you will notice that I put make certain words **bold**. With the exception of the word "bold" right there (and the section headings), if you see another word in bold it means you can find that word and its definition in the glossary at the back of the book. There are lots of new words to learn when it comes to American colleges and the admissions process, so the glossary should be your constant guide if you start to get confused.

The book is divided into three main sections:

Section I: Figuring Out Your College Preferences

Each chapter in Section I is focused on a different aspect of the college experience that may be important to consider such as the size of a school or its location.

At the end of each chapter, you will be able to select the features you prefer. And if you still can't figure it out, there is a "Not Sure?" quiz at the end of most chapters that will help you determine the best option for you. As you go through each chapter in Section I and start to figure out your preferences, you can start filling in these preferences on the College Match Profile Chart in Chapter 17 (page 270) because later in the book, this chart is going to help you build your college list.

The purpose of the first section is to help you figure out what you want out of your college experience.

Section II: Admissions and Applications

Section II is your guide to the American college admissions process. We'll talk about what college admissions officers are looking for, exploring the three areas where students are evaluated – academics, extracurricular activities, and personality. We'll talk about the tools admissions officers use to evaluate all three of these different facets such as teacher recommendations, personal essays, your transcript, and test scores.

We will also go through each component of the application process more extensively guiding you through the nuts and bolts of filling out a complete and impressive application.

Finally, we will talk about the application timeline exploring different admissions programs (such as early vs. regular decision) and covering when you should start preparing for the required tests like the SAT, ACT, and TOEFL. By the end of this chapter, you'll feel confident that you can get through this process successfully with less stress than you might think.

Section III: Finalizing Your College List

In the final section of the book, we will use the preferences you identified in Section I to create what I call your College Match Profile. Your College Match Profile is a list of all of the qualities you would want your ideal college to have. Once you have identified your list of preferences, you will start matching these preferences up to the list of qualities at each of the 176 colleges profiled in this section.

Using this method, you will be able to identify a list of eight to twelve specific schools that best meet your college preferences. These schools will form your college list, and in the remaining part of the chapter, we will talk about how you can continue to research the colleges on this list so that by the time you apply, you will be confident in your college choices.

Chapter 1
What is a Good Fit?

Sometimes when I tell students they need to consider colleges that are a "good fit" they look at me like I am crazy. They think the concept of "finding one's true match" is overly romantic. A school is a school, they say. It is a place for learning. If they look and see that the engineering program at a particular school is ranked highly, that is good enough for them.

It is true that a lot of students choose a school this way. Sometimes they get to college and are happy, and other times they are not. When you choose a school on the basis of one factor, you leave a lot up to luck. Do you like your peers? What about the culture of the school? Did you want to live in a city or in the middle of a cornfield? What about the academic philosophy? The teaching method? Did you know that you would have to take six classes at once? Perhaps all the students are required to take physical education classes, and you hate that. There may only be one dining hall on campus when you love variety. Maybe the school is religiously affiliated, and you don't feel you connect with your peers because you're not religious, or you belong to a different religion with very different values and practices. When you live at a college – especially a liberal arts college that by nature forces you to think about more facets of your education than the one subject you are studying – there is more to consider than the ranking of one academic department.

Okay, you may be thinking, fine if I have to live with limited eating options and students I do not get along with, at the end of the day, I'll end up with my degree and that is all I care about. When you are living day in and day out in a school you are unhappy with, especially when you don't have your family to come home to, and you are thousands of miles away from where you come from, you may feel differently. Engineering, physics, economics, statistics, or almost any subject you may study, are hard work, and you will do it better if you are comfortable with your surroundings. Furthermore, this sort of "it doesn't matter" attitude just seems unnecessarily self-destructive, even silly, considering how easy it is to pick a place you'll be happier. After all, when you have over 4,000 options as to where you go to school, you can probably find a place that would be better for you and give you an equivalent if not better education. So at least look. You may even find the process of looking fun.

No doubt the best way to look is to visit different colleges. Almost all American colleges offer student-led tours and information sessions hosted by admissions officers (the people who read applications and decide who gets accepted) to give prospective students a sense of the community and school offerings. For seniors in high school, many colleges offer guests the opportunity to eat in one of the dining halls and attend classes so that they can get a better sense of the students and culture of the campus. And sometimes, there are even opportunities to stay overnight in one of the dorms with a host student who will give you a more complete sense of the full experience.

If you have the opportunity to visit a few schools this way, do it. Not only will you learn about a particular school, but you may have a better sense of things you want or don't want on the other schools on your list. Perhaps you visit Connecticut College, a small school in Connecticut with under 2,000 students (or just under 500 per class year) and think – "This place feels too small. I feel like everyone knows each other." Well then you can narrow your list down to medium- and large-sized schools. Or perhaps your reaction to Connecticut College is that you love the sense of community there, which you feel is particularly strong because the campus is small and cohesive, and the social scene seems entirely focused on campus life. This is an attribute you can look for in other schools as well as you form your list of possible schools.

For me personally, I took my first college tour at Yale University when I was 13 years old. I decided to take a tour of the college, and one of the first places my tour guide took me to was Saybrook College, one of the twelve residential communities where Yale students live (despite its name, it is not a separate college from Yale but rather a dorm that is called "Saybrook College"). From the moment I stepped into the Saybrook College courtyard, I was in love. The gothic style building made me feel like I was in Harry Potter. Outside, students were sitting on the grass working on problem sets for class and one student was lying in a hammock reading. My tour guide explained that from the moment students arrived at Yale, they were assigned to live in one of twelve communities, called "residential colleges," all with a unique identity.

These residential colleges were more than a place to live. They were a full community. Each college had its own dining hall, its own gym, its own library. Each of these residential communities competed against other communities in intramural sports and each had their own traditions, annual formals, lecture series, and so on. This created a huge sense of pride among students, and created a system which allowed students to be a part of a strong small community within the context of a large university with lots of resources.

I fell in love with this idea, and as I created my own college list in the coming years, this realization had a significant impact on me. I knew I wanted to live in a largely residential campus. I also knew that while I was attracted to medium and larger schools where there were always tons of options, I also wanted a smaller community that I could feel a part of. Residential systems like Yale's that made a medium-sized large university feel smaller were perfect. And I soon found out that there were many school besides Yale – Harvard, Rice, The University of Chicago, among others – that had similar systems. I also knew from visiting Yale that I wanted to be in a school that had outdoor space where I could sit outside and study in the grass. Originally I had put New York University (NYU) on my list in part because I thought it would be incredible to go to school in New York City, but when I found out that it didn't have any grassy outdoor space on campus (students use a public park when they want to hang out outside), I knew that was a deal breaker.

The important thing is to realize the features that make *you* really excited about college. When I thought of being in a small community within a big one, and when I imagined reading through my textbooks while sprawled out on a grassy courtyard, I felt excited about going to college. And although these features are not directly related to the academic experience (I had a list of things important to me in that arena as well), I know they influenced my ability to be happy and do my work effectively as well.

Finding Your "College Match Profile"

I know that not everyone has the opportunity to visit many colleges, and especially if you are coming from abroad, you may not be able to visit any colleges before you start applying. While you cannot completely supplement the experience of stepping onto a campus yourself and getting that feeling where you *feel* inspired by the place, the College Match Profile Method can at least break down the decision process into the most important points to consider. As you think about these points, you will start to figure out what is most important to you and the kinds of schools you are looking for.

I have created eleven categories that are important to consider. These are meaningful differences that exist between colleges and that can have a large impact on the feel of a campus, the culture, and the academic experience you ultimately have.

Here are those categories:

- **School Type** (college or university)
- **School Funding** (public or private)

- **Campus Structure** (island, street-side, or integrated)
- **Surrounding Area** (rural, town, suburb, small city, city)
- **Region** (New England, Mid-Atlantic, South, Pacific Coast, West, Midwest)
- **Size** (very small, small, medium, large)
- **Curriculum Type** (core, loose core, distribution requirements, open)
- **Residential Type** (high residential, medium residential, low residential)
- **Selectivity** (S1-S6)
- **Financial Aid** (the best, excellent, good, some, none)
- **Prestige** (most prestigious, prestigious, no prestige rating)

Every school featured in this book will have a profile made up of one characteristic for each of the eleven categories on this list. So for example, after working through the book, you may know you want a private university, medium-sized, and with distribution requirements (if you don't already know what this means, no worries: that's covered in Chapter 8).

As you keep reading, you may add to your list that a high level of prestige is important as is good financial aid for international students. The sum total of this list of preferences is your College Match Profile. If you flip to the end of the book, you can look up the schools that appear on the medium-sized list and see if they also are rated as "most prestigious," "best financial aid," etc. to identify good match schools.

You will uncover your College Match Profile naturally as you read through Section I. At the end of every chapter, you will see a summary of the characteristics we discussed in that chapter, and you will be asked to select one or more of those characteristics to add to your College Match Profile. For instance, in the chapter about campus types, you will be asked to select whether or not you prefer an island, integrated, or street-side campus (we will cover the definition of those terms in that chapter). If by the end of the chapter you know that you like the idea of being at an island campus, for example, you will fill out that preference on the College Match Profile Chart in Chapter 17 (page 270).

Once you have finished Section I, the College Match Profile Chart will be complete, and it will reveal your College Match Profile. Again, this profile is a list of your ideal college preferences and could look like the example below.

Example College Match Profile:

School Type: College
School Funding: Private
Campus Structure: Island
Surrounding Area: Town or Small City
Region: New England or Mid-Atlantic
Size: Small or Medium
Curriculum Type: Loose Core
Residential Type: High Residential
Selectivity: S-2, S-3, or S-4
Financial Aid: Best Aid, Excellent Aid, Good Aid, Some Aid, and No Aid for International Students
Prestige: Most Prestigious, Prestigious, No Prestige Rating

In page 281, you will find a master list of characteristics of 176 colleges around the United States. You can use your profile to match up schools that meet some or all of your personal preferences.

If your College Match Profile matched the example above, you would see, for instance, that the following schools would match your profile perfectly:

Lafayette College
Union College
Bates College
Bucknell University
Colgate College
Connecticut College

In addition, a number of other schools would match your College Match Profile in ten of the eleven categories and may also be worth considering. These additional options include:

Middlebury College
Knox College
St. Olaf College
Trinity College
Wheaton College (MA)
Beloit College
Gettysburg College
Hobart and William Smith Colleges

I will explain how to use your College Match Profile in further detail in Section III, but the purpose of the profile is to give you a defined set of preferences so you can start identifying specific schools to add to your college list. Not every school on your list will need to match your profile exactly, but this system is designed to give you a starting point so that you can identify the schools that best match your preferences.

The system I've outlined above is the best way to use this book because you will start building your college list after you've figured out all of your preferences. However, I know it might be tempting to start identifying schools before you finish all of Section I. At the end of every chapter in that section, I have included a list of every school that fits into each one of the categories discussed. These category charts can be useful because if you read through the list of schools for each of your preferences, you may start to notice that certain schools keep showing up in your preferred categories. If you start to notice that you are seeing "Vassar College" or "Colorado College" all the time, you may want to put a note for yourself next to the names of those schools on the master list of colleges and their features on page 281 to give yourself a reminder to check those schools out in more detail later.

Designations: Things that Make Colleges Stand Out

I have also identified areas in which certain colleges particularly stand out which I've called **designations**. These are areas that make up a school's identity. Schools are given a designation when there is an identifying factor that is integral to a school's sense of pride and that is a fundamental aspect of the school's culture. It does not mean that schools without a designation in say, humanities, couldn't offer you a great education with a humanities major, but it just means that humanities isn't quite as core to the overall self-identity, culture, and pride of the school.

The designations I've considered include:

Sports	Economics
Athletic	Business
Outdoors	Humanities
Artistic	Engineering
Social Activism and	Hard Sciences
Community Service	Environmental
Government and	Awareness and
Politics	Activism
Serious Academic	Pre-med
School Spirit	Architecture
Religious	International
Entrepreneurship	Student Body
Techie	Greek Life
Music	College Town
Theater	Housing
Journalism	Single Sex
Quirky	Writing

After you've identified your preferences within the eleven basic categories, which reveal your fundamental college preferences, you can begin to filter your list down by finding schools with designations that match your interests. So if you find 20 schools that match your College Match Profile or come close to matching your profile preferences, start looking for schools that perhaps have a theater and economics designation if those are your interests. These designations can help you rank the schools on your list, but remember they only indicate where a school shines particularly strongly. A school that has a music designation may be superb in music, and music may be a strong part of the campus culture, but it doesn't mean the others schools on your list that don't have a music designation don't offer solid music programs; they may have perfectly fine music offerings but simply have other even stronger programs or identities in other areas. The goal of the designations is not to make you eliminate a school that lacks any given quality, but instead to give you a more nuanced picture of the strengths and culture at each school.

Building on Your Base

After reading this book, I would encourage you to continue your research. There are many other great resources. The best is probably on the colleges' websites themselves. Most websites will have a section for prospective students. There you can often learn about the details of the curriculum, view a list of majors and student clubs, take a virtual tour of the campus, read the course catalogue, see pictures of the residential buildings, read about current students, find the application requirements, and more.

Other resources you may want to check out include College Confidential (www.collegeconfidential.com), which has probably the best college discussion board online. This is a website that is not affiliated with any particular college but that has boards where students around the country and the world discuss colleges they are interested in. Often, current students from various colleges post on the site as well so if you have a particular question about student life, the academic program, food, and other relevant topics, it is a great place to get information. Every year when the admissions decisions come out, students post their admissions results, so if you want to see the profile of students getting in (obviously you don't see the full picture from a self-reported forum post, but it does give you an idea), you should check in at **early decision** time in mid-December or in late March when most of the **regular decision** responses are released (we will talk about both early and regular decision in Chapter 16).

The Princeton Review has some good information on its website (www.princetonreview.com) as well. You can look up almost any college there, and find a quick list of statistics on the school, information about student life, demographics, etc.

US News & World Report publishes their annual college rankings each year, which you can access for free. I am not a huge fan of their methodology of determining rankings, however, in the process of developing rankings, they do collect a lot of data. You can access some basic data for free, but you can also register for their College Compass service ($30/year) where you can find a huge amount of data on each individual school on your list. I used College Compass as one of my main research tools for this book, and it is probably the most comprehensive set of data I found. You can find detailed statistics on the admissions rates for early and regular decision applicant pools, SAT and ACT ranges, average amounts of aid for international students, percentage of students participating in Greek life, most popular majors, among many other informative data points.

Another useful resource is Unigo (www.unigo.com) which is a website where you can read reviews directly from current students about their experiences at all of the major colleges and universities around the country.

And probably my favorite source of information, and this is a book that I recommend to all of the students that I have counseled is the *Insider's Guide to Colleges*, which is a book published annually by Yale students, and it contains full reviews of hundreds of colleges. Each profile features a number of quotes from current students, and they tend to give you a very vivid picture of student life and the culture of each individual school profiled.

Chapter 2
Is an American College for Me?

Coming to college in the United States from another country is a huge decision. You are deciding to move hundreds or even thousands of miles away from your friends, family, and culture. You are likely going to be making a huge financial investment. And you are embarking on a journey that will likely change who you are and how you see the world. You are not alone in thinking that this is something you want to do. Over 800,000 students come from abroad every year to study, and hundreds of thousands more try (often not succeeding because of logistical or financial complications).

For decades, the United States has been seen as an attractive place to come to college. There are three main reasons I most often hear about why students feel coming to the United States is important. The most common reason is prestige. Students believe that by studying here, they will return to their countries with a credential that will make it easier for them to secure a more prestigious and well-paying job. The second reason is the academics. Many times, students believe that the quality of the instruction in the United States is better than at the universities in their home countries. They want to have access to world-class professors and sometimes just an educational system that lacks institutional corruption. Finally, there are a number of students that are attracted to the United States for the unique college experience American colleges offer. Let's take a closer look at each of these three reasons.

Prestige

A lot of students tell me that if they attend college in the United States, when they return home, their degree will be more respected. As a result, it will be easier to get a well-paying and prestigious job. Similarly, they believe that if they want to work for a multi-national corporation, a degree from an American university will be more valuable and well regarded. And finally, they are convinced that if they want to work in the United States after graduating or attend a masters or PhD program here, it will be easier with a degree from an American institution.

All of these things are likely true. American universities are generally well respected throughout the world, and in many countries, a degree from one opens doors. In some countries, getting a degree from a foreign institution is regarded as far superior than getting a degree domestically (especially if you come from a country with high levels of institutional corruption). But even if you come from a country where the university system is just fine, getting a degree from an American university will prove your proficiency in English (which may be valuable if you are a non-native speaker) and be recognizable to most recruiters at multi-national corporations who are familiar with the American university system.

If your main motivation for choosing an American university is that you think the degree will land you a better job when you return home (or allow you to stay in the United States afterwards if that is what you want to do), that is a fine reason to choose to come here. However, on its own, I don't think getting a job is a sufficient enough reason to warrant moving overseas to earn your degree. If this is your only for wanting to study in the US, read on. If you don't make sure the academics and overall experience at an American university is a good fit for you, you might be disappointed.

Academics

Many times when I've asked students why they are considering college in the United States, they've said it is because they want to attend one of the "best" universities in the world. What they are really saying is they want to get the best education possible, and they believe that an American university will provide that for them.

I frequently run into students who are confident that an American university will provide them with a superior academic experience than what is available in their country. And it might, but it depends not only on the educational system in the country they are coming from, but also on the student and what they are looking for in their education. When I ask students why they believe an American education is far superior to one in their own country a common answer I hear is that American universities appear on lists of international university rankings more than universities in any other country. This is true, but I caution you to be careful before you jump to the conclusion that you will get a better education here just because of these rankings.

Worldwide university rankings are often focused on the amount of research being produced by the university, the number of faculty members who have won prestigious international awards like the Nobel and Pulitzer prizes, and the size of the university's endowment. While a school with those things may have a positive "trickle down" effect on undergraduate students, they are not as directly important to undergraduates as other facets of student life like the type of curriculum, quality and diversity of the student body, and the resources being devoted to undergraduates. These are the things that will matter a lot more to you and your academic experience so I'd encourage you to look more broadly than rankings when deciding if an American university is right for you from an academic perspective.

If you live in a country known for institutional corruption where students often bribe their professors or where there are massive strikes that shut down universities for months at a time, American universities may have a clear advantage. Neither of those problems is common here. If you try to bribe your professor (or anyone for that matter), you will be at best expelled and at worst thrown in jail. And while students may protest for things they care about, universities do not get shut down over such things. Our university system is for the most part fair and reliable.

Another academic advantage American universities have is that the high cost of our universities does often translate into higher cost spent per pupil at our schools. It does vary significantly by school but in general, American colleges offer students significant support in the way of advising and counseling that may not be available in other countries. Furthermore, additional funding per pupil often supports more resources such as first-class telescopes, impressive libraries, student health services, ample study and social spaces and other facilities that cannot be supported to the same degree at universities in countries where less money is available.

As you weigh the decision of whether or not the academic value of an American university is really worth it to you, you should consider how the American education system is structured and how it compares to the system in your country. When you decide to come to college in the United States, you will most likely be entering a 4-year degree program. By the end of that degree program, you will graduate with a "major" in some particular field of your choosing.

Many students coming from abroad find that American universities offer unparalleled academic flexibility. At most American colleges, you will also be encouraged to take more than half of your courses outside of your primary field of study. Many schools allow you to take up to 70% of your courses in unrelated fields to your major. In addition, at American colleges, you often have the option of pursuing a double major (i.e. so you graduate with two focus areas even if they are unrelated) or earn a "minor" (a secondary focus area). Plus, most schools allow students to change their field of study as late as their second or even third year of school.

Remember that because of our tradition of **liberal arts**, most American colleges will require or at least highly encourage you to pursue courses in subjects unrelated to your major. There are some colleges in this country that do not have liberal arts philosophies, but they tend to be very specialized institutions such as music conservatories, art schools, and some technical colleges. You can get a music degree, art degree, or technical degree from a liberal arts college. In fact, many of the liberal arts schools featured in this book have music schools, art programs, and technical divisions within them but still encourage their students to take classes in other fields. This book does not focus on these smaller specific institutions in part because they are in general considered less prestigious (with a handful of notable exceptions such as Julliard and Rhode Island School of Design) and more limiting. Students who study music at a liberal arts school often go on to become doctors, but it would be very rare for someone to go on to become a doctor, lawyer, or academic after getting a degree from one of these specialized schools.

Some students who come to study here from abroad are very excited about the idea of liberal arts, but it isn't something that is right for everyone. Frankly, students in other countries without a liberal arts philosophy come out of their undergraduate years more prepared to be engineers, doctors, and lawyers than American students (many of whom, especially in technical subjects, need to go to graduate school before they are employable). Eventually, American students become great doctors, lawyers, scientists, etc., but it may take longer because so much of their time during their undergraduate years is spent studying fields unrelated to their future profession.

Do not make the assumption that just because you go to a prestigious American college you will be a better engineer (or whatever it is you want to do) because you will learn more in your classes here. That is not necessarily the case. With a broader liberal arts education, your time will be more divided studying other areas and pursuing extracurricular activities. So by the end of your undergraduate years, you will probably know less math than some of your peers at non-liberal arts colleges in other countries. But, if you believe that improving your writing skills, your critical thinking abilities, gaining leadership experience, and making great friends and connections will help you be an engineer in its own right, then maybe it will make you a better engineer to come to school in the United States.

If your primary motivation for coming to the United States is that you don't want to stay in your country where there is institutional corruption or pervasive striking, those are understandable reasons. However, you should still consider whether or not a liberal arts philosophy sounds appealing to you. If you do not want to take classes outside of your main field of study, you may want to look into studying in the United Kingdom, Australia, or in other countries that offer corruption-free and stable universities but don't have as much of a liberal arts legacy. But if you love the idea that in the United States you are allowed to take classes in whichever areas interest you and that the system affords you enough flexibility to change your mind about what you want to study usually well into your second or even third year, choosing to come to the United States for academics may be an excellent reason.

Overall Experience

Americans are known for their strong attachments to their colleges. Many of us see college not just as a stepping-stone to what we do next but also as a transformative experience that made us who we are. If you are attracted to coming to the United States for college because you think it would be a more meaningful experience than what is offered in your own country, that is an excellent reason to make the decision to come here.

You'll notice that lots of the most prominent members of American society speak about college in a way you don't hear about as much in other countries. Lots of Americans will know where the president went to college. Barack Obama has discussed his time at Columbia and Harvard Law and George W. Bush would often reference his time at Yale. Most people know that even though they both dropped out, both Mark Zuckerberg and Bill Gates went to Harvard. Both of their businesses started while they were students, and in the case of Mark Zuckerberg, Facebook was created directly in response to improving campus culture. Michael Dell has talked about starting Dell while at the University of Texas at Austin. Hillary Clinton has discussed being involved with the student government at Wellesley and how it influenced her decision to go into politics.

Americans feel a unique attachment to their colleges. Many successful Americans attribute their time in college as the time they discovered their passions and got set on whichever path led them to success. And they are usually referring to more than their academic experience. They will mention classes that transformed their lives, but they also talk about their residential situation, the activities they were a part of, and the people they met as being fundamental part of an overall life-changing experience.

The college experience in the United States is designed to be transformative. The following facets of the American university system make many graduates feel attached to their school in ways typically not found in other countries:

- Tradition of liberal arts which gives students a freedom to explore a wide variety of fields while in college and discover new passions
- A rich residential and social experience
- Exposure to diversity via students who come to these institutions from all around the country and the world
- Extracurricular emphasis where undergraduates are encouraged to participate in many things – art, music, sports, politics, theatre, student government, community service, etc.

These non-curricular facets make the American university unique. In many other countries, students do not live on campus. Universities don't offer many extracurricular activities, and there are few if any social organizations. Additionally, as we discussed in the previous section, students are encouraged to study one narrow subject, and that is it. The primary purpose of higher education is to prepare for a career – the experience is a means to an end.

If you aren't excited about the American college experience, you should think about if the benefits of prestige and/or academics outweigh the high monetary cost of an American education. But if you want to come here in part because you want to live at school; be surrounded by a diverse group of people; explore your interests; and have the chance to participate in many different types of activities, I think that is a phenomenal reason to make the choice to study in the United States. Students who choose an American college for this reason tend to be happiest with their choice. They not only pursue the most opportunities once they are here, but they make the most friends and build the best networks. Eventually, this could turn into a job, a fellowship, or another opportunity.

Before we proceed, take a moment to think about which of the reasons for coming to school in the United States – prestige, academics, and overall experience – resonate with you. You'll want to hold onto that thought as you proceed through the rest of this book. Depending on your answer to the question of "Why do I want to come to school in the United States?" you may choose schools with different attributes for your college list so keep this thought in the front of your mind as we continue.

Section I
Your College Profile

The key purpose of this book is to help you figure out what type of school you are looking for, and give you the tools you need to build your **college list**, the list of schools to which you are planning to apply. The following chapters are divided into sections based on the critical categories that distinguish one school from another. These categories represent fundamental differences between each of the schools assessed in this book. These categories will make a material impact on your college experience. As you go through each chapter, think carefully about what kind of environment to which you gravitate. Most people will find that for many if not all of these categories, they have a preference. There may be a few areas where you are not sure. You do not have to have a firm preference for each one, but you will likely be able to at least find a few characteristics you would be happy with and eliminate some characteristics you don't want.

After you finish each section, circle the categories you are interested in and put them into the College Match Profile Chart in Chapter 17 (page 270) which will eventually reveal your College Match Profile. You will also find a list of schools at the end of each section that fit into each of the categories discussed. These charts are included to help you get a sense of where some of the schools you may be already thinking about fit and so that you can start to notice patterns if certain schools keep appearing on the list of your preferred characteristics. Each school's full profile is revealed in the back of the book beginning on page 281.

I have selected 176 colleges and profiled them based on these characteristics so that by the end of this book you can match the schools you are interested in to the schools that match your profile. Given the scope of this book and the fact that there are over 4,000 schools in the United States, not all schools are profiled. The 176 schools were selected very deliberately. They are all residential 4-year campuses (rather than 2-year colleges, predominantly commuter, or online schools) that are welcoming to international students. Furthermore, they all have been influenced by the liberal arts tradition and represent what are generally considered to be the most respected and well-known institutions in the country. There is some diversity when it comes to selectivity and admissions standards, but for the most part these schools are targeting students with solid academic preparation for college.

I made the decision to focus on this group of schools because most students who are serious enough to travel across the world for their studies are academically qualified enough to succeed at some or all of these schools. It is not to say, however, that all of the other colleges this country offers should be dismissed. In fact, some of the small, less prestigious, and regional institutions will offer fantastic scholarships to international students in an effort to increase diversity on campus.

If you are interested in schools outside those profiled in this book, the methodology we explore in this book should be applicable to additional universities, and you can apply the College Match Profile Method to other schools as well. In addition, I continue to profile additional schools regularly on my website at www.thecollegematchmaker.com.

In addition to finding good match colleges, creating a solid application is something you will also need to consider. Even if you find a list of eight to twelve schools that match your personality preferences, you still will need to make sure that your application is competitive enough to gain admission to at least some of these schools. We will touch on selectivity in Chapter 10 and then discuss the application process in greater detail in Chapter 14. If you are looking for more extensive resources on how to create the perfect application, I have recommended some additional resources at the back of the book on page 371.

In a similar fashion, financial aid may also affect your college list. We will talk about financial aid for international students in Chapter 11, but there are other resources you may want to seek on this topic as well. I have also included a list of some of the best ones on page 374.

And a final word before we begin... as I touched on before, the best way to know if a college is right for you is to visit. You can narrow down your list considerably from using this method, and you will increase your odds of finding a school that works for you, but there is nothing that will replace the experience of stepping onto a campus, walking through the quad, talking to the students, and getting a gut feeling that it is the right place. Being an international student, this is not always possible, but if you have the opportunity to visit these schools even after you've applied before you make your final decision, it can make a big difference.

Chapter 3
Colleges vs. Universities

As you begin your college search, one of the first things to consider is whether or not you would prefer attending a college or a university. What's the difference? It can be more complicated than it may first appear.

A **university** is an institution of higher learning and research. It includes both undergraduate and postgraduate students as well as researchers and scholars whose primary focus is contributing to the body of knowledge in their field. A **college** refers specifically to the undergraduate portion of a university, or to a school that only offers bachelor's degrees (4-year degrees).[1]

When you apply to school in the United States, regardless of whether you end up choosing to attend a college or a university, you will apply to receive a bachelor's degree. After your 4-year degree is complete, you will need to apply to a graduate program if you are interested in pursuing further study to receive either a masters degree or PhD. Some students who choose to study at universities for their bachelors degree may apply for a program at the same school they attended for their bachelors degree, but the majority will end up applying to

---

[1] Another kind of "college," a community or junior college, may only offer an associate's degree, awarded after two years of post-secondary study. For the purpose of this book, however, "college" will refer to schools that offer 4-year bachelor's degrees with the exception of Deep Springs College, a 2-year school.

schools elsewhere, and most graduate students at any given university attended other colleges and universities prior to studying at their current institution.

Your decision to attend either a college or a university should not be based on whether or not you want to continue your studies after you complete your bachelors degree; it is equally easy to attend graduate school regardless of which option you choose. However, your decision to pick one school type over another should come down to your own personal preferences about what kind of environment you would like to be in. We'll talk about the two different environments in a moment, but first, let's clarify a few common points of confusion.

First of all, some universities have schools within them formally called colleges and others do not. Harvard University, for example, is a university that includes medical, law, business, and other graduate degrees and programs, but undergraduate students (i.e., those who have not yet received a bachelor's degree) go to "Harvard College," just as undergraduate students at Yale University go to "Yale College," which are both parts of the greater university. Some universities, like Princeton University or the University of California at Berkeley, do not refer to their undergraduate contingencies formally as "X College" but it would still be appropriate to say for instance "I went to Princeton for college" when referring to one's undergraduate years.

Another thing that can be confusing is that some universities will have the word "college" in their official name referring to both undergraduate and graduate components even though they are full universities. Dartmouth College, for instance, is a full university with a business school, engineering school, medical school, and offering other postgraduate degrees in a number of fields. However, because it was originally founded as a college, it has kept its original name. Students and faculty will acknowledge they are at a university but when you ask which one, they will say "Dartmouth College."

Some colleges are not associated with a university at all. They are institutions that exist for the purpose of educating undergraduates and granting bachelor's degrees. In a couple of instances, they may offer one or two masters programs (awarded for 1-2 years of study beyond the bachelors degree) or house a couple of small research labs, but undergraduate education is the primary focus and purpose of the institution. Most of these schools do not have the word "university" in their names at all. You always refer to Amherst, for example, as "Amherst College." There is no such thing as "Amherst University."

However, to make things even more confusing, there are a couple of colleges that have "university" in their name. Wesleyan University has 2,870 students and is definitively focused on undergraduate education. It does have a few graduate programs that in total enroll an additional 197 students. These additional graduate students are the reason Wesleyan keeps "university" in its name, but for all intents and purposes this school functions like a college devoted to undergraduate education. These misnamed institutions are the exception to the rule, but luckily I have sorted out everything out for you at the list at the end of this chapter, so you can see the definitive classification of each school featured in this book.

Should You Pick a College or a University?

So why does this distinction between colleges that are part of universities and those that are not matter? Both of these models produce schools with very different cultures and strengths and many students find they are better suited for one or the other.

Here are some of the big points to consider.

Colleges that are part of universities tend to:

- Offer larger campuses with more students
- Employ the most famous scholars and researchers rather than the best teachers
- House labs and research projects where groundbreaking work is being conducted

None of these tendencies is universally true, and none is all good or bad. One thing some people complain about at universities, for example, is that although there are more course offerings, sometimes the classes (or sections of classes) are taught by Teaching Assistants (TAs) who are graduate students rather than full professors. Additionally, although a university-related college may employ superstar professors, these people may not be teaching introductory classes, or teaching undergraduate students at all. Some universities will employ the most famous professors to teach introductory courses, but often when this is the case, these classes are huge, sometimes with hundreds or even thousands of students.

On the flip side, because universities have graduate students who are being taught at the highest level in their fields, undergraduate students often have the ability to join upper-level courses for graduate students by the time they become **upperclassmen** (i.e., third and fourth year students). And at that level, sometimes they can get into a small seminar with the best-of-the-best scholar in that field.

Additionally, there are opportunities to be a part of the groundbreaking work that goes on in a university. For instance, research labs that are working on finding the cure to cancer will frequently take on undergraduate assistants. And of course, being in an environment where students may encounter students in medical school, law school, business school, PhD programs, and the like, many of whom have had work experience in all sorts of fields before coming back to school, means that universities can be a great place to find mentors.

In contrast, colleges that are not part of universities tend to:

- Offer smaller campuses with fewer students
- Focus completely on undergraduates (by definition)
- Hire professors because they are the best teachers rather than because they are widely published or widely renowned researchers

Colleges exist for the sole purpose of giving their undergraduate students a good education. Classes are generally smaller than those at colleges housed within larger universities, and the professors that teach them are there because they have a passion not just for their field but also for teaching. It is not to say that these professors never publish their own papers or do original work, but typically those things are secondary to their role as teachers.

Although at many colleges there may not be as many opportunities to see cutting edge research up close, the advantage is that everything that is being done is dominated by undergraduates so sometimes there end up being more opportunities in other ways. For instance, if a professor does decide to conduct a small research project, every student involved will be an undergraduate so undergraduates will be able to hold more substantial positions than they might be able to find at a university lab where they are competing with graduate students. And at a college, all of the music and theater programs are for undergraduates. If you want to be in a play or get into a performing group, you are not competing with graduate students who focus on these fields.

This is not to say that at large research universities undergraduates don't have activities just for them or ample research opportunities, but at a college it can feel easier to star in *the* fall musical on campus or be *the* head researcher for a project. At a college, it may be easier to feel like you play a critical role in helping to define the campus culture.

College Match Profile: School Type

Students who attend universities during their undergraduate years and students that attend pure colleges all can go on to go to graduate school and do whatever they want. Because of this, I've heard some students point out that they chose a college because they can always go to a university for graduate school, but they can't do things the other way around. That is true, but at the same time, I've heard students who chose to go to a university for their four undergraduate years say that if they hadn't had the opportunity to work with a certain researcher and take certain high level courses in their field, they wouldn't have discovered their passion for the field they are studying in graduate school.

Some students walk onto a university campus and feel inspired by the amount of stuff that is happening, the energy of the place and people – not just undergraduates, but also medical students, doctoral candidates, Nobel Prize winning scientists, etc. – going off in every direction doing different things. They get a burst of energy as they realize how many opportunities lay before them both during their four undergraduate years and in the world beyond them. By comparison, a smaller college might feel small and just won't make their heart race the same way.

But a different student might visit a university, feel overwhelmed, like maybe they'd get lost, and feel like everyone is anonymous. By comparison, a college may feel like a tight and nurturing community that will support them, and actively make an effort to help them find their passions. This smaller, more nurturing environment may give them newfound confidence and be just what they need to make them *want* to do something in the world beyond college.

Divide up our top politicians, business leaders, artists, and the like and you will find that they have come from a good mix of college and universities, so this is not a distinguishing factor that is associated with future success. Ultimately, there is no better choice, just one that might be more suited for your personality and preferences.

Select whether you think you would prefer a college or a university. Most students will find that they have an inclination towards one or another although if you feel like you could be happy at either one, it is also okay to select both school types. As a reminder:

College – An institution of higher learning that focuses exclusively on undergraduate students (i.e. students pursuing 4-year programs to earn their bachelor's degrees).

University – An institution of higher learning that includes undergraduates, graduate students, and research faculty members.

Preferred School Type (college or university?):

_____

If you are not sure which you prefer, check out the "Not Sure?" quiz on the next page to help you figure it out.

After you've identified your choice, flip to the College Match Profile in Chapter 17 (page 270) to record your selection and start the process of revealing your College Match Profile.

NOT SURE?

If you are not sure about whether you prefer a college or a university, consider the following questions:

1) Which of the following statements do you most agree with?

   a) One of my biggest priorities in college is having professors who really care about teaching me.
   b) One of my biggest priorities in college is going to a school where by the time I'm an upperclassman, there will be opportunities for me to work with top-notch research faculty members in their fields.

2) Would you rather...

   a) Not be able to take a class in a subject that interests you because your school doesn't offer courses in that field. You can, however, study this subject over the summer at another college if you choose or create a self-directed independent plan of study and gain course credit studying the subject matter independently under the mentorship of a professor.
   b) Get stuck in a large lecture course with 1,000 students. During class, there are not many opportunities to get your questions answered by the professor. You do get to break into a section of 15 students once a week led by a graduate student who is there to answer your questions about the course material. And, if you choose, the professor holds office hours once a week where you can drop by to ask him your questions directly if you feel so inclined.

3) Thinking about being in some classes with students who are in law school, medical school, business school, or earning their PhDs, makes me feel...

   a) Intimidated. Or, at least I would rather be in a class with people my age. It is not because I'm not smart enough to handle being around graduate students, but I'd feel more comfortable speaking my mind and sharing with the class if everyone was an undergraduate. Ultimately, I'd perform better in a classroom filled with my peers.
   b) Excited. It would be great to find mentors in peers that are in the next stage of life. Also, some of them might be able to offer me research opportunities.

NOT SURE? (cont.)

Count up your choices on the previous page.

If you picked two or more A choices, look for **colleges.**
If you picked two or more B choices, look for **universities.**

If you do not feel like you have a particular inclination towards either one, it is okay to include both colleges and universities in your college profile.

Before you move on to the next section, fill in your preference for a college or university (or both) on the College Match Profile Chart in Chapter 17 (page 270) to reveal your College Match Profile.

Colleges

Amherst College
Bard College
Barnard College
Bates College
Beloit College
Bennington College
Bowdoin College
Bryn Mawr College
Bucknell University
Carleton College
Centre College
Claremont McKenna College
Colby College
Colgate College
College of the Atlantic
College of the Holy Cross
Colorado College
Connecticut College
Cooper Union
Davidson College
Deep Springs College
Denison University
DePauw University
Dickinson College
Franklin and Marshall College
Furman University
Gettysburg College
Goucher College
Grinnell College
Hamilton College
Hampshire College
Harvey Mudd College
Haverford College
Hendrix College
Hobart and William Smith Colleges
Kalamazoo College
Kenyon College
Knox College
Lafayette College

Lawrence University
Macalester College
Middlebury College
Mount Holyoke College
New College of Florida
Oberlin College
Occidental College
Olin College
Pitzer College
Pomona College
Reed College
Rhodes College
Sarah Lawrence College
Scripps College
Sewanee: The University of the South
Shimer College
Skidmore College
Smith College
Soka University of America
St John's College Annapolis
St. John's College – Santa Fe
St. Lawrence University
St. Mary's College of Maryland
St. Olaf College
Swarthmore College
Thomas Aquinas College
Trinity College
Union College
University of Richmond
Vassar College
Wabash College
Washington and Lee University
Wellesley College
Wesleyan University
Wheaton College (IL)
Wheaton College (MA)
Whitman College
Willamette University
Williams College

Universities

American University
Arizona State University
Boston College
Boston University
Brandeis University
Brigham Young University
Brown University
California Institute of Technology
Carnegie Mellon University
Case Western University
Clark University
Clemson University
Colorado School of Mines
College of William and Mary
Columbia University
Cornell University
Dartmouth College
Duke University
Emory University
Eugene Lang at The New School
Florida State University
Fordham University
George Washington University
Georgetown University
Georgia Institute of Technology
Harvard University
Illinois Institute of Technology
Indiana University – Bloomington
Ithaca College
Johns Hopkins University
Lehigh University
Loyola University Chicago
Marquette University
Massachusetts Institute of Technology
Michigan State University
Northeastern University
Northwestern University
New York University
Ohio State University
Ohio Wesleyan University
Penn State University

Pepperdine University
Pratt University
Princeton University
Purdue University
Rensselaer Polytechnic Institute
Rice University
Rutgers – New Brunswick
Southern Methodist University
Stanford University
Stony Brook University – SUNY
Syracuse University
Texas A&M University
Tufts University
Tulane University
University of California – Berkeley
University of California – San Diego
University of California – Davis
University of California – Irvine
University of California – Santa Barbara
University of California – Santa Cruz
University of California – Los Angeles
University of Rochester
University of Texas – Austin
University of Chicago
University of Colorado – Boulder
University of Connecticut
University of Delaware
University of Florida
University of Georgia
University of Illinois
University of Iowa
University of Maine
University of Maryland – Baltimore County
University of Maryland – College Park
University of Massachusetts – Amherst
University of Miami

Universities (cont.)

University of Michigan – Ann Arbor
University of Minnesota – Twin Cities
University of New Hampshire
University of New Mexico
University of North Carolina – Chapel Hill
University of Notre Dame
University of Pennsylvania
University of Pittsburgh
University of Rochester
University of Southern California

University of Vermont
University of Virginia
University of Washington
University of Wisconsin
Vanderbilt University
Virginia Polytechnic Institute
Wake Forest University
Washington University in St Louis
Worcester Polytechnic Institute
Yale University
Yeshiva University

Chapter 4
Public vs. Private Schools

Of the approximately 4,000 colleges and universities around the country, about half offer two-year degrees and the other half offer four-year degrees. This book is focused on the schools offering four-year degrees where students end up graduating with a bachelor's degree, which in the United States takes four years. Students who attend two-year programs receive associate's degrees and will need to transfer to a four-year school and typically gain two more years of credits before they can receive a bachelor's degree. Of the colleges and universities offering four-year degrees, 25% are public, and 75% are private. Public and private schools have very distinct characteristics and having a sense of which one you prefer can have a big impact on your college search.

Public Colleges and Universities

Public schools, also known as "state schools," are predominantly funded by the individual state they are in (e.g., New York, California, or Michigan), while private schools are mostly funded through independent means. Because significant state funds are used to support public universities, meaningful differences between public and private choices often arise. Since the actual money that supports much of a public university comes from that state's tax base, students who are residents in the particular state of a given state college or university usually pay in-state tuition, i.e., a reduced tuition rate. Students from other states or other countries usually pay a higher out-of-state rate. While usually a substantial figure, this non-resident rate is still typically lower than the cost of tuition at many private schools.

Given the financial incentives and, sometimes, laws that require a minimum percentage of in-state students (students that have legal residency in that particular state), public universities tend to have a large percentage of in-state students who choose to attend, often making up the majority of the student body (though there are some exceptions to this). As an international student, this is something to be aware of insofar as you should realize that the student body at a state school may not be quite as geographically diverse as at many private schools.

Another feature of public universities is that on average, they are bigger institutions than private colleges. There are small public universities such as the New College of Florida and the College of William and Mary that basically look, feel, and function more similarly to a private school, but the largest universities in the country are all public schools. The largest school nationally, Arizona State University, has over 72,000 students, including 58,000 undergraduate students. Just to put that into context, Harvard University, which is considered a fairly large private university, enrolls a total of approximately 20,000 students with only about 6,500 undergraduates.

Large State Flagship Universities

A massive college campus like Arizona State basically looks like a city, with shuttles taking people everywhere because it is too big to walk and enormous sports stadiums packed to the brim. You can really only find this kind of size and scale at a public university. The sports culture at many public universities in the US is a huge part of life. Most states have a flagship state university (and sometimes several), and these schools are home to the state's pride and joy in terms of football, basketball, and the like.

The University of Michigan, University of North Carolina at Chapel Hill, Ohio State University and Pennsylvania State University are all examples of these types of flagship schools. The best student athletes in the state (often who end up going to play professionally straight from college) almost all want to go to play for the team at their state college. These schools are the recruiting spots for the NFL and NBA athletes (our professional football and basketball leagues), so many of the top professional athletes across the United States played for a flagship public university team. The athletes at many flagship public universities are treated like royalty often earning substantial scholarships, getting first pick for housing and courses, and getting followed around the campus by a bunch of their "fans" (often fellow classmates).

Many kids grow up dreaming of going to their flagship state school. In part because of the sports culture, there is a huge amount of school pride and school spirit you'd be hard-pressed to find at a private school, and this is something that lasts for life. I live in Boston (in the state of Massachusetts), which is a 12-hour drive and several states away from Michigan. But there are several bars in my neighborhood that are known as "Michigan bars" where every week during the basketball season dozens of University of Michigan alumni gather to watch their basketball team on television (the games at many state schools are nationally broadcast). They could not dream of missing a game even now that they are ten years or more out of school. It is a lifetime attachment.

Academically, large flagship state schools often attract top-notch faculty members, including Nobel Prize winners, Pulitzer Prize winners, and internationally renowned researchers. These are research universities, and it is a point of pride to have some of the faculty doing cutting-edge research. Certain departments may stand out at each individual school, and most of the large flagship schools have some field or multiple fields in which they are known to be one of the best nationally or even worldwide. Indiana University – Bloomington, for instance, is known for having some of the best music faculty in the country. University of Illinois – Urbana-Champaign has a great engineering program. University of Maryland – College Park stands out in government and politics (in part because of its proximity to DC).

That said, given the sheer size of these institutions, both the quality of the overall faculty and the quality of the students may be more of a mixed bag than that at private schools. In some states, for instance in Texas, there are laws in place that say that any Texas high school student in the top 10% of their high school class (based on grades) automatically gains admission to any state school, including the flagship university, The University of Texas – Austin. This means students who go to high schools that may not be as rigorous will automatically gain admission despite the fact that other metrics such as their writing ability, scores, and extracurricular involvement may not be as competitive.

Even in states where these kinds of laws do not exist, the size of big state schools typically means that getting admitted is not as competitive as at the top private universities, especially for in-state students. It is for this reason that many public universities offer an "Honors Program" or an "Honors College." Basically, these schools select a subset of the undergraduate student body at the time of their application (some schools allow you to apply after you enroll in the university) and give these students special academic opportunities. Sometimes, they are given the option to take specific classes with the most eminent faculty not offered to the entire student body. Sometimes, they can choose to live in dorms separate from other students so that they are in a more scholarly community. Sometimes, these students are also awarded financial incentives like merit scholarships. These programs try to create the experience of a smaller selective school within a large public university.

The biggest advantage of state schools is that they usually are substantially less expensive than private colleges even for out-of-state and international students (often times the sticker price is half that of a private college and sometimes even less than half even for out-of-state and international students). On some occasions, a select group of international students may even get a tuition waiver, which allows them to pay in-state tuition instead of out of state pricing to make the sticker price even less.

In addition, given their large size, public universities can make a lot of sense for someone looking to have tons of academic options both in terms of courses and extracurricular offerings. These schools tend to draw some amazing faculty members, have some standout departments, and can offer honors programs that offer an experience more similar to that at a top private university. And because state schools are known for unparalleled school pride and interest in school sports, many students feel connected to their school for life making for powerful alumni networks you can tap into for jobs and introductions for the rest of your life.

Keep in mind that by choosing a flagship state university you are choosing to attend a large school that is publicly funded, which means that there will be larger variation of quality among the student body. Not everyone will be at the same academic level, and you will go into each class needing to prove yourself. Given the financial incentives for in-state students, a large percentage of the student body will come from in state (which also means down the road when you are tapping into the alumni network, a disproportionate percentage of the alumni will be tied to that specific geographic area).

Another major point to consider is that state schools have the reputation for being bureaucratic. Because the government funds these schools, you are subject to the rules of the system. Exceptions are usually not made for you if you miss a deadline or forget to turn in a form. And state schools are notorious for imposing class size limits so that you may be shut out of certain classes you want to take if you are not majoring in that subject or if you are an underclassmen (first or second year student).

Overall, the students who do best at large public universities are usually highly motivated students who know how to take advantage of being in a huge environment with lots of resources but probably not a lot personal attention. There are great mentors to be found if you look for them, but they won't necessarily come to you. If you want to talk to a professor, you will need to set up a meeting. If you want advice on what to take next semester, you will need to call your advisor and ask to talk. And you'll need to make sure to turn your course schedule in on time or risk not being able to take classes that semester. The students that have the best experiences at big state schools tend to be very independent and self-motivated.

Plenty of students do get lost in these schools and that is one of the reasons, along with the more mixed quality of the student body and bureaucratic policies, that state schools on average tend to have a much higher dropout rate than private schools. However, students who are excited about a culture of strong school spirit, who will put themselves out there to form a strong community of peers, and who will take the initiative to reach out to faculty members and alumni, can have a great experience at a state school and save some money.

Other Public Universities

What I've just described above is the experience at the major flagship state colleges, the premiere college in each state (some states have a couple of flagship colleges). This book features a number of schools in this category. In addition to the big flagship state schools, however, most states offer secondary public universities that are part of their public university system. These are universities that are usually less competitive to get into but give slightly less competitive students the opportunity to go to college. Occasionally, these secondary state universities will excel in a couple of departments. However, most of the time, they are generally regarded as a tier below the flagship schools. In many states, students who attend these secondary universities and do well academically will try to transfer to the flagship university for their final two years so they can obtain their degree under the flagship school's name.

Often, states will have a transfer policy that says that students from these secondary state schools will automatically gain admission to the flagship school if they earn above a certain GPA. If you cannot gain admission to the flagship state school you would like to go to right away, this may be something to look into, although this book does not feature many secondary state colleges. You can usually find a list of all of these secondary state school options on the website of the flagship university or by searching for "Ohio university system," "Arizona university system," etc.

Public Liberal Arts Colleges

Before I get into private colleges, I wanted to mention that there is a small subset of state schools that are small liberal arts colleges rather than universities. These are very rare (there are only a handful in the country), but there are two that I've featured in this book, the New College of Florida and St. Mary's College of Maryland. Neither of these schools is considered to be secondary to the major flagship universities in each state. Equally competitive students (and sometimes more competitive students) choose these colleges because they are looking for a small private college experience at a public school price. Like all public options, these schools have a substantially reduced tuition rate and attract a higher percentage of in-state students than do most private colleges. Unlike other state colleges, they do not support the same kind of massive sports teams and accordingly do not have the same kind of wild school spirit. But, students at these schools tend to get substantially more personal attention and these schools are designed to focus on the undergraduate experience.

Private Colleges and Universities

Private schools come in a more diverse array of models just because they are privately funded and have more flexibility to be what they choose to be. The first thing that many Americans would say if you brought up private colleges would be "expensive"! Private colleges do have a reputation for being wildly expensive. And while it is true that most of them are more costly than public colleges, and that the priciest colleges in the country are all private colleges, this is not always the case. In fact, there is a subset of private colleges that are highly discounted or even free because of large endowments funded by private donors.

Olin College in Massachusetts, which specializes in engineering, pays for 50% of the tuition through an endowment for every single student that enrolls. Deep Springs College in California is the only two-year college featured in this book, is a great option because it is entirely free for both years. The school is incredibly small (just 26 students) and competitive, but the caliber of the students is excellent, and most of the students go on to finish their degrees by transferring into their third year at some of the best colleges in the country (Harvard, Yale, Cornell, Amherst, and their equivalents all frequently enroll Deep Springs alumni). Cooper Union in New York City is another completely free school offering four-year degrees in engineering, the fine arts, and architecture.

The other thing to keep in mind is that colleges offer financial aid, which means the advertised price is often much higher than the actual price for most students. Most private colleges today offer aid to at least half of their student body. If you are a US citizen, even if you live out of the country, you should be eligible for a combination of aid through the federal government as well as aid offered directly through your school. If you are not a US citizen, you won't be eligible for federal aid, but at many schools, even private schools, you still may be eligible for some aid either through direct need-based grants through the college or university or through merit programs.

At a handful of private schools, the school will actually supplement whatever you can't get in federal funding as a non-US citizen with their own grants so that your tuition will be reduced significantly. We will discuss these options more in Chapter 11, but the key point to be aware of now is that the sticker price does not always reflect what you actually pay. The advertised price alone is not a good reason in and of itself to wipe a school off your list.

Aside from the fact that on average, private colleges are more expensive than public colleges and that the average private college is smaller than public options, private colleges can be hard to generalize. You have probably heard of the Ivy League schools, technical institutes, and small liberal arts colleges. These are all different kinds of private colleges that you will find throughout the United States.

Private Universities

The first type of private school we will talk about is the private university. Like all universities, private universities typically have both undergraduate and graduate divisions. They exist not only for the purpose of educating all of these students but also to house faculty conducting innovative research.

Because of the research being conducted on campus, private universities tend to be great places for students to get hands-on research opportunities. Some universities may have faculty members come in for short-term appointments directly from big business jobs or from working in politics, and this can mean students have great access to internships and jobs based on these connections.

In general, private universities are smaller than public universities, although there are some exceptions. The advantage of being privately funded is that these institutions tend to be less bureaucratic and more student-focused. However, the quality of the faculty and the student body is not necessarily better – it depends on the school.

You may have heard of the Ivy League, which is a grouping of eight private universities on the East Coast – Harvard, Yale, Princeton, Brown, Cornell, Dartmouth, Columbia, and The University of Pennsylvania – known to be some of the best universities in the country. The Ivy League was originally an athletic conference (they were a subset of schools that competed against each other in sports), but over time, the term has evolved to refer to the superb faculty all-around, top-notch student bodies, and significant endowments of these institutions. For undergraduates, these schools are strong in a wide variety of fields and typically encourage students to take classes in multiple disciplines including the hard sciences, the humanities, the social sciences, and the arts. The philosophy is to teach students how to think rather than how to master a particular field although even at these schools, students do come out with some sort of a major or field of focus.

If you are interested in a private university, I would encourage you to think beyond the Ivy League. While the schools within it are excellent and attract incredible faculty and students, the term "Ivy League" means little more than the name of an athletic conference, and there are many other schools such as Tufts, Johns Hopkins, and Stanford that offer equally impressive students, staff members, and resources.

Technical Institutes

The second type of private school is the technical institute such as the California Institute of Technology ("Caltech") and Rensselaer Polytechnic Institute ("RPI"), which are private schools designed to give students in-depth expertise primarily in engineering and the hard sciences. Technical institutes are a type of university that attract top-notch student bodies including some of the best math and science students, and they attract all-star faculty members doing cutting-edge research. But, unlike the Ivy League and Ivy League-comparable private universities, they devote the majority of their resources toward their technical fields. While they usually still offer classes in the social sciences, humanities, and arts (and typically require that students take some classes in all of these areas), their stated goal is to train the future scientists, engineers, and computer programmers of the world so the other fields are treated more as extras. So for instance, writing classes are still taught, but the majority of students will view writing useful insofar as it will help them learn to clearly articulate their ideas in scientific papers, grant proposals, and so forth.

It is worth nothing that many technical institutes do offer students the option to major in history, English, and other non-technical fields, but the students who pursue these options are in the minority at these schools. And, anyone who attends a technical institute, regardless of their chosen major, will be required to gain significant technical training as a base requirement.

Small Liberal Arts Colleges

The third type of private institution is the small liberal arts college. Small liberal arts colleges are colleges like the ones discussed in the previous chapter, rather than universities. They are focused almost entirely on undergraduate education. In general they are small- to medium-sized. Like the Ivy

League schools, but perhaps even more so, the liberal arts college is focused on providing students with a broad education that will expose them to a number of fields. They are designed to help students develop general thinking and writing skills that will allow them to thrive in any field they go into, and perhaps more importantly, help students understand their own values and goals.

Different liberal arts colleges have different philosophies on what the best approach is to achieving these aims. Some schools, like Amherst College, Hamilton College, and the University of Rochester, have absolutely no requirements in terms of what types of courses students take outside of the requirements for each student's major; they give student free reign to explore what interests them and use their four years to find their passions and develop skills as they see fit. Other schools, like St. Johns' College in Annapolis, MD and Santa Fe, NM, take the exact opposite approach, prescribing each and every class a student takes from start to finish. They believe that reading key works from the Western Canon exposes students to core ideas that will help them learn how to think and how to form their own values. And they believe there is value to having every student on campus read the same material at the same time so there is a common set of ideas being discussed and worked out in and outside of the classroom.

Most liberal arts schools fall somewhere in the middle of these two approaches in terms of requirements, requiring that students take a set number of courses in different fields but allowing them to pursue some sort of a major focusing more intensely on a particular subject and giving them time to take electives in any field they want. Even so, each liberal arts school will have its own take on the best way to implement a liberal arts philosophy.

At Colorado College, for instance, students only take one class at a time so they can devote themselves fully to something for a set amount of time before moving on to another topic in four weeks. And some schools have a January term where students can take non-credit courses or in some cases courses for credit in unique subjects or in locations around the world to add to the more conventional course offerings they take during the main academic terms.

The advantage of the small liberal arts college is that all of the energy is devoted to a student's development. Regardless of their academic philosophy, they tend to be nurturing places that go to great lengths to make sure students have a strong support network of peers, advisors, and plenty of resources so that they have a fulfilling experience. As such, they tend to have high graduation rates.

What is important to consider, though, when it comes to a small liberal arts school is that often this type of academic philosophy does mean that students come out without a whole lot of technical preparation in a specific field. Although most American colleges have some liberal arts components, the small liberal arts colleges tend to have the strongest liberal arts philosophy. This can make getting one's first job a challenge. While some students find jobs that require the critical thinking skills a broad liberal arts education develops (including jobs as journalists, paralegals, management consultants, lab research assistants, etc.), there may not be as many jobs right off the bat for young graduates of small liberal arts colleges as for graduates with a newly minted technical degree.

It often takes a few years before this type of education pays off. Students may have a harder time finding their first job, but a few years in, the broad range of experience and critical thinking skills a liberal arts education develops helps these students gain an edge getting promotions and earning management positions.

In addition, these liberal arts students typically have one of the highest rates of admission to graduate schools. Lots of students from small liberal arts colleges go on to law school, medical school, business school, and PhD programs. The top graduate programs often actually prefer liberal arts students with a broad educational background over students with more specialized degrees. And many students from liberal arts colleges go on to be leaders in their fields.

So the downside to a private liberal arts college is that in the short-term, it is more challenging to get a job right out of school, and students often feel that they didn't end up with any directly applicable knowledge for their careers. The value of these types of degrees may not become apparent for many years after graduating, but if you don't believe it is there, just look at how many well-known physicians, lawyers, politicians, businessmen, and actors attended liberal arts institutions, and you will see that clearly there must be something to it.

College Match Profile: School Funding

As you start to figure out your College Match Profile, think first whether the big public university experience with the huge and diverse array of academic options, massive school pride, and strong alumni networks appeals to you or whether the smaller size, more consistent quality, but more expensive private schools, sound more appealing. If you decide you are interested in the private route, think a bit more about whether you would prefer a private university, a technical institute, or a small liberal arts college.

Public School – Colleges or universities that are predominantly funded by the government.

Private College/University – Colleges or universities that do not receive the majority of their funding from the government and are administered independently.

Preferred School Funding Type (Public or Private?):

_____

Fill in your preference on the College Match Profile Chart in Chapter 17 (page 270) to reveal your College Match Profile. If you're still not sure of your preference, take the "Not Sure?" quiz on the next page, and then come back to fill in the blank.

NOT SURE?

If you don't have an immediate preference for a private or public school, consider the following questions.

1) On a scale of 1 to 5 (1 being the least and 5 being the most), how much is cost a consideration in your college choice?
2) On a scale of 1 to 5 (1 being the least and 5 being the most), how much do you enjoy attending sporting events?
3) On a scale of 1 to 5 (1 being the least and 5 being the most), how self-directed are you?
4) On a scale of 1 to 5 (1 being the least and 5 being the most), how willing are you to deal with bureaucratic policies that require you to fill out lots of paperwork to get things done and may keep you out of classes if you don't follow proper procedures?
5) On a scale of 1 to 5 (1 being the least and 5 being the most), how comfortable are you being in a large environment where there are thousands of choices?
6) On a scale of 1 to 5 (1 being the least and 5 being the most), how comfortable are you being in a school environment where there is huge diversity in the academic abilities and qualifications of the students attending the university?

Add up the numbers you chose for each of the questions above.

If you scored a 21 or above, a **public** college or university would likely be the best fit for you.

If you scored below a 12, a **private** college or university would probably be the best fit.

If you scored between 13 and 20, you would likely be able to find good fits at both **public** and **private** schools.

Fill in your preferences in the College Match Profile Chart in Chapter 17 (page 270) to reveal your College Match Profile.

Public Colleges and Universities

Arizona State University
Clemson University
Colorado School of Mines
College of William and Mary
Florida State University
Georgia Institute of Technology
Indiana University – Bloomington
Michigan State University
New College of Florida
Ohio State University
Penn State University
Purdue University – West Lafayette College
Rutgers University – New Brunswick
St. Mary's College of Maryland
Stony Brook University
Texas A&M University
University of California – Berkeley
University of California – San Diego
University of California – Davis
University of California – Irvine
University of California – Santa Barbara
University of California – Santa Cruz
University of California – Los Angeles

University of Colorado – Boulder
University of Connecticut
University of Delaware
University of Florida
University of Georgia
University of Illinois
University of Iowa
University of Maine
University of Maryland – Baltimore County
University of Maryland – College Park
University of Massachusetts – Amherst
University of Michigan
University of Minnesota – Twin Cities
University of New Hampshire
University of New Mexico
University of North Carolina – Chapel Hill
University of Pittsburgh
University of Texas – Austin
University of Vermont
University of Virginia
University of Washington
University of Wisconsin – Madison
Virginia Polytechnic Institute

Private Colleges and Universities

American University
Amherst College
Bard College
Barnard College
Bates College
Beloit College
Bennington College
Boston College
Boston University
Bowdoin College
Brandeis University
Brigham Young University
Brown University
Bryn Mawr College
Bucknell University
California Institute of Technology
Carleton College
Carnegie Mellon University
Case Western Reserve University
Centre College
Claremont McKenna College
Clark University
Colby College
Colgate College
College of the Atlantic
College of the Holy Cross
Colorado College
Columbia University
Connecticut College
Cooper Union
Cornell University
Dartmouth College
Davidson College
Deep Springs College
Denison University
DePauw University
Dickinson College
Duck University
Emerson College
Emory University
Eugene Lang College at The New School
Fordham University

Franklin and Marshall College
Furman University
George Washington University
Georgetown University
Gettysburg College
Goucher College
Grinnell College
Hamilton College
Hampshire College
Harvard University
Harvey Mudd College
Haverford College
Hendrix College
Hobart and William Smith Colleges
Illinois Institute of Technology
Ithaca College
Johns Hopkins University
Kalamazoo College
Kenyon College
Knox College
Lafayette College
Lawrence University
Lehigh University
Loyola University Chicago
Macalester College
Marquette University
Massachusetts Institute of Technology
Middlebury College
Mount Holyoke College
New York University
Northeastern University
Northwestern University
Oberlin College
Occidental College
Ohio Wesleyan University
Olin College
Pepperdine University
Pitzer College
Pomona College
Pratt Institute
Princeton University
Reed College

Private Colleges and Universities (cont.)

Rensselaer Polytechnic Institute
Rhodes College
Rice University
Sarah Lawrence
Scripps College
Sewanee: The University of the
South
Shimer College
Skidmore College
Smith College
Soka University of America
Southern Methodist University
St. John's College – Annapolis
St. John's College – Santa Fe
St. Lawrence University
St. Olaf College
Stanford University
Swarthmore College
Syracuse University
Thomas Aquinas College
Trinity College
Tufts University
Tulane University
Union College

University of Chicago
University of Miami
University of Notre Dame
University of Pennsylvania
University of Richmond
University of Rochester
University of Southern California
Vanderbilt University
Vassar College
Wabash College
Washington and Lee University
Washington University – St.
Louis
Wellesley College
Wesleyan University
Wheaton College (IL)
Wheaton College (MA)
Whitman College
Willamette University
Williams College
Worcester Polytechnic Institute
Yale University
Yeshiva University

Chapter 5
Campus Structure and Surrounding Area

You will likely be in college for at least four years, and this means you will be spending a lot of your time on a college campus. Most likely you will live, eat, take classes, and socialize on the grounds of your college. This is a marked difference from the way students in many countries experience college. In many countries, college is primarily a place to take classes. Yes, there is the occasional social or extracurricular event, but at the end of the day, a college is a couple of buildings that students go to when they have class and then they go home. As you start to develop a list of colleges to consider, I would make the campus structure a key point to take into account because in the United States, it will make a big difference to the way you live.

Island Campus

Some college students come home for the summer and are shocked to see people who are outside of the age range of 18-22 other than professors. Kids? Elderly people? They've practically forgotten they exist. The majority of top US colleges have an **island campus**, college grounds that are completely separated from the outer world. Sometimes, there is a gate surrounding the campus, other times just a grassy lawn or a bunch of buildings all facing inwards towards a central core, but either way, there is a definitive physical separation between the campus and the greater world.

On island campuses, everything you need on a daily basis is within these grounds. Classes, dorms, dining, social spots, and the like are contained within this world. Of course, at some island campuses students may decide to live off-campus or go out to town for dinner on a weekend if they so choose, but upon leaving the campus grounds either to go to one's off-campus apartment or on an excursion, there is a definitive sense of leaving the world of college behind.

In some cases, like at Hampshire College, there is absolutely nowhere students can walk to from the campus grounds besides a few rural homes and to the woods (which the students love because they feel like they have their own wooded paradise). If students want to leave the campus, they either need to drive or take a bus to the nearest town to get somewhere. Hampshire College is an example of a school that is an island campus in a **rural location**, which means the school is not located within a short drive of a major city and is not within walking distance of the center of a town.

That said, getting to retail and entertainment establishments outside the school is not always a major ordeal at some island campuses. Princeton University, for instance is located within the bustling town of Princeton, New Jersey, which has plenty of great shops and restaurants. Students can walk to these shops and restaurants easily from the campus – they are only a few blocks away. However, there is a definitive sense of where the campus starts and where it ends. You are aware of the exact second you step off campus, and given the layout of the campus (basically a big rectangle with everything associated Princeton contained within it), students who don't make an active effort to go to town, never have to see it. It isn't a part of daily life unless students make it a part of their life, and that reality impacts the campus culture.

Princeton is an example of an island campus in a **town location**. Island campuses can even be found in the middle of large cities. Emory University in Atlanta and Georgetown University in Washington DC are such examples.

Island campuses, regardless of whether they are in a rural location, a town, **suburb** (a town that is within a short drive of a major city), in a **small city** (a legally-designated city with under 100,000 people) or **city** (over 100,000 people), have a unique atmosphere. They are closed off bubbles, little academic worlds on their own. Regardless of whether you are sitting on the quad or in the library, many students at these schools describe the feeling of being almost anywhere across campus as feeling like they are home. Because the campus is closed off, students say they feel safe and protected, a part of a strong community.

Social life on island campuses is often focused internally, either through events held on school-owned property like a school-operated pub, student center, coffee house, or fraternity / sorority houses. Students on island campuses need to make an extra effort if they want to go out to a restaurant or see a movie that isn't associated with the college. It isn't unusual to hear a student comment that they haven't been "off campus" for weeks and need to get away.

On occasion, especially when island campuses are located in rural locations or in small towns, you'll hear students say that they feel stuck within the gates and miss seeing cars, working people, children, and everything else they know is out there. They miss shopping and Mexican food and have to make a special excursion (often without a car) to get these things. Being inside an island campus can be wonderful, but getting out can be more of a pain than on other types of campuses.

Street-Side Campus

The opposite of the island campus is the **street-side campus**. This is the most common type of college campus at universities around the world but actually the least common type within the United States. Street-side campuses are campuses located within a town or city (usually a city) where the campus is comprised primarily of one or more buildings that sit alongside stores, houses, and municipal buildings. The campus begins when you walk into one of the buildings. When you walk out, you are back in the town or city.

These types of campuses typically have very little if any green space. If students want to congregate outside, perhaps the campus offers a small green lawn in the courtyard of a building or between two adjacent buildings, but standing in these spaces there is no sense of "This is it! I'm finally on the campus." You feel more like you are in the side or backyard of a building where perhaps you are waiting to go in for your next class. A lot of your social life will take place at the nearby coffee shops, restaurants, public parks, and other amenities that the town and city offer.

Your life at a school like this will be in large part influenced by the place you are in, not just the school you are in (in contrast, on an island campus, it is easy to forget the culture of the place you are in and just focus on the culture of the school). Spending so much time out in a city or town often inspires students at street-side campuses to take part in the community around them either through community service or taking jobs or internships in the area. Access to these things tends to be very easy.

New York University (NYU) is perhaps the most classic example of a street-side campus in the United States. Located in the middle of Greenwich Village in New York City, the campus is in one of the densest neighborhoods in the country. As such, students often joke that there is "no campus." When you walk out of class, the building next door might be a Cuban restaurant or a clothing boutique. You do not walk around the area and think, "I'm here. I'm at NYU." Instead, you walk into a building and think, "I'm in the architecture building." Many students find the close interaction with Greenwich Village exciting. They like being able to easily switch modes between being in class and hanging out in their favorite coffee shop next door.

The down side to a street-side campus is that it does not foster the same type of community as the island campus. It is more likely that students will live in housing that is not affiliated with the university, especially as they become upperclassmen. Social life tends to be directed more towards the amenities a city or surrounding town offers rather than on-campus activities. And, because there are fewer spaces for students to congregate, many students devote time and energy to being a part of the town or city rather than contributing to campus life. Extracurricular activities, while likely available, will not be as central to the culture of the school. As an NYU student once pointed out to me, "Why would I go to a campus play when I could just take a quick subway ride to see a Broadway show?" Of course seeing a Broadway show is awesome, but it is a different experience than one might have at an island campus where the main stage production on-campus is a big thing (an NYU student might counter back that the best acting students at NYU are on Broadway, so it is basically the same thing).

Integrated Campus

The third type of college campus is the **integrated campus,** which is the middle ground between the two types we have examined. The integrated campus is located within a suburb, town, or city (not in a rural location) and is within close proximity to commercial life. Whereas on an island campus, you have to make an effort to leave the campus and see other people besides affiliates of the school and their guests, at an integrated campus seeing people out and about in the world is a part of daily life. Perhaps you pass a bookstore and a dentist's office on your walk from history to anthropology class. Perhaps you always stop for a slice of pizza at a local pizzeria on your way back to your dorm at the end of the day. That said, unlike at a street-side campus where that is also the case, students on an integrated campus will still have large parts of the campus that feel distinctly "on campus," usually some sort of large central quad and grassy areas around the dormitories and some of the academic buildings. The grounds may not be as large as on some island campuses or as private, but they do give students the feeling that they are on their own turf.

An example of an integrated campus is Harvard University. Harvard's campus is almost perfectly integrated into Harvard Square, a popular shopping and eating destination in the Boston area. Harvard Yard is the central core of the campus. Surrounded by brick gates, you walk inside and are surrounded by stunning Georgian architecture around large grassy quads. Students take some of their classes in this area, and the **freshmen** (first year students) live here, but for other classes, upperclassmen housing, the university hospital, counseling center, and other critical parts of the campus students need to walk right through the middle of Harvard Square passing groups of tourists, street artists, shops, bars, restaurants, usually a few homeless people, and the entrance to the T, Boston's metro system. In between all of these things, many of Harvard's buildings are integrated seamlessly. Some are right in the middle of everything but have hidden private courtyards in-between. There is plenty of space for students to nap in the grass reading a book, but at the end of the day, you cannot live on the campus and forget that you are in the middle of a city.

Integrated campuses tend to be middle grounds in terms of the amount of energy devoted inwards to extracurricular activities and on-campus social life. Integrated campuses have a good amount of on-campus space to host all sorts of events. That said, there are other options very close by to compete for students' attention. Integrated campuses offer options but lack the same degree of community strength and peacefulness associated with an island campus. They offer opportunities for being a part of the outside world on a daily basis, but don't quite make students feel like they are residents of a city rather than members of a campus community. NYU students, for instance, will say, "I live in New York City and attend NYU" whereas Harvard students will say "I go to Harvard, so I live in Harvard Square." The distinction is subtle but important. At integrated campuses, just as on island campuses, students identify strongly with their campus community and prize that community culture above the place they are living in; on street-side campuses, the campus culture matters less than the urban culture.

College Match Profile: Campus Structure and Surrounding Area

In this chapter, you will want to figure out both your preferred campus type(s) and your location type(s). Both categories will be important to consider as you create your College Match Profile.

Campus Structure

First, choose which type of campus you prefer:

Island – The type of campus that is physically enclosed or separated from the surrounding communities.

Street-Side – A type of campus that has both grassy enclosed areas and parts of the campus that are entwined in the surrounding neighborhood.

Integrated – The type of campus that has both grassy enclosed areas and parts of the campus that are entwined in the surrounding neighborhood.

Preferred Campus Structure (Island, Street-Side, or Integrated):

_____

Fill in your preference(s) for preferred campus type in the College Match Profile Chart in Chapter 17 (page 270) to reveal your College Match Profile. If you're still not sure of your preference, take the "Not Sure?" quiz on the next page, and then come back to fill in the blank.

NOT SURE?

If you aren't sure which campus structure type is right for you, consider the following questions:

1) A college campus should be a place where...

   a) A grassy oasis filled with my peers. It is a place I can feel safe hanging out in at 2 pm or 2 am any day of the week.
   b) I can sit in the grass and read during the day but where within a couple of minutes, I can meet my friends at a local café for lunch.
   c) I feel like I'm living in the middle of an exciting city.

2) When I walk to class, I want to see...

   a) My classmates and my professors. I like the idea of being in a truly academic environment.
   b) Mostly my classmates, but some normal people too who are going to work, taking their kids to school, or just out enjoying their day. I don't want to forget about the outside world.
   c) Mostly people in the streets of the city. I want to see people from all walks of life and just be one person in the middle of a diverse city street.

3) At 2 am Saturday, I imagine myself...

   a) Studying at the campus library or lying out in the grass with my friends talking.
   b) Going out to dinner with my friends and then maybe go to an on-campus party or hang out in one of our dorm rooms talking until late.
   c) Living it up in the city. We'll check out a new restaurant, go to a professional play or comedy show or find a dance club.

Count up your answers above.

If you selected mostly A choices, your best fit is an **island campus**.

If you selected mostly B choices, look for an **integrated campus**.

If you picked mostly C choices, look for a **street-side campus.**

Fill in your preferences on the previous page and on the College Match Profile Chart in Chapter 17 (page 270) to reveal your College Match Profile.

Schools with an Island Campus

American University
Bard College
Beloit College
Bennington College
Boston College
Brandeis University
Bryn Mawr College
Bucknell University
Centre College
Claremont McKenna College
Clemson University
Colby College
Colgate College
College of the Atlantic
College of the Holy Cross
Colorado College
Connecticut College
Cornell University
Deep Springs College
Denison University
DePauw University
Emory University
Fordham University
Furman University
Georgetown University
Georgia Institute of Technology
Goucher College
Grinnell College
Hamilton College
Hampshire College
Harvey Mudd College
Haverford College
Hendrix College
Hobart and William Smith Colleges
Ithaca College
Kalamazoo College
Kenyon College
Knox College
Lafayette College
Lehigh University
Macalester College
Michigan State University
Middlebury College
New College of Florida

Occidental College
Olin College
Penn State University
Pepperdine University
Pitzer College
Pomona College
Princeton University
Purdue University – West Lafayette
Reed College
Rensselaer Polytechnic Institute
Rhodes College
Rice University
Sarah Lawrence College
Scripps College
Sewanee: The University of the South
Skidmore College
Smith College
Soka University of America
St. John's College – Annapolis
St. John's College – Santa Fe
St. Lawrence University
St. Mary's College of Maryland
St. Olaf College
Stanford University
Stony Brook University
Swarthmore College
Texas A&M University
Thomas Aquinas College
Trinity College
Tufts University
Tulane University
University of California – San Diego
University of California – Davis
University of California – Irvine
University of California – Santa Cruz
Union College
University of Connecticut
University of Florida
University of Georgia
University of Maine

Schools with an Island Campus (cont.)

University of Maryland –
Baltimore County
University of Maryland –
College Park
University of Massachusetts –
Amherst
University of Miami
University of New Hampshire
University of New Mexico
University of Notre Dame
University of Richmond
University of Rochester

Vassar College
Virginia Polytechnic Institute
Wabash College
Wake Forest University
Washington and Lee University
Washington University – St.
Louis
Wellesley College
Wheaton College (IL)
Wheaton College (MA)
Whitman College

Schools with a Street-Side Campus

Barnard College
Boston University
Cooper Union
Emerson College
Eugene Lang College at The
New School

George Washington University
New York University
Shimer College
Yeshiva University

Schools with an Integrated Campus

Amherst College
Arizona State University
Bowdoin College
Brigham Young University
Brown University
Bryn Mawr College
California Institute of Technology
Carleton College
Carnegie Mellon University
Case Western Reserve University
Clark University
College of William and Mary
Colorado School of Mines
Columbia University
Dartmouth College
Davidson College
Dickinson College
Duke University
Florida State University
Franklin and Marshall College
Gettysburg College
Harvard University
Illinois Institute of Technology
Indiana University – Bloomington
Johns Hopkins University
Lawrence University
Loyola University of Chicago
Marquette University
Massachusetts Institute of Technology
Mount Holyoke College
Northeastern University
Northwestern University
Oberlin College
Ohio State University

Ohio Wesleyan University
Pratt Institute
Rutgers University – New Brunswick
Southern Methodist University
Syracuse University
University of California – Berkeley
University of California – Santa Barbara
University of California – Los Angeles
University of Chicago
University of Colorado – Boulder
University of Delaware
University of Illinois
University of Iowa
University of Michigan
University of Minnesota – Twin Cities
University of North Carolina – Chapel Hill
University of Pennsylvania
University of Pittsburgh
University of Southern California
University of Texas – Austin
University of Vermont
University of Virginia
University of Washington
University of Wisconsin – Madison
Vanderbilt University
Wesleyan University
Willamette University
Williams College
Worcester Polytechnic Institute
Yale University

Surrounding Area

Now that you've figured out your campus type preference, you'll want to pick your preferred surrounding area from the following list:

Rural – You cannot walk to a commercial area from the campus and the campus is not located within a short drive to a large city. Rural locations typically provide easy access to outdoor recreational activities.

Town – You can walk or bike to a small commercial area near the campus that will usually provide you with some combination of coffee shops, restaurants, bars, a grocery store, and convenience store for basic essentials. However, this commercial area is not within a short drive to a large city.

Suburb – You may or may not be able to walk to a small commercial area from campus, however, you are within a 45-minute drive from a major city. The area immediately surrounding the campus is primarily residential.

Small City – The campus is located within the city limits or within walking distance of the city limits of a legally designated city with a population of between 25,000 and 100,000 people.

City – The campus is located within the city limits or within walking distance of the city limits of a legally designated city with a population of over 100,000 people.

Preferred Surrounding Area (Rural, Town, Suburb, Small City, City)

_____

Fill in your preference(s) in the College Match Profile Chart in Chapter 17 (page 270) to reveal your College Match Profile. If you're still not sure of your preference, take the "Not Sure?" quiz on the next page, and then come back to fill in the blank.

NOT SURE?

If you aren't sure which surrounding area(s) you'd prefer, answer the following questions:

1) I plan to...

   a) Spend most of my time on campus participating in student life and would like my peers to do the same... I like the idea of being a part of a campus community.
   b) Spend most of my time on campus, but I would like to go to the big city every month or so because I think it is healthy to get off campus every once in a while.
   c) Spend most of my day on the campus, but once or twice a week I'd like to study at the local bookstore or coffee shop for a change of pace.
   d) Get off campus once every week or two to go out to dinner, see a play, or do something in the city.
   e) Go to as many museums, theater productions, clubs, and/or ethnic restaurants as I can. I love exploring new neighborhoods and being a part of a busy metropolis.

2) There is something appealing about the idea of...

   a) Going to a school in a quiet and reflective place where I can really focus on this stage of my life. I want to build deep friendships, develop academically, and learn about my own goals and passions.
   b) Living in a different society than what I'm used to back home and experiencing life in an American city. Constant stimulation makes me the most motivated.

3) If I could spend four years living anywhere, I'd choose...

   a) A spirited town with a handful of its own local hangouts, bizarre traditions, and a unique culture unlike anywhere else. The people there have local pride and encourage everyone to participate in the community.
   b) A city where I could always find new parks and restaurants, but by the end of my four years it would feel like home. I'd have my own neighborhood and community, but even outside of it I would know my way around without using a map and would have visited all of the major neighborhoods.
   c) A place where I would never run out of new neighborhoods to check out and places to see. Although I would have a neighborhood that became mine, by the end of four years much of the city would still feel new and exciting.

NOT SURE? (cont.)

4) Is there such a thing as making your own fun?

    a) When people say you should "make your own fun" they usually are saying there isn't anything exciting to do. Fun to me means culture, which means good food, professional art and sports, educated people, and the other sorts of amenities found in an urban environment.

    b) Sure I'd participate in activities my college hosted like formals and movie nights. But I also like creative activities like organizing themed parties with my friends, taking camping trips, ice skating, doing art, etc. I don't find it difficult to stay entertained no matter where I am, and I find it fun to find new things to entertain myself.

    c) I'm all good with making my own fun most of the time, but if you tell me that I can't get to a city regularly it would be too extreme. I don't like feeling like I'm in a bubble.

Below is a list of the different location types. Put a check mark next to each type depending on your answers as I've outlined here.

Rural:
Suburb:
Town:
Small City:
City:

Question 1: If you answered A, give yourself a check next to **rural**. If you selected B, check off **suburb**. For C, check off **town**. For D, check off **small city**. For E, pick **city**.

Question 2: For A, check off **rural**, **suburb**, and **town**. For B, check off **small city** and **city**.

Question 3: For A, check off **town** and **rural**. For B, check off **small city**. For C, check off **suburb** and **city**.

Question 4: For A, check off **city**. For B, check off **rural** and town. For C, check off **suburb** and **small city**.

Count up your check marks. The option(s) with the most check marks are your best match options. In this category, it is likely that several types of surrounding areas may suit you. You may decide to consider your top several options in your College Match Profile.

Put these preferences into the College Match Profile Chart in Chapter 17 (page 270) to reveal your College Match Profile.

Schools in a Rural Location

Bard College
Bennington College
Colby College
Deep Springs College
Denison University
DePauw University
Hamilton College
Hampshire College
Kenyon College
Sewanee: The University of the South
St. Lawrence University
St. Mary's College of Maryland
Thomas Aquinas College
University of Connecticut
University of Maine

Schools in a Town

Amherst College
Beloit College
Bowdoin College
Bucknell University
Carleton College
Centre College
Claremont McKenna College
Clemson University
Colgate University
College of the Atlantic
College of William and Mary
Dartmouth College
Davidson College
Dickinson College
Gettysburg College
Grinnell College
Harvey Mudd College
Hobart and William Smith Colleges
Middlebury College
Oberlin College
Pitzer College
Pomona College
Princeton University
Scripps College
Smith College
St. Olaf College
University of Massachusetts – Amherst
University of New Hampshire
Virginia Polytechnic Institute
Wabash College
Washington and Lee University
Williams College

Schools in a Suburb

Boston College
Brandeis University
Bryn Mawr College
California Institute of Technology
College of the Holy Cross
Colorado School of Mines
Furman University
Goucher College
Haverford College
Hendrix College
Michigan State University
New College of Florida
Ohio Wesleyan University
Olin College
Pepperdine University
Purdue University – West Lafayette
Sarah Lawrence
Soka University of America
Stanford University
Stony Brook University
Swarthmore College
Tufts University
University of California – Irvine
University of California – Santa Barbara

Schools in a Suburb (cont.)

University of Maryland –
Baltimore County
University of Maryland –
College Park
University of Miami
University of North Carolina –
Chapel Hill
University of Notre Dame

University of Richmond
University of Rochester
Wake Forest University
Washington University – St.
Louis
Wellesley College
Wheaton College (MA)

Schools in a Small City

Bates College
Connecticut College
Cornell University
Franklin and Marshall College
Indiana University –
Bloomington
Ithaca College
Kalamazoo College
Knox College
Lafayette College
Lawrence University
Penn State
Purdue University – West
Lafayette
Rensselaer Polytechnic Institute
Rutgers University– New
Brunswick
Skidmore College
St. John's College – Annapolis

St. John's College – Santa Fe
Texas A&M University
University of California – Davis
Union College
University of Delaware
University of Florida
University of Georgia
University of Illinois
University of Iowa
University of Michigan
University of Vermont
University of Virginia
University of Wisconsin –
Madison
Vassar College
Wesleyan University
Wheaton College (IL)
Whitman College

Schools in a City

America University
Arizona State University
Barnard College
Boston University
Brigham Young University
Brown University
Carnegie Mellon University
Case Western Reserve University
Clark University
Colorado College
Columbia University
Cooper Union
Duke University
Emerson College
Emory University
Eugene Lang College at The New School
Florida State University
Fordham University
George Washington University
Georgetown University
Georgia Institute of Technology
Harvard University
Illinois Institute of Technology
Johns Hopkins University
Loyola University Chicago
Macalester College
Massachusetts Institute of Technology
Marquette University
New York University
Northeastern University
Northwestern University
Occidental College

Ohio State University
Pratt Institute
Reed College
Rhodes College
Rice University
Shimer College
Southern Methodist University
Syracuse University
Trinity College
Tulane University
University of California – Berkeley
University of California – San Diego
University of California – Santa Cruz
University of California – Los Angeles
University of Chicago
University of Colorado – Boulder
University of Minnesota – Twin Cities
University of New Mexico
University of Pennsylvania
University of Pittsburgh
University of Southern California
University of Texas – Austin
University of Washington
Vanderbilt University
Willamette University
Worcester Polytechnic Institute
Yale University
Yeshiva University

Chapter 6
Parts of the United States

The United States is a large country. In terms of land, we are the fourth largest country in the world, and in terms of population, we are third. This means that the United States offers a wide variety of climates and cultures, and some may be more suited to your preferences than others.

It would take you about five days to drive across the United States from east to west and about six hours by plane (it is actually closer to fly to London from the East Coast than to fly across the country from coast to coast). Going north to south is no short journey either and will require at least several days. The continental United States (every state except Alaska and Hawaii) contains four distinct time zones and six climate zones. Whether you want to live in tropical weather, have four seasons and snow, be near the ocean, the mountains, the desert, or where it rains all the time, there are options for you.

Culturally, you may decide you want to be in an area that has a well educated, sophisticated population or perhaps you would prefer to be in a more rural, working class community so you can enjoy the benefits of a slightly slower and less expensive pace of life that you may feel is more conducive to your studies. The first step is to get a handle on the major regions of the country so you can assess appropriately.

Keep in mind that the United States is divided into 50 distinct states. States range in size dramatically in terms of both area and population. Colorado, Texas, California, and other states especially in the Midwest and the western parts of the country are massive in size. In fact, they are bigger than many countries across the world in terms of area. Texas is just a bit bigger than France. California is a tad bit bigger than Germany. New Mexico is bigger than Italy. Each state has its own state government that regulates many of the laws within it. Many of these things won't matter to you much as a student, but policies related to financial assistance at public universities and driving laws may be different depending on the state you are in. Furthermore, the sports culture, religiousness, cuisine offerings, and political activism may range dramatically from one area to the next. Where you end up will have a huge impact on your experience so make sure you have a bit of an understanding of the stereotypes of each region.

The regional characteristics in the sections that follow are, to some degree, stereotypes. Keep in mind, though, that a stereotype is just a generalization. In a country of over 300 million people we have a lot of diversity, and you will find a mix of people everywhere. However, there are reasons why these stereotypes exist, and understanding them a bit will help you figure out where you'd like to be.

New England

When people imagine the American College, they often picture a school in New England. New England is home to many of the oldest colleges in the United States including Harvard, Yale, Dartmouth, and Brown, which were all founded in the 17th and 18th centuries. New England was one of the first settled parts of the country and remains an area greatly shaped by its history. New England has developed a reputation for very strong community life. The landscape is dotted with quaint towns with historic main streets, community events and festivals, and a large sense of local pride. New England is the most educated part of the country with the highest percentage of college grads of any other region. It is also one of the wealthiest regions. And while this is not true of every part of New England (especially the rural parts), both the average income and the cost of living throughout the region is substantially higher than in most other regions.

Notable Locations in New England

New England has a variety of urban, rural, and suburban options. Although the small towns are what many people associate with New England, many New Englanders also live near cities.

Boston. The largest city in New England is Boston (in the state of Massachusetts), which is home to 4.5 million people within its metro area. With over 100 colleges, Boston is also home to more colleges and universities than any other city in the world. The Boston area has over 250,000 college students studying within it at any given time making it a lively college community. Just a few of the colleges featured in this book in the Boston area include Harvard University, Massachusetts Institute of Technology (MIT), Brandeis University, Emerson College, Tufts University, Wellesley College, Olin College, Northeastern University, Boston College, and Boston University.

As one of the oldest cities in the country, the city of Boston itself is very dense and pedestrian-friendly. You can walk from Chinatown, to the high-end shopping neighborhood, to the North End (home to lots of great Italian restaurants), the Seaport (lots of seafood), across the Boston Common and the Public Gardens (a gorgeous public park in the middle of the city) in less than an hour. And if you don't want to walk, the public transportation system, comprised of a subway system ("The T"), bus routes, and commuter rail lines that serve the entire metro area, is excellent.

There is a ton to do especially for college students. Boston is known for its British-style pubs, lively theater, arts, and sports scene, and the city is located right on the ocean. You can take public transportation to the beach, but if you drive an hour out, you can be on Cape Cod or on the North Shore, where you can find some of the most highly sought after beaches in the country. The mountains of New Hampshire, Vermont, and Maine are only a couple of hours away by car, so skiing and hiking are very accessible. And, although Boston offers almost all the urban amenities one could want, for a bigger city experience, New York City is an easy weekend trip. It takes about four hours to get there by bus, which you can pick up in downtown Boston and take right into New York for $15 each way.

Other New England Small Cities and Towns. New England also has a number of classic New England towns that offer urban amenities within close proximity of the beautiful landscape the area provides. Hartford, Connecticut (Trinity College); New Haven, Connecticut (Yale University); Providence, Rhode Island (Brown University); Burlington, Vermont (University of Vermont); and Northampton, Massachusetts (Hampshire College, Mount Holyoke College, Smith College, University of Massachusetts – Amherst, and Amherst College) are just a few.

New England Climate

Some people love the climate in New England, and others can't imagine living with it (i.e., it is not for people that hate the cold). New England states offer a true four seasons, a distinct spring, summer, winter, and fall. Fall is the glory season in New England. There is no other part of the country that compares. New England is a lush region with lots of greenery and trees over the summer. Come fall, between September and November, the trees turn bright colors that make the landscape breathtaking. Tourists come from all over the country and the world to see it.

At college campuses, fall coincides with the start of the year, and students take advantage of the stunning landscape by spending lots of time outside. Although the weather starts to cool down, it is still nice enough to enjoy the outdoors although usually with a pumpkin spice latte (the most popular fall drink for many college students) and a scarf. The imagery associated with the American fall holidays, Halloween and Thanksgiving (in October and November respectively), comes straight out of New England. Pumpkins surround the landscape and also mean the emergence of pumpkin flavored ice cream and pumpkin pies. Apple orchards are at their peak, and apple cider, apple pie, and apple crisp are some of the other foods that emerge.

Winters are cold. Between December and March there is snow and lots of it. Often it lasts for three or four months straight. The snow is beautiful and allows for residents to partake in all sorts of winter sports like skiing and ice skating. However, it does mean that it is cold, and people tend to stay indoors much more during this time of year than at other parts.

From April to June the weather warms up, and the colleges become alive. This is the time of year where students, having been spending time indoors for months, come outside and fill the campus with as many outdoor activities as possible. Most schools host spring concerts or picnics. Professors occasionally hold class outside, students sitting in the grass. Summers though, if you decide to stick around, are hot and humid. Most days the temperature is nice enough that you can sit outside comfortably, but there are always a few days of summer (and some years several weeks) where the temperature hits about 90° Fahrenheit (32° Celsius), and people tend to stay inside with air conditioning.

The weather extremes New England offers provide endless variety, but if you are scared of the cold, or just plain dislike it, it might not be the best fit. While across a year you will have plenty of warm sunny days, if you hate the cold it will be hard to go through three to four months of it.

If you think you can handle that though, New England is a beautiful, historic, and culturally interesting region filled with tons of great colleges. It can be an ideal place to go to school.

States within New England

- Massachusetts
- New Hampshire
- Rhode Island
- Vermont
- Maine
- Connecticut

Schools in New England

Amherst College
Bates College
Bennington College
Boston College
Boston University
Bowdoin College
Brandeis University
Brown University
Clark University
Colby College
College of the Atlantic
College of the Holy Cross
Connecticut College
Dartmouth College
Emerson College
Hampshire College
Harvard University
Massachusetts Institute of Technology

Middlebury College
Mount Holyoke College
Northeastern University
Olin College
Smith College
Trinity College
Tufts University
University of Connecticut
University of Maine
University of Massachusetts – Amherst
University of New Hampshire
University of Vermont
Wellesley College
Wesleyan University
Wheaton College (MA)
Williams College
Worcester Polytechnic Institute
Yale University

The Mid-Atlantic

The Mid-Atlantic is located just south of New England along the eastern coast of the Atlantic Ocean. This portion of the country is one of the most densely populated and consists of a number of metropolitan areas including some major cities, including New York City, which is the largest city in the country; Washington DC, the nation's capital; the historic city of Philadelphia; and the cities of Pittsburgh and Baltimore.

As a whole, the Mid-Atlantic is one of the most affluent areas of the country. Maryland, one of the states in this region, is, in fact, the wealthiest state in the country in terms of per capita income, and every other state in the region is within the top 20 wealthiest states in the country by per capita income. As a whole, the Mid-Atlantic region tends to be moderately to highly educated with the urban areas and suburbs being the most highly educated.

Notable Locations in the Mid-Atlantic

New York. New York is the largest state in the Mid-Atlantic region in terms of both land and population. New York City, while the biggest city in the country with approximately 19 million people within the metropolitan area, only dominates a small portion of the state. To drive from one side of the state to the other would take approximately seven hours.

The northern and western parts of the state are largely rural and less affluent, although these portions are dotted with a handful of smaller cities. Many of these cities are past their prime. They were old industrial towns that largely have lost their industry. Buffalo, the biggest of these cities, has high rates of poverty today but still maintains a population of over a million people within the metropolitan area and has made efforts to revive and diversify its economy. Other smaller cities within New York include Albany, Rochester, Syracuse, Ithaca, Poughkeepsie, Utica, Binghamton, Niagara Falls, among others. These small cities and the regions in between are rich with colleges, many of which are over one hundred years old founded during the glory days of this part of the country.

While the cities they surround are not filled with the amenities of a booming metropolis, most still offer at least a couple of neighborhoods where students can find adequate shopping and some good restaurants offering both American and ethnic cuisine. The last time I was in Poughkeepsie, for example, I was surprised to find excellent Thai and Indian restaurants just a few blocks from Vassar College's campus given the city's lackluster reputation. There may not be a ton of options, but it isn't the middle of nowhere.

One of the best things about this part of the country is that northern and western New York are also filled with many natural gems including a large number of lakes, forest preserves, and gorges creating easy access to the outdoors for students.

The key thing to remember before I move on to the next section is that "New York" and "New York City" are not the same thing. A school in "New York" could be anywhere in the massive state. You might be hours and hours away from New York City, and there may be no way to get there without a car. The state of New York offers many great features besides the city such as fantastic forests, mountains, and waterways. However, if you want to be in New York City, be careful not to put schools on your list just because they are in the state of New York. If being in New York City is what you want, look for schools that are in "New York City" or schools that I've listed as being in a "suburb" that are in the state of New York. All of the schools that I've listed as suburban in the state of New York, such as Sarah Lawrence College (located in Bronxville, New York which is about twenty miles from New York City) are within a short drive or train ride of New York City. Every year, students arrive at schools in the rural parts of New York and are shocked because they thought they picked a school in the middle of the city so make sure you pay close attention to exactly where a school is.

New York City. New York City is home to a number of top colleges. As a city, New York offers incredible diversity, world-class arts, food, cultural venues, a phenomenal public transportation system, 24/7 activity, and everything one would expect from a major global city. It is also very expensive in just about every sphere, with the possible exception of some bargain shops and inexpensive eateries that may take some effort to find.

Considering the prices and the density of the city, students in New York, especially those that are in schools in Manhattan (which is the most expensive and dense section of the city), tend to live in tiny dorm rooms and apartments, often in small rooms shared with other students. But given the stuff to do out in the city at any hour of the day, most of them don't care.

If you are considering colleges in New York City, make sure you look up specifically where the college is. Schools in Manhattan include New York University, Columbia, and Eugene Lang, and these schools have the most urban atmospheres. But there are other schools like Pratt Institute and Fordham University that are technically in the city but are located in other boroughs. (New York City is made up of five administrative divisions, or boroughs – Manhattan, The Bronx, Brooklyn, Queens, and Staten Island – and each has its own character.) These schools may feel less like your impression of New York City immediately surrounding the campus since most movies about New York City are filmed in Manhattan, but they are easily accessible to Manhattan by public transportation.

New Jersey. New Jersey is the state located directly south of New York. The northern part of the state consists of small cities and suburbs that basically function as an extension of New York City. Students in these areas can easily take the bus or train into the city at any time. Piscataway/New Brunswick where Rutgers University is located and Princeton University in Princeton, New Jersey are both in this part of the state. Southern New Jersey serves an extension of the Philadelphia metropolitan region, providing access to another major urban area.

Pennsylvania. Pennsylvania is the second largest state within the Mid-Atlantic in terms of landmass. Although Philadelphia and Pittsburgh are major cities, much of the rest of the state is rural. Economically, Pennsylvania is the least wealthy state within the Mid-Atlantic. However, certain parts of the state, most notably Philadelphia, are prosperous. Philadelphia historically was one of the most important cities in the country, and today it still offers incredible historic sites, diverse food options, arts, culture, and nightlife. The University of Pennsylvania is located in the heart of Philadelphia and Swarthmore College, Haverford College, and Bryn Mawr College are all nearby.

Pittsburgh, the other major city in the state, is not as prosperous as Philadelphia but in recent years has begun a revival. The neighborhoods surrounding the University of Pittsburgh and Carnegie Mellon University are vibrant student communities and provide an urban university experience equal to that of schools in the major cities. Many colleges in the state tend to cluster near the Pittsburgh and Philadelphia metropolitan areas, but there are a few exceptions such as Penn State University, the flagship public university of the state, and Gettysburg College, which are located in more remote parts.

Maryland and Washington, DC. Maryland and Washington, DC ("DC") on the southern portion of the Mid-Atlantic, contain a dense corridor of colleges. A conglomeration of several major metropolitan areas (including DC itself, plus Baltimore and Maryland's capital, Annapolis), the area is densely populated and well educated.

DC, the nation's capital, is a diverse city filled with people from all around the country and the world, drawn to the area for its booming economy, government and public policy jobs, and the unparalleled political scene. The city itself is a popular college destination given its solid public transportation system, fantastic cuisine, diverse nightlife, and a huge number of museums (more than in any other US city), the majority of which are free. The opportunities to intern with think tanks, work at your country's embassy, or work for a non-profit or NGO are also plentiful. Georgetown University, George Washington University, and American University are located right within the city limits. The University of Maryland – College Park, University of Maryland – Baltimore County, Goucher College, and St. John's College – Annapolis are also within driving distance.

Mid-Atlantic Climate

The weather in the northern portion of the Mid-Atlantic (New York and northern Pennsylvania) is similar to New England, with four seasons and a fair amount of snow (northwest New York near Buffalo actually gets some of the highest snowfall in the country).

The southern part of the Mid-Atlantic in DC and Maryland is slightly warmer in the winter, and while it usually does snow, it usually only happens a few times a year and doesn't last more than a few days. Spring starts earlier (usually in March) but by mid-summer it gets really hot and humid. DC is scorching hot and humid in August to the point that it is frequently uncomfortable to be outside during the middle of the day. Most schools won't start until the end of August or early September, so you may miss the worst part of summer if you go home or get an internship elsewhere during the summer. And even if you decide to stick around, every building is air-conditioned so if you stay indoors, you will be perfectly comfortable. By fall, it cools down again and the weather stays pleasant typically until late November or even early December.

States within the Mid-Atlantic:

- New York
- New Jersey
- Delaware
- Pennsylvania
- Maryland
- Washington DC (technically a district, not a state)

Schools in the Mid-Atlantic

American University
Bard College
Barnard College
Bryn Mawr College
Bucknell University
Carnegie Mellon University
Colgate University
Columbia University
Cooper Union
Cornell University
Dickinson College
Eugene Lang College at The New School
Fordham University
Franklin and Marshall College
George Washington University
Georgetown University
Gettysburg College
Goucher College
Hamilton College
Haverford College
Hobart and William Smith Colleges
Ithaca College
Johns Hopkins University
Lafayette College
Lehigh University

New York University
Penn State University
Pratt Institute
Princeton University
Rensselaer Polytechnic Institute
Rutgers University – New Brunswick
Sarah Lawrence College
Skidmore College
St. John's College – Annapolis
St. Lawrence University
St. Mary's College of Maryland
Stony Brook University
Swarthmore College
Syracuse University
Union College
University of Delaware
University of Maryland – Baltimore County
University of Maryland – College Park
University of Pennsylvania
University of Pittsburgh
University of Rochester
Vassar College
Yeshiva University

The South

The South refers to the area in the southeastern and central southern portion of the United States. This region has perhaps one of the most distinctive cultures within the country consisting of one of the widest ranges of dialects and a distinctive cuisine (traditionally including fried chicken and fried just about anything, barbeque, greens, sweet potato and pecan pie, cornbread, grits, and many other foods we often call "comfort foods").

Although there are a number of large metropolitan areas within the South, the identity of the region is often associated with its rural character. Historically, this was the part of the country that was largely agricultural. The cities developed much later than in New England and the Mid-Atlantic and are therefore considerably more spread out and sprawling. They were designed with cars in mind. They are less pedestrian-friendly, and while most of the larger ones do offer some sort of bus system in the prime areas, the vast majority of people get around by car.

Overall, economically the South is less affluent than New England and the Mid-Atlantic. The four poorest states in the country are in this region. These four states are also some of the least educated states in the country and none of them contain any colleges featured in this book so we won't dwell on them.

That said, there are some parts of the South with strong industry and some of the nation's finest colleges, as well as pockets with highly educated and sophisticated populations. Richmond, Virginia and Chapel Hill, North Carolina are some examples, and both are fantastic and walkable college towns within the South.

Notable Locations in the South

Atlanta. With over 5 million people within the metropolitan area, Atlanta (in the state of Georgia) is a major city with booming industry and a very diverse and international population.

As is characteristic of most southern cities, it is relatively spread out, but it does have better public transportation than most cities in the region and a couple of pedestrian friendly neighborhoods within the urban core. Still, most people in Atlanta own cars or find ways to be transported in them. Atlanta, besides being the location of Emory University and Georgia Institute of Technology, is known for its nightlife and music scene and great food (including both southern cuisine and ethnic options). The city also is home to some great museums including the world's largest aquarium.

Nashville. Nashville (located in the state of Tennessee), home to Vanderbilt College, is a city of just under two million people nationally famous for its live music scene. Downtown Nashville is filled with live music venues that bring in some of the best-known national musicians, many of whom live in Nashville (the country music industry is based in Nashville).

New Orleans. New Orleans (located in the state of Louisiana), home to Tulane University, is often referred to as the most unique city in the United States. New Orleans historically was located in a territory controlled by the French, and so it developed its own unique culture. The quaint French Quarter looks like it comes straight out of Europe. Little balconies on ornate homes look down on packed streets filled with tourists and locals who at all hours of the day are enjoying the city's famed nightlife, including world famous Dixieland jazz, and restaurant scene, known for its distinctive and fabulous food.

Miami. Miami (located in the state of Florida), home to the University of Miami, is known for its gorgeous beaches, vibrant nightlife, shopping, strong Latin American influence (you hear lots of Spanish everywhere in this city), and its tropical climate.

Texas. Texas is a massive state on the US-Mexico border that stands out from the rest of the South due to its size and history. Texas, for a short period of time in history, was actually its own country, and some residents would still like it to secede from the rest of the USA. Texans typically have a deep sense of Texas pride over their unique culture that has developed from its independent history.

The stereotype of Texas is that everything is big there. The same stores that exist everywhere else in the country – supermarkets, chain restaurants, clothing stores, and the like – but in Texas they are built in buildings twice as big. Restaurants are massive. Food portions are massive. Private homes are massive. Even the cars are massive. The landscape itself, which is mostly flat and relatively dry (so there isn't a huge density of trees), feels massive because from most places you can see for miles in any direction.

Texans also cherish and uphold the image of the cowboy as a part of their past. A lot of people really still do wear cowboy boots and cowboy hats in their everyday life. There are rodeos even today that you can go and watch. In keeping with that theme, steak and steakhouses are very popular.

Football is also a huge part of the Texas culture. High school football games are a social activity for many small Texas towns. College teams are even more important. People follow the scores of local college games even if they are not in any way affiliated with the college.

Perhaps this description of Texas sounds one-dimensional, but the state actually has a lot of diversity. The big Texas cities like Dallas, Fort Worth, Austin, Houston, and San Antonio all actually have large international populations and the diverse culture that comes with them. Given that Texas sits right on the border with Mexico, Mexico especially has a very strong influence. In some neighborhoods, you hear Spanish more than English.

In the past couple of decades, a number of major companies have moved into Texas given the state's favorable laws towards business, and, as a result people from all over the country and the world have flocked to the state, increasing diversity further. Texas cities are growing in population faster than in almost any other region. The people coming in bring a diversity of values and perspectives. Though Texans love their culture, in these cities with large "transplant" populations many still appreciate ethnic food, an active arts scene, and exposure to the other cultures that have migrated to the area.

As far as college towns are concerned, one should keep in mind that in Texas, sprawl is even more extreme than in other parts of the South. It was not a state designed with walking in mind. Many students at Texas universities have cars or make sure to have friends with cars. It is a part of the culture. There are a few exceptions such as the city of Austin.

Austin. The city of Austin (with a population just under 2 million in the metropolitan area and the state's capitol), is probably the most walkable city in the state and a fantastic college town. The city is home to the University of Texas – Austin, the state's flagship state university campus, which is located right downtown. Students can walk to restaurants, bars, cafes, bookstores, live music venues and anything a student could need. Austin's downtown is offbeat, quirky, and known to be the place where all the Texas misfits congregate. It has a unique character that appeals to college students because of its independent streak.

Austin is also known as a national tech hub, an area that draws entrepreneurs from around the country and fosters start-ups (Dell is perhaps the most well-known tech company based in Austin). For college students interested in being a part of the tech culture, there is constant activity on that front. Music, film, and art are also plentiful in Austin and probably best showcased during Austin's annual South by Southwest festival of music, film, and interactive art, which draws an audience of about 20,000 people from all over the country to Austin each spring.

Climate in the South

Weather in the South varies due to the large size of the area it covers. However, in general, weather in the South is much warmer than in New England and the Mid-Atlantic year-round. In the northern portion of this region (northern Virginia), the weather is comparable to Maryland and DC, but in southern Virginia, the Carolinas, and down to Georgia, the weather gets considerably warmer. The summers are hot and humid but the fall and spring are long with comfortable temperatures. Winters do get cold enough to require a jacket, but temperatures are not usually below freezing during the day. Most winters will have a couple of sprinklings of snow, but it is usually not much more than that, and it melts quickly.

Further south in Florida and Texas, the weather is even warmer. Southern Florida is in the tropical zone, and the weather there stays warm all year. Even in January, the coldest month of the year, the average temperature in southern Florida is 74° Fahrenheit (23° Celsius) during the day and 62° Fahrenheit (17° Celsius) at night. Texas is drier than in Florida and not tropical but the weather is still warm year-round and in most parts, snow comes not much more than once or twice every decade.

States within the South

- Virginia
- West Virginia
- North Carolina
- South Carolina
- Georgia
- Florida
- Louisiana
- Arkansas
- Mississippi
- Oklahoma
- Texas
- Kentucky
- Tennessee
- Alabama

Schools in the South

Centre College
Clemson University
College of William and Mary
Davidson College
Duke University
Emory University
Florida State University
Furman University
Georgia Institute of Technology
Hendrix College
New College of Florida
Rhodes College
Rice University
Sewanee: The University of the South

Southern Methodist University
Texas A&M University
Tulane University
University of Texas – Austin
University of Florida
University of Georgia
University of Miami
University of North Carolina – Chapel Hill
University of Richmond
University of Virginia
Vanderbilt University
Virginia Polytechnic Institute
Wake Forest University
Washington and Lee University

The West

The western portion of the United States is known for its large landmass filled with true wilderness – this is the area of the country that has huge expanses of land that is still untouched. The southwest (which includes the states of Utah, New Mexico, Arizona) is filled with massive deserts, vibrant colors created when the sun hits the brown landscape (creating epic sunsets), and a Native American influence.

Further north, while still drier than the East, the landscape becomes wet enough for evergreen and Aspen forests along the Rocky Mountains, the nation's largest mountain range. Colorado, Utah, and parts of Wyoming and Idaho are known to offer some of the best skiing in the country. Hiking, mountain biking, whitewater rafting, and other mountain sports are a huge draw to the area bringing in thousands of tourists from across the country and the world and playing a large part of the appeal to many local residents as well.

Some of the colleges within this region are located in small towns right on the edge of the wilderness, providing students with unparalleled access to outdoor recreation. Others are located within booming college towns and cities.

Urban areas in this part of the country vary from cities like Phoenix in Arizona that are mostly sprawling and car-dependent to others like Boulder in Colorado that offer a slightly denser urban experience.

Notable Locations in the West

Boulder. Boulder, Colorado is considered to be one of the best college towns in the country. Located right at the edge of the Rocky Mountains and filled with a huge number of parks and forested land open to the public for recreation, it is a small city of approximately 300,000 within the metro area, but it is centered around a lively downtown with the first pedestrian-only mall in the United States.

This central corridor in downtown Boulder is comprised of a cobblestone street filled with restaurants with outdoor seating, lively coffee shops, bars, and retail stores and is always packed with street musicians and artists. Down the street, you'll find a park through which flows the Boulder Creek that hosts a massive weekly farmer's market. It is also in this spot that walking and biking trails that span the city create easy access for people to come to the city center without a car (there is also a very good bus system).

The University of Colorado – Boulder is the flagship state school and fits seamlessly into the city's downtown. Students are a huge part of the local culture of activism. Boulder is also located within a 45-minute drive of Denver, the biggest city in the state of Colorado with a metropolitan area of 2.5 million offering the artistic and cultural opportunities of a large city and access to one of the biggest airports in the country – making the region easily accessible to other parts of the country and the world. Colorado School of Mines is located just a short drive from both of these cities as well.

Santa Fe. Santa Fe is another gem, this one hidden within the hills of New Mexico. This small city is home to the tiny Saint John's College – Santa Fe campus, and students enjoy rolling hills filled with evergreen forests leading down to one of the oldest cities in America originally settled by the Spanish and still filled with Spanish architecture different from what you'd see anywhere else in the country. The town is known for its stunning crafts, jewelry, and a nationally-recognized arts scene (Santa Fe has more art galleries per capita than in any other city in the country). The University of New Mexico is located just 45 minutes away from Santa Fe (accessible by car or train) in the larger city of Albuquerque.

Climate in the West

The weather in the West varies significant place to place due to the landmass it covers and the varying elevations of different regions. Arizona is the furthest state to the south and has a true desert climate with dry air, sunny days, and hot temperatures year-round. In the city of Phoenix (where Arizona State University is located), for example, the average high in the heart of winter is 67° Fahrenheit (19.5° Celsius) but in July, the warmest month of the year, the average high is a striking 106.1 degrees (41.2 degrees Celsius). The elevations in most of Colorado and New Mexico make them cooler. They too are known for clear sunny skies, but temperatures do get cooler in the winter although the sun helps people not feel the cold as much during the daytime. In Denver, Boulder, Santa Fe and Albuquerque, snow falls during winter but the sun usually melts it within a day. That said, mountain towns tend to be at higher elevations and are therefore cooler in winter; in these parts, the snowfall is high and sticks through the season (which supports the skiing industry). Summers throughout this region are warm and sunny allowing residents to fully enjoy summer recreational activities such as whitewater rafting, hiking, rock climbing, and mountain biking.

States within the West:

- Utah
- New Mexico
- Colorado
- Nevada
- Idaho
- Montana
- Arizona
- Wyoming

Schools in the West

Arizona State University
Brigham Young University
Colorado College
Colorado School of Mines

St. John's College – Santa Fe
University of Colorado – Boulder
University of New Mexico

The Pacific Coast

The Pacific Coast is comprised of the states that sit along the Pacific Ocean. This includes California, the largest state in this region by area and population, and Oregon and Washington to the north. In terms of affluence, these states are comparable to New England and the Mid-Atlantic. The cost of living on the Pacific Coast (especially California) is higher than in most parts of the country but there is a strong economy filled with lots of highly ambitious, talented, and well-educated people. This also means there is a concentration of universities.

Compared to New England and the Mid-Atlantic, the Pacific Northwest is known for its more "laid back" mentality, a slightly slower paced and relaxed lifestyle. Although people do work very hard, there is an emphasis on taking time to pursue outdoor activities like surfing (especially popular in southern California), hiking, and skiing.

California

California's Mediterranean-like climate allows it to be a major center of agricultural production. The produce grown in California make it unparalleled throughout the country, and thus the state is known for its high quality of food (and food-conscious culture). Avocados, grapes, artichokes, strawberries, arugula, broccoli, carrots, cherries, and garlic are just a few examples of some of the foods grown throughout the state that are abundantly available. The wine regions of Sonoma and Napa counties are internationally recognized as producing some of the best wine in the world.

If California were a country, it would be the seventh richest country in the world. Southern California surrounding Los Angeles, the nation's second largest city, is the center of the national entertainment industry (film, television, and video games). Northern California, San Francisco and Silicon Valley, is the tech hub of the country housing thousands of small tech start-ups as well as the tech giants like Google, Facebook, Yahoo, HP, Apple, and more. The economy, natural assets of the state, and proximity to Asia have attracted a large number of immigrants over the years. Today, it is one of the most diverse states in the country. There is a sizable population of immigrants from Japan, Korea, China, India, Vietnam, and the Philippines. The proximity to Mexico also means there is a fair amount of Latin American influence, especially in the southern part of the state. This has had a large impact on the cuisine and ethnic food is particularly appreciated.

Southern California. Los Angeles and San Diego are located in the southern part of California. Both cities are known for their sprawl, and both rely on car transportation given the lack of a comprehensive public transportation system. There are a couple of neighborhoods that are a bit more pedestrian-friendly including Los Angeles' Westwood neighborhood (where UCLA – the University of California, Los Angeles – is based), but they are few and far between. Still, both cities provide students with close access to the outdoors, plenty of opportunities for internships, and are known for having "perfect" weather year-round (it doesn't get cold, but it also rarely gets uncomfortably hot). Many colleges in this book are in Southern California including the Claremont Colleges (Scripps, Pomona, Harvey Mudd, Pitzer, and Claremont McKenna), Occidental College, the University of California – Los Angeles and the University of California – San Diego, just to name a few.

Northern California. San Francisco, and the surrounding Bay Area including Palo Alto (home to Stanford) and Berkeley (home to the University of California, Berkeley) – consistently ranks as one of the best places for young people in the country in national surveys. The city of San Francisco itself is set on stunning hills packed with quaint and historic homes overlooking the San Francisco Bay and Golden Gate Bridge. This city is a true exception to the lack of density and walkability in many of the country's southern and western cities. It feels as dense as the cities of the Northeast and has a pretty reliable public transportation system made up of streetcars and BART, the metro system. There is also a commuter rail system that will take people from Palo Alto where Stanford University is located (about a 45 minute journey) and other regions right into the heart of the city.

San Francisco has some incredible neighborhoods including a phenomenal Chinatown, North Beach (the city's Little Italy), Russian Hill filled with stunning houses and views of the Bay, the Mission (some of the city's best restaurants), among many others each with unique character. Across the Bay from San Francisco, it is a short drive to Berkeley, where the University of California, Berkeley is located. Berkeley also retains an urban and pedestrian-oriented culture and is known for its countercultural vibe, great food, and the great quantity of political activists and artists who roam the streets of the downtown right at the entrance to the university.

Oregon and Washington

The northern part of the Pacific Coast, Oregon and Washington, are known for their incredibly lush landscapes, almost constant misty rain (which happens most days of the year), the stunning ice-capped Olympic Mountains, and an eco-conscious, techie culture. Home to temperate rainforests, a rugged coastline, and hundreds of islands, the coasts of Washington and Oregon are stunningly beautiful and offer a number of recreational opportunities.

The cities of Portland in Oregon and Seattle in Washington are also a major draw to the area.

Seattle. Seattle is a nationally recognized tech hub and the area houses the headquarters for Amazon, Microsoft, and Boeing. Seattle, where the University of Washington (the state's flagship university) is located, is known for its outstanding coffee and quirky coffee shops, high quality ethnic food (like California, this area has attracted a number of immigrants from Asia), and its music scene that has been the birthplace of many national rock and alternative rock bands (perhaps most famously Nirvana in the early 90s). Seattle is a city with a young vibe, and it attracts a lot of college students and students right out of college, especially those interested in high tech, music, and the outdoors.

Portland. Portland, where Reed College is located, is a slightly smaller city than Seattle but attracts a similar crowd of techie, smart, and artistically-oriented hipsters. It too attracts plenty of college-aged students and recent graduates who are stereotyped to spend lots of time hanging out at local coffee shops and pubs that serve local craft beers.

Climate on the Pacific Coast

Due to the large size of the Pacific Coast, there is huge diversity when it comes to climate. However, none of the major cities in this region get regular snow. Most of southern California is sunny and warm (but rarely hot) all year long. The last time the city of Los Angeles even got a sprinkling of snow was in 1962. If you hate the cold weather but also don't like extreme hot, Los Angeles and San Diego are great places to be.

Weather in northern California is unusually unpredictable but mild. The saying, "If you don't like the weather, just wait a few minutes" may well have originated around the San Francisco

Bay. The region is susceptible to a large number of micro-climates where it can be raining in one place and not raining just down the street. In general, however, the weather in the largely populated parts of northern California is not one of extremes. The temperature doesn't vary much regardless of the time of year; it does not snow, but it also doesn't get very hot. In San Francisco, the average high in January (the coldest month of the year) is 57° Fahrenheit (14° Celsius) and in September (the warmest month of the year) is just 70° Fahrenheit (21° Celsius). Nights in San Francisco proper tend to be slightly cool year-round even when the day is relatively warm so residents usually bring a light jacket with them regardless of the time of year. Snow, if you want it, is easy to get to on a weekend trip. It is about a 3-hour drive to Lake Tahoe, one of the most popular skiing destinations in the country.

Both Portland and Seattle have wet climates and during about eight months of the year are known to be both misty and grey, as the sky is almost always covered with a thick layer of clouds. Still, it is rare even in the heart of winter that the temperature goes below freezing (except on the mountains), so as long as you have a light waterproof jacket, you shouldn't get too cold. The sun comes out in summer, and the rain lessens to some degree. This is a short period of the year, but it is glorious. The temperature is warm enough to be comfortable but rarely hot, and the clearer skies allow for stunning mountain and water views from many parts.

States on the Pacific Coast

- California
- Oregon
- Washington

Schools on the Pacific Coast

California Institute of Technology
Claremont McKenna College
Deep Springs College
Harvey Mudd College
Occidental College
Pepperdine University
Pitzer College
Pomona College
Reed College
Scripps College
Soka University of America
Stanford University
Thomas Aquinas College
University of California – Berkeley
University of California – San Diego
University of California – Davis
University of California – Irvine
University of California – Santa Barbara
University of California – Santa Cruz
University of California – Los Angeles
University of Southern California
University of Washington
Whitman College
Willamette University

The Midwest

The Midwest consists of the middle portion of the country starting just west of New York and Pennsylvania and ending at the Rockies to the west. This area, characterized by large, expansive, flat and fertile plains (although there are some pockets of hills here and there), is the agricultural heart of the USA. The area is also characterized by the Great Lakes, five massive lakes located within the northern portion of the Midwest each larger than many states, and is home to phenomenal sand dunes, beaches, and harbors.

When many people think of the Midwest, they think of small town America. While not highly prosperous, the smaller towns they imagine are filled with friendly and approachable residents, many of whom are actively involved with their churches and communities. To an extent, there is some truth to this stereotype, but there are also some very urban and cosmopolitan parts of the Midwest (as well as a few bustling and rather sophisticated small cities and towns).

Chicago. The city of Chicago is the largest city in the Midwest and the third largest city in the country with 9.5 million residents within the metropolitan area. Chicago is home to a number of colleges and universities including the University of Chicago, Northwestern University, Loyola University Chicago, Illinois Institute of Technology, Shimer College, among many others located within the metropolitan area. If you like New York City, Chicago is probably the closest other city in terms of feel. For this reason, many people refer to Chicago as "The Second City" (and, indeed, until the 1980s when it was overtaken by Los Angeles, it was the second largest city in the country). Chicago is famous for its architecturally stunning skyscrapers, distinctive cuisine (known for its diversity of ethnic options, innovative chefs, and local favorites like Chicago pizza and hot dogs), music scene (especially jazz and blues), and diverse, ground-breaking theater and arts in general.

The city has an extensive public transportation network, and it is easy to get by without a car. One of the most remarkable parts of Chicago is its waterfront along Lake Michigan, one of the Great Lakes. Chicago is set along 18 miles of the lake, and the lakefront is filled with parks, soccer fields, tennis courts, waterfront snack bars, a bike path, and stunning (as well as free) sandy beaches.

Madison. Other cities in the Midwest include the college town of Madison, the state capital of Wisconsin, and home to the University of Wisconsin – Madison. The downtown area of the state's flagship school is a lively and pedestrian-friendly, filled with shops and restaurants and within close proximity of three small lakes, giving residents great recreational opportunities.

Minneapolis-St. Paul. Minneapolis-St. Paul, known as the "Twin Cities," are two adjacent cities in the state of Minnesota representing a metropolitan area of approximately 3.5 million people. Macalester College is located in St. Paul and the University of Minnesota – Twin Cities is in Minneapolis. Carleton College and St. Olaf College are about a 40-minute drive from the cities in the quaint and bustling little town of Northfield. Both Minneapolis and St. Paul are known for a strong arts scene, the Mall of America (the largest shopping mall in the country and the most visited mall in the world), and very cold winters (but both cities have developed infrastructure to make them livable). The cities are also filled with several dozen small lakes surrounded by parks (the state of Minnesota has over 10,000 lakes).

Detroit and Ann Arbor. Detroit, in the state of Michigan, was once considered a major city and was home to the country's automotive industry. Today, the city is economically depressed and largely abandoned. Much of it feels post-apocalyptic, with completely abandoned streets of Victorian houses. That said, some of the suburban areas surrounding the city continue to thrive, and there are some great colleges within the area. Ann Arbor, a small city of its own just half an hour from Detroit, is perhaps one of the nicest college towns in the country. Home to the University of Michigan, the state's flagship school, the town houses over 43,000 students. While the downtown area is relatively small, the main streets have a feeling of an urban cosmopolitan city with trendy bars, diverse restaurants, and charming coffee shops surrounded by neighborhoods of unique and historic houses.

Other Notable Midwestern College Towns. Other cities of note in the Midwest include St. Louis, a historic city on the Mississippi River known for good music and food and home to Washington University in St. Louis. In addition, Milwaukee in Wisconsin; Cleveland, Toledo, and Columbus in Ohio; and Indianapolis in Indiana, are mid-sized cities with urban amenities and several colleges.

Climate in the Midwest

The weather in the Midwest is comparable to the weather in New England with four distinct seasons including a cold and snowy winter lasting three to four months, warm summers, and a beautiful fall season with crisp air and colorful foliage.

States within the Midwest

- Michigan
- Ohio
- Indiana
- Illinois
- Wisconsin
- Minnesota
- Kansas
- Missouri
- Iowa
- North Dakota
- South Dakota

Schools in the Midwest

Beloit College
Carleton College
Case Western Reserve University
Denison University
DePauw University
Grinnell College
Illinois Institute of Technology
Indiana University – Bloomington
Kenyon College
Knox College
Lawrence University
Loyola University Chicago
Macalester College
Marquette University
Michigan State University
Northwestern University
Oberlin College
Ohio State University
Ohio Wesleyan University
Purdue University – West Lafayette
Shimer College
St. Olaf College
University of Chicago
University of Illinois
University of Iowa
University of Michigan
University of Minnesota – Twin Cities
University of Notre Dame
University of Wisconsin – Madison
Wabash College
Washington University – St. Louis
Wheaton College (IL)

College Match Profile: Region

Different regions have unique cultures and climates. Select which of the regions you are comfortable with from the options below:

New England
Mid-Atlantic
The South
The West
Pacific Northwest
Midwest

Preferred Region (New England, Mid-Atlantic, The South, The West, Pacific Northwest, or Midwest):

_____

Fill in your preference(s) in the College Match Profile Chart in Chapter 17 (page 270) to reveal your College Match Profile. If you're still not sure of your preference, take the "Not Sure?" quiz on the next page, and then come back to fill in the blank.

NOT SURE?

If you are not sure what region to pick, consider the following questions:

1) What kind of weather do you prefer?

    a) I don't mind dealing with snow and cold for a few months of the year. I like the idea of living in a place that has four distinct seasons. I appreciate variety.
    b) As long as it is sunny most days, I don't care much about how cold it is.
    c) It is okay if it is a little cool, but if it is snowing it is generally too cold for me. And I don't like it when it gets too hot. I prefer climates that stay comfortable for most of the year.
    d) If it snows once or twice a year I can deal with it, but generally I prefer things to be warmer. Hot summers are fine by me.

2) What do you like to do during a free weekend?

    a) Walk around and explore a new neighborhood/city
    b) Go hiking, skiing, or something outdoorsy
    c) Do something artistic/cultural in a big city
    d) Go to the beach
    e) Stay on campus and relax

3) Do you prefer historic buildings or more modern architecture?

    a) I like the look of historic towns. They are more beautiful than newer areas and tend to be friendlier to pedestrians.
    b) I prefer when everything is new and modern. Newer areas are designed with cars in mind, so it is easier to park. Plus, newer buildings tend to have more modern amenities.
    c) I like the option of seeing some historic buildings since they are pretty, but it is nice when there are also lots of newer buildings mixed in. These jumbled towns and cities may look inconsistent, but I like the variety.

NOT SURE? (cont.)

4) How do you feel about hills?

    a) I prefer to be somewhere flat because it is easier to walk and bike.

    b) I like the look and feel of hilly places even if it means walking up and down hills.

    c) I like the idea of being near mountains because I like participating in outdoor activities that require hills and mountains (hiking, skiing, mountain biking).

5) I see myself as...

    a) Pretty laid back and relaxed... I don't usually get stressed out

    b) Very ambitious. I like to be around other people who are always thinking about who they are and where they want to go in life

    c) Serious about school but not at the expense of an active social life.

Below is the list of all of the regions: Give yourself a check mark next to each of the areas as you go through each question based on the instructions below the list.

New England:
Mid-Atlantic:
The South:
The West:
Pacific Coast:
Midwest:

Question 1: If you chose A, give yourself a check next to **New England**, the **Mid-Atlantic,** and the **Midwest**. If you chose B, check off the **West**. If you chose C, give yourself a check for the **Pacific Coast**. For D, check off the **South**.

Question 2: If you chose A, give yourself a check for **New England** and the **Mid-Atlantic**. If you chose B, check off the **Pacific Coast** and the **West**. If you chose C, check off **New England**, the **Mid-Atlantic**, the **Pacific Coast**, and the **Midwest**. If you chose D, check off the **South** and the **Pacific Coast**. If you chose E, check off the **South**, the **West**, and the **Midwest**.

NOT SURE? (cont.)

Question 3: If you chose A, check off **New England**, the **Mid-Atlantic**, and the **South**. If you chose B, check off the **West** and the **Pacific Coast**. If you chose C, check off the **Midwest** and the **South**.

Question 4: If you chose A, check off the **Midwest**. If you chose B, check off the **South**, **Mid-Atlantic**, **New England**, **Pacific Coast**, and the **West**. If you chose C, check off the **West**, **Pacific Coast**, and **New England**.

Question 5: If you chose A, check off the **Pacific Coast** and the **West**. If you chose B, check off **New England** and the **Mid-Atlantic**. If you chose C, check off the **South** and **Midwest**.

Count up your check marks from the list on the previous page. The region with the most check marks is your best match region. I recommend you consider your top couple of regions, since most people find they could be happy in several parts of the country.

Input the regions you would consider into the College Match Profile Chart in Chapter 17 (page 270) to reveal your College Match Profile.

Chapter 7
Picking the Right Size School

The size of the school you choose will affect a number of factors in your college experience. Size affects who you know on campus, the sense of community, the amount of gossip, and the type of social atmosphere. Size also affects the amount of social gathering space, the number of social offerings, the diversity of extracurricular activities, and the amount of classes and majors available. Larger schools tend to have the most options because they have the students to support more options. Small schools, on the other hand, may have fewer options but have the tightest communities.

It can be hard to get a real sense for your size preferences without visiting schools and trying to see what sizes feel right, but we will cover the different reactions students commonly have to different-sized schools in this chapter, and at the very least this should give you an idea about the kinds of feelings and experiences you can expect at differently sized colleges.

You can also use the size of your high school as a frame of reference; however, keep in mind that colleges will have many more buildings than a high school even if they are the same size. Since unlike the vast majority of high schools, colleges house students and have libraries, fully-equipped labs, athletic facilities, and separate academic departments, often each in its own building, most college campuses will be at least twice as big in terms of physical space as an equivalently sized high school.

Very Small Schools

The smallest college I'm aware of, and the smallest college featured in this book, is Deep Springs College, an alternative two-year college in rural California with a total of 26 students. With this sort of size, every student is out of necessity going to get to know every other student very well. I classify schools with under 1,250 students as **very small**. The means that each **class** – the students in each year (e.g. everyone graduating in 2020 would be the "Class of 2020") – would have approximately 300 students or fewer. At this size or smaller, chances are that by the end of one's four years you will know everyone's name. The advantage is that this often means that there is a strong sense of campus community and class cohesion. The down side is that it is nearly impossible to escape people you don't like and don't want to see constantly – nor can you expect to discover new friends on a regular basis, or change your group of friends drastically. And whether these things matter to you or not, if you choose to go to a very small school, you should be aware that these environments can often mean that everyone knows your business (i.e., there will be lots of gossip). This can be a good or a bad thing, depending on what your business is, of course, and how you like to lead your life.

Very Small Schools

Bennington College (688)
California Institute of Technology (997)
College of the Atlantic (330)
Cooper Union (880)
Deep Springs College (26)
Harvey Mudd College (783)
Haverford College (1,205)
New College of Florida (832)
Olin College (355)
Pitzer College (1,084)
Sarah Lawrence College (1,235)
Scripps College (945)
Shimer College (140)
Soka University of America (140)
St. John's College – Annapolis (475)
St. John's College – Santa Fe (375)
Thomas Aquinas College (370)
Wabash College (906)

Small Schools

Schools with over 1,250 students but no more than 4,000 are classified as **small** schools. These are schools that are just large enough where you might not know everyone's name within your class, but between you and your friends you collectively know or at least recognize the majority of students. Gossip still exists but not to the same extent as at very small schools.

The other main advantage of this kind of school is that awards are a bit less competitive than at larger schools. By graduation, many colleges will recognize students with the best final paper or thesis in each given field. Regardless of the size school you choose, there will be one captain of each sports team, one president of each club, and one student selected each year from the college to attend an inter-collegiate conference. Smaller schools may offer slightly fewer opportunities than larger schools in numbers, but because the ratio of students to opportunities per student is higher, the number of awards and recognitions granted per student is often higher at smaller institutions.

Small Schools

Amherst College (1,817)
Bard College (2,051)
Barnard College (2,504)
Bates College (1,753)
Beloit College (1,359)
Bowdoin College (1,839)
Brandeis University (3,588)
Bryn Mawr College (1,322)
Bucknell University (3,536)
Carleton College (2,055)
Centre College (1,344)
Claremont McKenna College (1,264)
Clark University (2,352)
Colby College (1,863)
Colgate University (2,871)
College of the Holy Cross (2,926)
Colorado College (2,008)
Connecticut College (1,926)

Davidson College (1,790)
Denison University (2,336)
DePauw University (2,336)
Dickinson College (2,386)
Emerson College (3,675)
Eugene Lang College at The New School (1,511)
Franklin and Marshall College (2,365)
Furman University (2,753)
Gettysburg College (2,597)
Goucher College (1,484)
Grinnell College (1,674)
Hamilton College (1,884)
Hampshire College (1,461)
Hendrix College (1,373)
Hobart and William Smith Colleges (2,292)

Small Schools (cont.)

Illinois Institute of Technology (2,800)
Kalamazoo College (1,379)
Kenyon College (1,667)
Knox College (1,430)
Lafayette College (2,488)
Lawrence University (1,525)
Macalester College (2,070)
Middlebury College (2,526)
Mount Holyoke College (2,322)
Oberlin College (2,930)
Occidental College (2,176)
Ohio Wesleyan University (1,821)
Pepperdine University (3,488)
Pomona College (1,607)
Pratt Institute (2,076)
Reed College (1,492)
Rhodes College (1,915)
Rice University (2,848)
Sewanee: The University of the South (1,478)
Skidmore College (2,660)

Smith College (2,664)
St. Lawrence University (2,398)
St. Mary's College of Maryland (1,901)
St. Olaf College (3,176)
Swarthmore College (1,552)
Trinity College (2,301)
Union College (2,241)
University of Richmond (3,074)
Vassar College (2,406)
Washington and Lee University (1,838)
Wellesley College (2,481)
Wesleyan University (2,940)
Wheaton College (IL) (2,508)
Wheaton College (MA) (1,616)
Whitman College (1,539)
Willamette University (2,103)
Williams College (2,052)
Worcester Polytechnic Institute (3,952)
Yeshiva University (2,869)

Medium-Sized Schools

Medium-sized schools have between 4,000 and 10,000 undergraduate students. These schools are just large enough that they lose the tight sense of cohesive community that both very small and small schools have (and correspondingly the gossip that goes with it), but they do not feel anonymous. If you walk across the campus between classes, chances are you will pass by someone you know and a handful of people you recognize, but most of the people you pass will be strangers.

There are pros and cons to this size. It is big enough that you will need to make an active effort to form a social community. If you don't try to make friends, you can easily get lost in the masses (whereas at a small school, you have to try very hard not to be noticed). But most people who make at least some effort will find fast friends in their dorm, in class, or in their extracurricular activities where they spend most of their time.

And once you do find a social group (or several), you'll form your own small community. But if you have a falling out with that community, there is a big enough pond to choose from that you can probably move to the other side of campus, find a new group, and never have to see your original group again. Hopefully that will not happen to you, but these schools are big enough that if need be, you can carve out a new identity, and other than pass members of your former life occasionally as you walk to class, you'll leave your past mostly behind you.

Medium-Sized Schools

American University (7,299)
Boston College (9,110)
Brown University (6,435)
Carnegie Mellon University (6,279)
Case Western Reserve University (4,386)
College of William and Mary (6,171)
Colorado School of Mines (4,169)
Columbia University (6,068)
Dartmouth College (4,193)
Duke University (6,655)
Emory University (7,656)
Fordham University (8,325)
Georgetown University (7,552)
Harvard University (6,658)
Ithaca College (6,281)
Johns Hopkins University (6,153)
Lehigh University (4,883)
Loyola University Chicago (9,723)
Marquette University (8,293)

Massachusetts Institute of Technology (4,503)
Northwestern University (8,600)
Princeton University (5,336)
Rensselaer Polytechnic Institute (5,394)
Southern Methodist University (6,249)
Stanford University (7,063)
Tufts University (5,255)
Tulane University (8,423)
University of Chicago (5,590)
University of Maine (8,778)
University of Notre Dame (8,475)
University of Pennsylvania (9,682)
University of Rochester (5,785)
Vanderbilt University (2,406)
Wake Forest University (4,815)
Washington University – St. Louis (7,259)
Yale University (5,405)

Large Schools

The more students you have, the more classes your school can support. **Large schools,** which have over 10,000 students, usually offer more majors, have greater breadth of departments, and offer more extracurricular options than smaller schools. Some large schools are massive – Arizona State, the largest school in the country – has over 58,000 undergraduates and offers over 250 majors and over 1,000 student clubs and organizations.

Some students find medium-sized schools and larger schools overwhelming. But keep in mind that there are some schools in this group that make an effort to create small communities within the larger context of the school. Universities that offer a School of Engineering, School of Nursing, School of Business, etc., which students are assigned to based on their major, can sometimes offer tight communities within these larger schools if they are run well. Similarly, schools with a strong residential system may create smaller communities within individual dorms or themed houses.

According to fans of large schools, the biggest pro is probably the number of opportunities a huge school supports. Large schools will support not only more classes and majors but more niche extracurricular activities, more study abroad programs, more "neighborhoods" on campus, and more potential friends to choose from. A lot of people find all these options really exciting; others find the amount of choice paralyzing and somewhat divisive since two students who meet randomly may have almost no common experiences. At the end of four years, you perhaps meet someone that lived on the opposite side of campus (where you maybe have never even been), studied entirely in a different school that you know nothing about, and participated in extracurricular activities you haven't even heard of. Going to a large university like this is kind of like living in a city. You will get to know your neighbors and your colleagues (i.e., your classmates in your department or your peers in your extracurricular activities), but most people will always be strangers to each other and anonymous in the eyes of the larger school community.

That is not to say that there won't be a few things that the majority of the campus feels tied to (especially at state schools, football often draws the campus together). On a personal level, however, anyone considering one of these large schools should consider that it is going to be very difficult to get to know the majority of people on the campus or even the majority of activities and programs the university offers. As with very small schools, this can be an advantage or a disadvantage, depending on who you are and what you want from your college experience.

Large Schools

Arizona State University (59,382)
Boston University (18,306)
Brigham Young University (31,060)
Clemson University (16,562)
Cornell University (14,261)
Florida State University (32,171)
George Washington University (10,464)
Georgia Institute of Technology (14,527)
Indiana University – Bloomington (32,371)
Michigan State University (37,454)
New York University (22,948)
Northeastern University (13107)
Ohio State University (43,058)
Penn State University (39,192)
Purdue University – West Lafayette College (30,147)
Rutgers University – New Brunswick (31,499)
Stony Brook University (16,003)
Syracuse University (14,798)
Texas A&M University (40,103)
University of California – Berkeley (25,774)

University of California – San Diego (22,676)
University of California – Davis (25,759)
University of California – Irvine (22,216)
University of California – Santa Barbara (18,977)
University of California–Santa Cruz (15,978)
University of California – Los Angeles (25,774)
University of Colorado – Boulder (25,805)
University of Connecticut (17,528)
University of Delaware (17,427)
University of Florida (32,776)
University of Georgia (26,259)
University of Illinois (32,281)
University of Iowa (21,999)
University of Massachusetts – Amherst (21,928)
University of Maryland – Baltimore County (10,953)
University of Maryland – College Park (26,487)
University of Miami (10,590)
University of Michigan (27,979)

Large Schools (cont.)

University of Minnesota – Twin Cities (34,469)

University of New Hampshire (12,811)

University of New Mexico (22,773)

University of North Carolina – Chapel Hill (18,503)

University of Pittsburgh (18,429)

University of Southern California (18,311)

University of Texas – Austin (39,955)

University of Vermont (11,211)

University of Virginia (15,822)

University of Wisconsin – Madison (28,933)

Virginia Polytechnic Institute (23,859)

College Match Profile: School Size

You will want to figure which of the following size types you are most comfortable with:

Very Small (up to 1,250 students)
Small (1,250-4,000 students)
Medium (4,000-10,000 students)
Large (over 10,000 students)

Preferred School Size (very small, small, medium, or large):

_____

Fill in your preference(s) on the College Match Profile Chart in Chapter 17 (page 270) to reveal your College Match Profile. If you're still not sure of your preference, take the "Not Sure?" quiz on the next page, and then come back to fill in the blank.

NOT SURE?

If you are not sure exactly which category best describes you, consider the following questions:

1) When I think of college, I...

   a) Imagine being part of a tight community where everyone knows each other, and though some people may be closer to each other than others, in general our whole class feels like a group of friends.
   b) Think it would be great to know the names of everyone in my class, but I'd still like to have a smaller social group that does its own thing.
   c) Don't want to know everyone in my class – I want to always have the opportunity to meet new people. However, it would be nice to see people I know as I walk to class.
   d) Don't want to know everyone in my class. I will hang out with my friends when I want to, but in general, I'd like to be able to walk through the middle of campus and feel relatively anonymous.

2) How do you feel about gossip?

   a) Gossip makes life exciting.
   b) I don't mind a little bit of gossip as long as it is done in moderation.
   c) Gossip can sometimes get out of control, so I think it is important that if things get out of hand, you can remove yourself from the situation.
   d) I strongly dislike environments where there is a lot of gossip.

3) When it comes to physical space...

   a) I think it would be great if most of the students hung out in the same couple of central locations... it would create a stronger sense of community.
   b) I prefer that there are at least a handful of different places I can eat and study. A little variety is good, but too much variety would be overwhelming and make me feel disconnected.
   c) I want to go to school where I don't get bored with the food options or choices for where I study or hang out. I don't want to stick to the same routine all the time – I like to change things up.

NOT SURE? (cont.)

d) I want to go to a school where I know I will never go inside all of the campus buildings. Every day, I will have the option of seeing or doing something completely new which will keep things exciting.

4) How do you feel about choice in what you study and do with your free time?

a) Quality over quantity. You can only take 30-40 courses in college anyway, so whether my college offers 80 or 8000 courses doesn't really matter to me. If the professors are good and focused on teaching me, that is really what matters.

b) I want to be able to choose my major based on my interests and pursue extracurricular activities that fit my personality. But I don't need 50 singing groups or six different women's soccer teams. A couple of good singing ensembles and an intramural and varsity soccer team is enough choice for me. Too many choices, and the community starts to feel divided.

c) I prefer an environment where I have lots of choices in terms of what I study and what extracurricular activities I pursue.

d) It would be cool to meet people who study things I haven't even heard or are in clubs I didn't even know the school had. Endless options and diversity make life exciting.

If you picked mostly A choices, look for a **very small school**.

If you picked mostly B choices, look for **small school** choices.

Mostly C options means you may be best suited for **medium-sized schools.**

If you had mostly D choices, choose a **large school.**

Your answers may have been mixed between categories – it is okay to consider several sized options if you have several you think could be good fits for you.

Fill in your preferences on the College Match Profile Chart in Chapter 17 (page 270) to reveal your College Match Profile.

Chapter 8
Academic Philosophies

There are a variety of reasons students choose to go to college. For some, it is the logical next step that will lead them to their careers. Others believe that there is a base of knowledge they want to build that they feel will help them in whatever career they choose. And some are looking to figure out their interests – they see college as a time of academic exploration.

You may have any one or a combination of these orientations. And depending on how you feel about this topic, some schools might suit you better than others. I will elaborate on the different types of academic philosophies that are common across the institutions featured in this book; however, I first would like to clarify something I think is of particular importance to note for international students.

In many countries, students are required from the time they are in their teens or even younger to pick a track to study. You are deemed, for example, to be good at the natural sciences and then are put on a science and math track in high school where you take the majority of subjects in this field. It is presumed that you will then specialize more by choosing biology, chemistry, physics, pre-med, or something similar when you get to college. Eventually you will graduate with a specialization that will land you a job in a related field.

This is the way education happens in most of the world, and thus it is understandable why so many students tell me "I want to be a doctor and therefore want to study pre-med." This is a **pre-professional approach** to education, and it is not entirely absent from the US educational system either. While we do not typically offer specialized tracks in high schools (with a few exceptions), there are colleges and universities that will offer, for example, a pre-med major for students who want to be doctors where the majority of students intend on becoming either doctors or nurses.

However, what often comes as a surprise to many international students is that, actually, in the United States, lots of students go onto medical school having studied English or philosophy or other seemingly unrelated subjects as their major. In fact, at most of the top universities in this country, pre-professional degrees like "pre-med" and "pre-law" are not even offered as majors. There will likely be related topics like "biology" and "political science" which many students will choose if they want to go into medicine or law respectively, but even with these options, students are still encouraged to study other fields during their undergraduate years.

Medical schools have entrance requirements so that students take some biology, chemistry and related topics before entering medical school, but at many American universities, you only need to take a fraction of courses in your field in order to major in that topic, or to go on to study that subject in a professional school. So if you want to study something like theater because you love it and then go to medical school, it is possible. At most schools, you will be able not only to fill the requirements for a theater degree but also leave room in your schedule to complete all of the prerequisites for gaining admission to medical school or law school or business school or whatever it is you want to do after graduation.

Similarly, many companies will hire students with majors that are not related to what the company does or even what its employees need to know. I knew people that got hired at Google doing computer programming who majored in philosophy (usually with some computer science courses here and there within their schedule) and chemistry majors who got a job in management consulting with major firms. What is especially surprising to many international students is that many graduate schools and companies actually view studying something different than the obvious choice to be an advantage. They often like that you can bring a unique perspective to the table and know that skills can be taught more easily than unique perspectives. Above all, they value the ability to think critically and communicate, both trademarks of a good liberal arts education.

Imagine you are applying to medical school as someone that majored in theater. You are asked to write an essay about how your undergraduate education prepared you for medical school. Your peers that majored in pre-med or biology talk about the rigor of their classes and some of the medical procedures they learned about that they found fascinating. Some of these essays will be thoughtful and interesting and some of these students will be admitted. You, however, write an essay about how your acting classes have helped you learn to interact with different types of people and make you comfortable being around people from all sorts of backgrounds. You have still taken all of the prerequisites in biology, chemistry, and physics required in the application process, and you have earned good grades. They know you are academically capable of succeeding in their program. But what you offer that some of the biology students don't is a perspective that may allow you to be a great doctor. Your success as a theater major perhaps will translate into a superb bedside manner, a personal quality medical schools really care about.

Now you could also decide that you really want to major in biology. And that is also a fine choice that could get you into medical school or serve you well elsewhere in life. But even if you do pick that major at a US college, you will have some option to take classes in other fields. In fact, on average, classes devoted to your major only take up about one third to one half of your total coursework. If you want to take some theater classes, Spanish, or history as well as other types of science classes, those can be a part of your education as well.

A lot of students find this idea of taking classes outside their field of focus freeing. You are not necessarily stuck in one specific thing nor do you have to study exactly the thing you want to do for the rest of your life. And if you don't know what you want to do after college, that is also okay. Many students use college as a time of academic exploration, and in a lot of fields employers and professional schools embrace students who pursued a broad education.

There are a few exceptions to this. Most notably, students who want to be engineers tend to need to major in some form of engineering as undergraduates. There are a few programs that allow students who studied an unrelated field to begin an engineering program after college but this is one field that tends to favor students that start early. Nevertheless, even in engineering programs, students are typically given enough room in their schedules, and may even be required, to take some classes in other fields.

While some schools or programs may have a more pre-professional focus than others, at the end of the day, the majority of colleges in this country and all of the schools featured in this book have been influenced by the tradition of **liberal arts**. If I were to try to define liberal arts specifically, a lot of people would criticize my definition. Lots of colleges advertise that they offer "a true liberal arts education," and they all mean different things. It is a term that is not entirely agreed upon. However, the common thread of every liberal arts model I've seen is that it is an approach to education that results in students being exposed to more fields than those directly related to their major.

The way that students allocate time in college between a major, university requirements, and electives (classes that students choose) is determined by the school's academic philosophy. Finding a school that has a compatible academic philosophy with your own philosophy is probably one of the most important factors to consider when choosing a college. Regardless of which school you attend, you will be required to take a certain number of courses or earn a certain number of credits or credit hours. The distinction between whether your school counts courses or credits/credit hours is pretty trivial – it is really just a system of counting. What matters more is the subject matter that fills the time you spend in the classroom. What percentage of time do you spend studying your major? How much is spent taking on requirements necessary to graduate? How much can be spent taking electives? These ratios can vary significantly by school.

There is more to consider than the requirements for your prospective major and the prerequisites necessary to get into graduate school or get a specific job. Think about the kind of education you want and who you want to be surrounded by. Do you believe that there is a core set of classes every student should take in order to graduate from college? Or do you think that education is best when it is self-directed, and students only take classes they want to be in? Do you think that there are certain types of areas (e.g., quantitative-based and writing-intensive classes) every student should gain exposure to but no specific class that students should have to take in order to get an education in these areas? Do you want to be around students who are very focused on their field of study, or do you prefer to be around people who take classes in a wide variety of areas? You may be fine with several of these models. But many students are not, and one of the most helpful things you can do in choosing a school is to know which of these models make sense for you.

Columbia University, for example, requires its students to take a set of specific core classes in order to graduate. For many students, this is one of the main ways Columbia stands out from its peer institutions that have looser requirements. Most students who choose schools with core curriculums say that they appreciated the solid educational foundation these curriculums provide and like the fact that a consistent core provides a connection between all the students on campus, all of whom participate in the same program (regardless of their major). However, every so often I run into Columbia students who picked Columbia because they wanted to go to an Ivy League school in New York City (Columbia also stands out from other Ivy League schools because of its location), and they tell me that they did not enjoy the core requirements and found them to be a drag, taking up their time from classes in the fields they most wanted to study. You get from your education what you want to get. If you don't value the subject matter your school wants you to study, then you are probably better off finding a school that has a different system of requirements or a school that requires students to take subjects only in the fields you care about.

There are as many academic philosophies as there are colleges. I've never seen two schools with exactly the same system. And over time, schools will modify their own philosophies. It is usually an ongoing debate on any given campus as students, teachers, and administrators all weigh in on how to structure the best education. Because of this diversity, it is difficult to just say there are four different academic philosophies. But looking across the board, I do notice that most colleges tend to have philosophies that fall into one of four genres: open curriculum, distribution requirements, loose core, and core curriculum.

Open Curriculum

The first kind of curriculum we will discuss is the **open curriculum**. Open curriculums are the rarest of the four curriculum types but perhaps the easiest understand. Just like the name suggests, the open curriculum has the fewest requirements of all four types. Other than the requirements for one's major, meeting a basic number of total classes, passing those classes with adequate grades, and in some cases taking one course designated as writing-intensive (a requirement a couple of schools with otherwise open curriculums have), there are **no requirements**.

Students who prefer this model feel that they don't want to take any classes or study any fields that they don't want to study. They don't want to take classes in areas that they aren't interested in, and sometimes more importantly, don't want to be in classes with peers that are not interested in the subject matter. They believe that education is most effective when students are in every class they take by choice. Of course, you may still have some requirements within the context of your major. If you get a degree in English, the department may say you need to take one class on Shakespeare and one class on 20th century literature, and a total of 12 classes in all. However, the college will not tell you that all students need to take a math and science class in order to graduate.

Students at these kinds of schools need to be very self-directed to get the most out of them. It can be easy to only take classes in things that you are good at or things that you already know interest you. If you want to stretch yourself academically, discover new interests, and build new skills, that responsibility is on you.

Contrary to what you may expect, most of the schools offering open curriculums are some of the most well regarded schools in the country. The schools that have adopted this system put tremendous trust in their students to make good academic decisions for themselves. Many of these schools report that most of their students end up taking a wide variety of courses despite the fact that there are no requirements to do so, but the point is that it is up to you how you want to design your education.

Along with schools with an open curriculum system, I have also included in this category several schools that do not have any university-wide requirements but may have departmental requirements. What I mean by this is that there is no one set of subjects or classes that every student in the university must take, but if you enroll in, say, the School of Engineering, that school may have specific requirements even outside of your major. For instance, you may have to take two humanities courses and two social sciences courses in addition to your engineering work. At the same university, however, students enrolled in another school like the School of Architecture may not have any requirements outside of those required by their major. There are only a few colleges that have this system. On the following list, the University of Michigan, Lehigh University, and Carnegie Mellon University are the only schools with this departmentally determined system. For these schools, you will want to check the website of the specific school or department you are interested in to see if there are any general education requirements that must be taken outside of your primary field of study in order to graduate.

Schools with an Open Curriculum

Amherst College
Bennington College
Brown University
Carnegie Mellon University
Grinnell College
Hamilton College
Hampshire College
Hobart and William Smith
Colleges

Lehigh University
New College of Florida
Sarah Lawrence College
Smith College
University of Michigan
University of Rochester
Vassar College
Wesleyan College

Distribution Requirements

The second type of academic system we will talk about is the system of **distribution requirements**. This term refers to schools with course requirements designed to ensure that all students are exposed to a handful of different disciplines before graduation but still give students a huge amount of freedom in determining the classes they take.

A distribution requirement system divides a university's full course catalogue into usually three to six different broad categories such as "social sciences," "quantitative reasoning," "humanities," etc. Students are required to take a certain number of courses in each of these categories before graduation. The majority of the classes in the catalogue get a categorization, so at a medium-sized or large school you may have literally hundreds of options you could choose from in order to fulfill any particular requirement. If you don't want to take calculus to fill your quantitative reasoning requirement, you could probably take statistics or probability or sometimes even astronomy to fulfill that requirement. Similarly, if you don't want to take chemistry, physics, or biology you might be able to take a course on ecology, psychology, or geology to fulfill your science requirement. You have a lot of flexibility but will end up with some exposure to fields outside of your major by the time you graduate.

Schools with Distribution Requirements

Beloit College
Boston University
Bowdoin College
Bryn Mawr College
Colby College
College of the Holy Cross
College of William and Mary
Cornell University
DePauw University
Dickinson College
Florida State University
Franklin and Marshall College
Haverford College
Johns Hopkins University
Kalamazoo College
Kenyon College
Michigan State University
Middlebury College
Mount Holyoke College
Northwestern College
Oberlin College
Occidental College
Penn State University
Pitzer College
Pomona College

Princeton University
Rensselaer Polytechnic Institute
Rice University
Sewanee: The University of the South
Skidmore College
St. Lawrence University
Swarthmore College
Tufts University
University of California – Los Angeles
University of Florida
University of Massachusetts – Amherst
University of Maryland – College Park
University of Richmond
University of Virginia
University of Washington
University of Wisconsin – Madison
Wellesley College
Williams College
Worcester Polytechnic Institute
Yale University

Loose Core

The third type of curriculum, the **loose core**, is similar to the distribution requirements system but slightly more specific in laying out requirements. As with the distribution requirement curriculum, schools with a loose core ensure that all students graduate having taken courses in a range of disciplines. Also like the distribution requirement system, schools with a loose core do not require students to take any one specific course to graduate. However, the loose core system is a bit more narrowed down than distribution requirements. While schools with distribution requirements may tell you that you need to take two or three courses in three or six big, broad categories, schools with a loose core will delineate approximately seven to nine specific categories and tell you that you need to take one course in each one.

So, for example, whereas a school with a system of distribution requirements might have a category titled "Social Sciences," and you could take any anthropology, history, political science, or economics class to fulfill it, a loose core system may have a category called "US History and America's Role in the World," and you would need to select a designated course specifically related to that more defined topic.

Where this gets really tricky is that a lot of schools have hybrid curriculum types. There are some schools that have a system of distribution requirements (say they have five broad categories, and you need to take two courses in each), but they also have one or two additional categories that are more specific and similar to a loose core system. So, in addition to meeting the distribution requirements, you also are required to take one class in perhaps religion (from a list of five options) and one writing course (from a list of 20 thematic sections you can choose from). This kind of hybrid system is quite common, and I've classified any curriculum with a mix of multiple components as the type of the most restrictive requirement. So, in the case of the example above, the school would be designated as a loose core because there are some courses you need to take in more narrowed down categories, and you only have a handful of choices to choose from rather than a large chunk of the whole course catalogue.

In recent years, the loose core curriculum has become the most common curriculum type. Schools that in the past had distribution requirement systems have added narrowed down categories as new fields emerge that they deem important for students to understand. One of the most common additions you see added to curriculums every year is a requirement in taking some course about other cultures (some schools require both a western cultures and non-western cultures course), foreign language, and cultural identity. As the world becomes more globalized, this area is now considered to be vitally important, and many schools are making it a requirement for students to take at least one class in these areas prior to graduation.

While writing courses have been a core part of many colleges' curriculums for a long time, creating new writing seminars as a requirement for all students has been another common addition to curriculums at many schools. Many people consider writing to be one of the most essential skills one develops in college, and it is a skill that matters in almost any field. Because of this, many schools have developed introductory writing seminars required for all freshmen. Some schools will allow students to place out of these courses by taking a placement test or by receiving a certain score on the SAT or ACT, but at other schools, these kind of seminars are a must for every student regardless of prior writing experience.

If a school does have a writing requirement, look carefully at the specifics. Sometimes, like at Washington University – St. Louis and the University of Delaware, the freshman course is a specific course where everyone covers exactly the same material. However, the emerging trend has been to give students a choice of at least 10-20 themes so that you are studying a field that interests you while learning about writing. So, for instance, you could take "Writing about Psychology Research" or "Writing about Drama" and learn about something that fascinates you while mastering the fundamentals of academic writing.

Overall, the advantage of the loose core system is that it ensures that you are exposed to a wide variety of areas and develop a select group of specific types of skills, but it does not dictate exact courses you need to take. A loose core may require you to choose a course from as few as three and as many as fifty or more courses in a select group of fields, but you will not have to take one specific course (other than in some cases a writing course) if you don't want to.

Schools with a Loose Core

American University
Arizona State University
Bard College
Barnard College
Bates College
Boston College
Brandeis University
Bucknell University
Carleton College
Case Western Reserve University
Centre College
Claremont McKenna College
Clark University
Clemson University
Colgate College
Connecticut College
Davidson College
Denison University
Duke University
Emory University
Eugene Lang at The New School
Furman University
George Washington University
Georgetown University
Gettysburg College
Goucher College
Harvard University
Illinois Institute of Technology
Indiana University – Bloomington
Ithaca College
Knox College
Lafayette College
Loyola University Chicago
Macalester College
Marquette University
New York University
Northeastern University
Ohio State University
Ohio Wesleyan University
Purdue University – West Lafayette College
Rhodes College
Rutgers University – New Brunswick
Southern Methodist University

St. Mary's College of Maryland
St. Olaf College
Stanford University
Stony Brook University
Syracuse University
Texas A&M University
Trinity College
Tulane University
University of California – Berkeley
University of California – San Diego
University of California – Davis
University of California – Irvine
University of California – Santa Barbara
University of California – Santa Cruz
Union College
University of Colorado – Boulder
University of Connecticut
University of Delaware
University of Georgia
University of Illinois
University of Iowa
University of Maine
University of Maryland – Baltimore County
University of Maryland – College Park
University of Miami
University of Minnesota – Twin Cities
University of New Hampshire
University of New Mexico
University of North Carolina – Chapel Hill
University of Notre Dame
University of Pennsylvania
University of Pittsburgh
University of Southern California
University of Texas – Austin
University of Vermont
Vanderbilt University
Virginia Polytechnic Institute
Wake Forest University

Schools with a Loose Core (cont.)

Washington and Lee University
Washington University – St.
Louis

Wheaton College (IL)
Wheaton College (MA)
Willamette University

Core Curriculum

A **core curriculum** is when a college says specifically, "In order for you to be an educated person, you need to take these specific classes." It is not to say that the school doesn't allow students to take electives (although several core curriculum schools do not) or that the school doesn't have other requirements as well for specific majors or programs. The key is that all students will have specific common ground on which they all stand by the time they graduate.

Depending on the school, this common curriculum might mean that all students have read some of the same literature. Or perhaps they have learned the same writing techniques. Or they studied the same religion. Perhaps they all had to take linear algebra. If you choose a school with a core curriculum, it will be more important than at anywhere else that you look over the requirements and make sure that you are interested (or at least willing to study) the subject matter. At these kinds of schools, you cannot graduate without doing so.

Again, what distinguishes core curriculum schools from other models is that all students take some mandatory classes. Some of the schools I've identified as having a core curriculum may actually only require that you take one specific course and the rest of your requirements are distribution requirements. For example, at Whitman College, every entering freshman takes General Studies 145 & 146. This is a two-semester class that introduces students to the liberal arts by examining an interdisciplinary topic that varies each year. The course is an opportunity for students to learn about college writing, gain exposure to a wide variety of disciplines, and bond with their classmates. After this course, the rest of the graduation requirements are quite broad, but this kind of defined academic experience is enough to classify the college as having a core curriculum.

Columbia University is an example of a school with a core curriculum that has a moderate set of requirements. At Columbia, students take a mostly humanities-based set of six specific courses taught in seminar-style classes. In addition to taking these specific six courses, Columbia students still need to pass a science, foreign language, physical education, and global core requirement that they can satisfy by taking one of many courses.

On the extreme end, you have St. Johns College, a school with campuses in both Annapolis, Maryland and Santa Fe, New Mexico. St. Johns has a different type of core curriculum where almost every class students take before graduation is part of the core (there are only a couple of elective classes). St. Johns teaches the western canon from Homer to the great works of the 20th century. The philosophy of the school is that these works build off of one another, and students should be exposed to all of them.

Also included on the list of core curriculum schools below are a few schools that upon first examination may actually look more similar to loose core systems. The University of Chicago, for example, is one of the few schools I've designated as having a core curriculum that does not actually have one specific course that everyone shares. While the vast majority of colleges with a core do have at least one specific course every school takes, a few schools on this list have a philosophical orientation about creating a cohesive academic experience for all students without requiring all students take exactly the same class. Both the Humanities and Social Sciences Sequence of The Core at The University of Chicago offer students several course options, but across all options there is substantial thematic overlap and certain readings appear across course offerings. By strict definition, I would have classified the University of Chicago as a loose core as there is no specific course everyone takes, but in practice, students at Chicago have enough overlap in their coursework to create the type of community a core curriculum offers.

Moreover, the students, faculty, and administration all pride themselves on this "Core." For all these reasons, I've classified the University of Chicago (and a couple of other similar models) as core curriculum schools.

The key benefit of all of the schools I have classified as having core curriculums is the sense of community fostered when everyone shares some common background. Plus, many students find it a comfort to know that regardless of their choices, there will be some cohesiveness to their education. Someone else has done the legwork and said, "This is what you should take to get a good education," and then you as the student just need to focus on doing the work.

There are several schools that I have not classified as having core curriculums that you may want to look into as well if a core curriculum appeals to you. Some colleges that have other academic philosophies offer specialized programs that students can opt into if they want to have a core curriculum experience. 10% of Yale's freshman class, for instance, chooses to take part in its Directed Studies program, a core curriculum equivalent. Stanford offers a similar program called Structured Liberal Education (SLE), Boston University has an optional Core Curriculum, and St. Olaf College offers The Great Conversation program. Because these programs are optional, these schools do not gain the benefits that come from having everyone in their class share the same educational foundation, but they do provide a structured liberal arts curriculum to students that are looking for that kind of experience.

Schools with a Core Curriculum

Brigham Young University
California Institute of Technology
College of the Atlantic
Colorado College
Colorado School of Mines
Columbia University
Cooper Union
Deep Springs College
Duke University
Fordham University
Georgia Institute of Technology
Harvey Mudd College
Hendrix College
Lawrence University
Massachusetts Institute of Technology
Olin College
Pepperdine University
Pratt Institute
Reed College
Scripps College
Shimer College
Soka University of America
St. John's College – Annapolis
St. John's College – Santa Fe
Thomas Aquinas College
University of Chicago
Wabash College
Whitman College
Yeshiva University

After reviewing these different types, many students will find that they have a strong preference for one curriculum over another. I have encountered many students who after considering the different types feel completely set on an open curriculum or who decide that the only type of school they want is a school with a core curriculum. Others gravitate to the types in between, the loose core and distribution requirement systems, because they ensure well-rounded educations but provide some flexibility.

Regardless of the type you prefer, I highly encourage you to do some additional research on the curricula of the specific schools that end up on your college list. The difference between two schools even within the same category can be extreme. While both Harvey Mudd and Columbia University have core requirements, Harvey Mudd's core courses are focused primarily on math and science whereas Columbia's strength is in its humanities core courses. Similarly, whereas both Brown and Hampshire College have open curriculums of sorts, Hampshire requires each student to develop his or her own educational plan based on his or her particular academic goals and have this plan reviewed in a formal process, whereas Brown allows students to pick classes without this type of oversight.

These categories are a useful way to understand the conceptual framework of a curriculum, but once you are in the process of actually ranking your preferences on your college list, I recommend visiting each college's website for the specifics of their academic plan. Usually, if you google the college's name followed by the words "core requirements," "general education requirements," or "graduation requirements," you will find this information.

College Match Profile: Curriculum Type

Select which of the curriculum types you would consider:

Open Curriculum – A type of curriculum where colleges do not require students to take any classes outside of the requirements for their major.

Distribution Requirements – A curricular system that divides the course catalogue into three to six broad categories and requires students to take a specific number of courses from each category to graduate.

Loose Core Curriculum – A type of curriculum where students take courses from a set of specific categories in order to graduate but that requires no specific courses.

Core Curriculum – A curricular model based on the philosophy that every student at a college should take a common set of classes.

Preferred Curriculum Type (Open Curriculum, Distribution Requirements, Loose Core Curriculum, or Core Curriculum):

_____

Fill in your preference(s) on the College Match Profile Chart in Chapter 17 (page 270) to reveal your College Match Profile. If you're still not sure of your preference, take the "Not Sure?" quiz on the next page, and then come back to fill in the blank.

NOT SURE?

If you don't have an inclination right off the bat, try answering these questions to reveal your preference:

1) Which best describes you:

   a) I trust my own judgment, and I believe I should be responsible for taking control of my own education.
   b) In general, I think I make good decisions for myself in terms of navigating my education, but I appreciate mentors, advisors, and some guidance as I choose my courses and make academic decisions.
   c) I like the idea of being exposed to all sorts of different fields, but I don't want to get stuck in a class on a subject I hate.
   d) I get overwhelmed when I have to make too many choices. I would take comfort in the fact that my school was telling me to take certain courses so I wouldn't graduate with holes in my education.

2) If given the choice, you would prefer:

   a) To miss out on studying some important fields in order to take more classes in the things I know I'm really excited about.
   b) To have too many options rather than too few choices when it comes to choosing classes in the liberal arts.
   c) To always have more than one course option (and preferably at least a handful of options) when it comes to fulfilling requirements but not so many options that it reduces the value of my education. I want to make sure I graduate feeling like I've learned a little about a lot of things including the things the college thinks are important for me to know.
   d) To take one or two classes I might not end up liking rather than only take classes that I know I will love. If the college thinks certain subject matter is important to learn, it is worth studying it even if it isn't my favorite subject. College is a time to try new things, and you shouldn't knock a field until you at least give it a try.

NOT SURE? (cont.)

3) Which of the following statements best describes your feelings about a cohesive academic community?

   a) I'm not really sure what that means.
   b) I think it is important that students at least have some idea of what is going on at their college/university outside of their particular department.
   c) I want to be in classes with lots of students who major in different areas.
   d) I think there are certain things every student should learn while in college, and I think that it would be cool to have some common education with all of my peers.

If you selected two or more A choices, you are best suited for an **open curriculum**.

If you selected two or more B choices, look for a school with **distribution requirements**.

If you picked two or more C choices, a **loose core curriculum** is for you.

And if you chose two or more D options, look for schools with a **core curriculum**.

If your answers are split between multiple options, you may be open to several different categories so include whichever curriculum types you would like to consider in your College Match Profile.

Fill in your preference(s) on the College Match Profile Chart in Chapter 17 (page 270) to reveal your full College Match Profile.

Chapter 9
Residential Systems

You are going to end up living at college for at least four years, so while housing may seem like a trivial part of the decision, it is actually a factor that has a huge impact on your college experience. Where you live will dramatically affect your life, influencing how much time you spend on campus, who your friends are, where you study, where you sleep, how you eat, and, ultimately, how and where you spend most of those four years. Colleges have wildly different perspectives on residential life, and these could have a real impact on you, so this aspect of a school is just as important to consider as all of the other categories we've discussed.

On-Campus Housing

First, let's talk about what options exist. When most people imagine a college in the United States, they imagine a **traditional dorm**. A traditional dorm is a university-owned building designated for students' living quarters. Most colleges have some traditional dorms on their campus.

The exact policies of dorms can vary. Sometimes dorms are just for first-year students. Some dorms might be single sex and others co-ed. Some might be mixed class, which means they house students in different years of study rather than just freshmen or upperclassmen, others are substance free (no alcohol allowed), and others are designated as quiet dorms (no parties). Dorm buildings sometimes just contain student rooms, but most of the time there will be some common facilities such as lounges where students can socialize and watch TV and common kitchens that students can use if they want to cook. Sometimes, dorms are even connected to dining halls and cafeterias.

At most of the colleges profiled in this book, freshmen are highly encouraged or required to live on campus. If this is the case, incoming freshmen are most commonly assigned to a dorm randomly. Within these dorms, the majority of freshmen will be assigned at least one roommate who will share a bedroom with them. Usually, the roommate will also be a freshman and sometimes the whole dorm will be freshmen, but depending on the school and specific policies, students may be placed in a mixed-class building or floor.

The stereotypical freshman room consists of a small single room with two beds, two desks, and two closets or dressers. Many times, students will share a common bathroom with other students on their floor (a few schools are fortunate enough to have a bathroom for each room but this is a rarity).

Colleges usually try to make an effort to pair people with roommates with whom they will be compatible. Most colleges will have you fill out a questionnaire after you accept a college's offer of admission asking you to explain your sleeping and study habits, your degree of organization, and whether you prefer to be in a loud or quiet dorm. With this information, you will be assigned a roommate. Of course, when you are living in these kind of tight living quarters, sometimes rooming situations don't work out, and most colleges will consider moving your room if it does become a problem.

Occasionally, schools offer freshmen the option of living in singles. A single is a (usually very small) private room. If you are assigned a single, you will not have a roommate although it is still likely that you will share a bathroom with other students. There are many students who actually really don't want a single because they think having a roommate is part of the "college experience," so sometimes singles are not as difficult to get as students think. However, if you are going to request a single consider the fact that a lot of social life in college and especially during freshman year happens within the residential system. If you choose to live in a single, it will take a bit more of a proactive effort to get involved.

At some schools, freshmen will be assigned triples. Putting three students in one small room is tight, and the people I know who did this almost all said it was a challenge. You may want to ask a college how many one-room triples they assign as you consider your college options. If it has to happen, do some research on common spaces in the building and nearby libraries – you will likely want to do a lot of your studying outside of the room.

Some lucky number of freshmen at certain schools will be assigned to live in suites. At some schools such as Harvard and Yale, suites are the norm. At Harvard, a suite can be shared by anywhere between two and six students. But unlike the typical double or triple arrangement where multiple students share just one room, a suite consists of several adjoining rooms, usually including a private common room with several bedrooms off of it. These bedrooms might be singles or doubles, but either way, there is more flexibility about who sleeps where. If your roommate is sleeping, you can study in the common room and if certain suitemates tend to be less compatible than others, you can shuffle around the bedroom arrangements.

After freshman year is when you see a big divergence in the living systems at colleges. At some schools, students continue to live in dorms for the rest of their time at school (though if this is the case, they typically move to nicer living arrangements each year). At other schools, students are given more options outside of traditional dorms such as living in specialty housing, co-ops, fraternities and sororities, and school-owned houses. At many colleges, some upperclassmen opt to move off campus and live on their own in apartments.

Specialty Housing

Specialty housing has become an increasingly popular model in recent years, and many colleges have converted some of their traditional dorms into these sorts of options. Specialty housing allows students to live in a separate building or on a specifically designated floor of a dorm with other students who share their interests or lifestyle preferences. Foreign language specialty housing where everyone commits to only speaking Spanish, French, Chinese, etc. are popular, as are sustainability houses where special efforts are made to recycle properly, compost, and conserve energy. Some specialty housing is cultural. For example, there are international houses, Latino cultural houses, and Chinese cultural communities.

Co-op Communities

Co-ops are communities (usually housed within a dorm or in a university-owned house) which students elect to be a part of and in which students are required to pitch in on various chores each week. Typically, students do the cooking, cleaning, and management of this living community. Eating tends to be a big part of co-op culture, and oftentimes dinner is set at a specific time and residents usually eat together to create a tighter sense of community. Some co-ops have their own gardens where students grow produce to be used in the kitchens, and many are committed to a vegetarian lifestyle (though there are exceptions). Overall co-ops tend to create a very tight community but can also sometimes separate residents from life on the rest of the campus because of the time commitment required.

Fraternities and Sororities Houses

Fraternities and **sororities** also are a potential source of housing for upperclassmen. A fraternity or sorority (also known as "**Greek Life**") is a social organization deriving from the Latin for "brotherhood" and "sisterhood." Many colleges won't allow fraternities and sororities, but at others they are a critical component of social and sometimes residential life on campus.

Historically, fraternities have been all-male and sororities all-female, although today some schools offer co-ed fraternities. Most of the time, each of the fraternities and sororities are associated with a house on the campus where these organizations hold social events and sometimes live (some schools only allow non-residential Greek Life).

Regardless of the specifics, Greek Life is a controversial topic. On the one hand, it is known to produce deep bonds among students who participate. Students are members of these organizations for life, and they can provide a great support network for students within a large school. Fraternities and sororities are also known to do community service work as a part of their mission.

However, these organizations are also exclusive by nature – some students are invited to join and others aren't. Often the process of getting admitted to one can be painful and humiliating. Essentially, you need to prove that you are a good social fit for the group and that you will be loyal to them. This can be a simple process like attending a few parties and social events, but other organizations make it more difficult forcing students who are **"rushing"** (trying to get accepted) to embarrass themselves in a whole variety of creative ways to prove their worth.

The other negative stereotype of fraternities and sororities is that they are known host wild parties all the time. Again, this is not true of every fraternity and sorority, but it is true of many, and especially if you live in one, it is something to consider.

On-Campus Apartments, Townhouses, and Houses

Other on-campus options include **on-campus apartments**, townhouses, and houses. These are beginning to pop up more and more although they are usually reserved only for upperclassmen. These buildings are designed to function like an off-campus option but are owned by the college. They have their own kitchens, and students who choose to live in these arrangements are usually on a partial meal plan or no meal plan. A few colleges have bought up a number of the houses in the surrounding area and turned old Victorian homes into dorms. At Smith College, for example, gorgeous old homes are the primary form of housing on campus.

Housing Philosophies

You may end up choosing a school that offers all of these options. Some schools will give you the option of living in a traditional dorm, specialty housing, a fraternity/sorority, co-ops, and more.

Other schools are philosophically opposed to offering so many housing options. These schools believe that by splitting up students into so many different types of arrangements, they are segregating the campus.

There are schools that say that living around people with different backgrounds and interests is one of the most valuable parts of going to college. At the beginning of the book, I talked about Yale's residential system, which is strongly oriented around this philosophy. At Yale, entering students are all randomly assigned to one of twelve residential colleges, which they will be a part of for all four years. Because of the random nature of these assignments, each of these college communities is comprised of a diverse group of students with different interests and backgrounds; the idea is that each residential college community is a microcosm of the student body as a whole.

Physically, a residential college is similar to a dorm but with more features. Every college is structured around a central courtyard where residents pass through each day on the way to class. Each college has its own dining hall, library, gym, and late night café for shared student use. Each college is overseen by a Master, a professor who is given a large budget each year to organize social events for the college like formals, parties, trips, lectures, and sporting events. Examples of other colleges with similar systems include Rice, Harvard, Princeton, and the University of Chicago. These schools encourage that idea that being a part of a diverse community is critical to their campus culture and removing oneself from that community to live only with people with similar interests and backgrounds is discouraged.

Off-Campus Housing

There are a number of schools where many students elect not to be a part of the residential systems at all especially after their freshman year. This could be for a variety of reasons. Sometimes colleges just don't have enough space to host all of their students. In other cases, the local rental market makes living off campus less expensive than living in a dorm, and students elect to live off campus in order to save money. Other times, students move off campus because the on-campus housing isn't very good. Whatever the reason, if you choose to go to a school where a lot of students live off campus, there will likely be some effect on the campus culture.

On the one hand, living off campus provides students freedom and independence that some students really like. There are fewer rules, you may have more space, and a big plus to many is having a real kitchen so you can cook. Many students appreciate living in an apartment because it makes them feel like independent adults.

But there are some disadvantages other than worrying about paying rent. Living off campus usually affects the amount of time spent on campus and means that a subset of the student body is not as active in on-campus social life. Students living off campus are more likely to come to school to go to class in the morning and then go home in the afternoon removing themselves from afternoon and evening activities. It is not to say that they never participate in these things, but it does make things more difficult for them than for their peers who live right in the middle of everything. Oftentimes, students living off campus are no longer on meal plans so the social aspect surrounding dining is also lost.

Even if you do decide to stay on campus, if you attend a school where a lot of students live off campus, it may affect you. With a large subset of students away, there may be less vibrancy to on-campus life in terms of social activities and dining culture.

At Harvard, almost everyone lives on campus for all four years. This is because the housing options are nice, centrally located, much less expensive than the surrounding real estate, and a fundamental part of the campus culture. Most students would have trouble even imagining living off campus because they'd feel like they'd be missing out. They'd miss events, parties, lectures, and eating in the dining halls, places that also serve as one of the main venues for club meetings and study sessions.

At a school where a sizable percentage of students live off campus, a culture like this wouldn't exist. Social activities would more likely occur at off-campus apartments and students might care less about the campus dining culture, preferring to socialize at other types of venues like at student lounges and local restaurants.

As far as my own personal bias, I spent all four years living on campus and loved it. I met lots of interesting people, and I felt very much entrenched in my campus community. I felt like I was in the center of everything. So much was always going on just a few steps from my room. Study sessions, parties, lectures, and more. Simple things like meeting new people in the laundry room made me feel connected to my school, and I am very grateful for that experience.

Plus, with all the other things I was focused on, I was glad not to worry about paying bills each month (you just pay once at the beginning of the semester), cleaning up the bathroom (they sent someone once a week), and getting things fixed when they broke (I just made a phone call and someone came to fix everything). And when I wanted to get away from everything, I was still able to go out to eat at a restaurant or meet my friends at a local café in no way affiliated with the college.

All that said, I know plenty of people who will say just the opposite. They said they had enough of dorm living after freshman year and really enjoyed living more comfortably and independently after that in an off-campus apartment. They say they learned how to clean up for themselves and cook, and it was enjoyable to do that with their close friends. Plus, they said they really appreciated the idea that they had "gone home" after a long day of stress at school and could truly unwind.

I strongly advise students to check the percentage of students who live on campus when considering a school. This figure alone will tell you a lot about the student culture. You should also check to see if colleges guarantee housing for all four years especially if you prefer to live on campus since some colleges will force you to move into your own apartment if they do not have enough space to accommodate everyone.

College Match Profile: Residential Type

The colleges featured in this book vary dramatically in terms of the percentage of students living on campus. At some of the colleges profiled, the vast majority of students live on campus. At others, the campus is split between those living on and off campus. And there are a number of schools where the vast majority of upperclassmen students choose to live in off-campus housing. All of the colleges are divided into the three categories below:

High Residential – Schools where 80% or more of the student body lives on campus.

Medium Residential – Schools where between 50% and 80% of the students live on campus.

Low Residential – Schools where less than 50% of the student body lives on campus.

Preferred Residential Type (high residential, medium residential, or low residential):

_____

Fill in your preference(s) on the College Match Profile Chart in Chapter 17 (page 270) to reveal your College Match Profile. If you're still not sure of your preference, take the "Not Sure?" quiz on the next page, and then come back to fill in the blank.

NOT SURE?

Do you prefer a school where more students live on campus or off campus? If you don't know off the top of your head, consider the following questions:

1) Which of the following would I prefer:

  a) To attend a party at my friend's apartment about a 15-minute walk from where I live.
  b) To attend a party at a large social venue within a short walk from where I live.
  c) To attend a party downstairs from where I live where most of the attendees are residents of my building.
  d) I'm not really into parties.

2) How are you with handling money?

  a) I am very responsible with money, and I like the idea of paying my bills like a responsible adult.
  b) I don't like to think about money unless I have to.
  c) I'm pretty responsible when it comes to money, but if given a choice I'd rather not have to spend my time worrying about it.
  d) I'm fine with handling money if I need to handle it.

3) Who do you want to live with?

  a) I want to live with my closest friends in a place that we pick out together. We will pick out the perfect apartment and decorate to make it our own.
  b) I want to share a room/apartment with close friends or even maybe have my own room, but I also want to live near other people at my school so I have a wider social circle.
  c) I want to live with a large group of people that all share my interests. I can live with a small group of friends after college but I think college is a unique time where you can live with 30-40 people together that are all the same age with the same hobbies and interests.
  d) I don't plan on spending that much time wherever I'm living. I'd rather meet friends in my classes or extracurricular activities, and I like to study at the library or in cafes.

NOT SURE? (cont.)

4) Which of the following sounds most like you:

   a) I want to feel like I've come home after a long day of class and unwind.
   b) I don't want to have to walk more than 15 minutes from where I live to get to class or to any one of my friend's rooms.
   c) I want to be a part of a large social circle and have an active social life.
   d) I don't mind taking long walks to get where I need to go.

5) How do you feel about food?

   a) I love cooking and plan to cook a lot.
   b) I don't want to cook for myself, but I hope there are multiple options for where I eat every day. I also hope to eat with my friends and classmates.
   c) I don't want to cook for myself every day, but I think it would be nice to cook sometimes. And it would be great to eat with the same group of people most of the time.
   d) I prefer to eat by myself. I will cook if I need to, but eating out or at a dining hall would also be okay.

Count up the number of each letter you circled.

If you circled three or more A choices, you should look for a **low residential campus** (less than 50% of students living on campus).

If you circled more than four B and C choices combined, you should look for a **high residential campus** (more than 80% of students living on campus). If you fit into this category, more B choices than C would indicate that you prefer a community-based housing system like Yale, Rice, and Harvard. If you circled more C options, you would prefer a school that offers a wide variety of on-campus housing arrangements like co-ops, specialty housing, and on-campus apartments.

If you do not fit into one of the above categories (you either have mostly D answers or have a pretty even spread between A, B, and C options), look for schools that are **medium residential** (between 50 and 80 percent of students living on campus).

Fill in your preferences for residential type in the College Match Profile Chart in Chapter 17 (page 270) to reveal your College Match Profile.

High Residential Schools (More than 80% Living On Campus)

Amherst College (97%)
Barnard College (91%)
Bates College (92%)
Beloit College (94%)
Bennington College (95%)
Boston College (85%)
Bowdoin College (92%)
Bryn Mawr College (94%)
Bucknell University (86%)
California Institute of Technology (85%)
Carleton College (94%)
Centre College (98%)
Claremont McKenna College (94%)
Colby College (93%)
Colgate College (91%)
College of the Holy Cross (91%)
Columbia University (94%)
Connecticut College (99%)
Dartmouth College (86%)
Davidson College (100%)
Denison University (99%)
DePauw University (95%)
Dickinson College (95%)
Duke University (85%)
Franklin and Marshall College (97%)
Furman University (96%)
Goucher College (86%)
Grinnell College (82%)
Hamilton College (98%)
Hampshire College (90%)
Harvard University (97%)
Harvey Mudd College (99%)
Haverford College (99%)
Hendrix College (88%)
Hobart and William Smith Colleges (90%)
Kenyon College (98%)
Knox College (85%)

Lafayette College (92%)
Middlebury College (97%)
Massachusetts Institute of Technology (90%)
Mount Holyoke College (95%)
Oberlin College (89%)
Occidental College (80%)
Ohio Wesleyan University (90%)
Olin College (100%)
Pomona College (98%)
Princeton University (97%)
Sarah Lawrence College (85%)
Scripps College (95%)
Sewanee: The University of the South (96%)
Skidmore College (86%)
Smith College (95%)
Soka University of America (100%)
St. John's College – Santa Fe (82%)
St. Lawrence University (97%)
St. Mary's College of Maryland (86%)
Stanford University (91%)
Swarthmore College (93%)
Thomas Aquinas College (99%)
Trinity College (89%)
Union College (89%)
University of Notre Dame (80%)
University of Richmond (89%)
University of Rochester (86%)
Vanderbilt University (83%)
Vassar College (94%)
Wabash College (87%)
Wellesley College (93%)
Wesleyan University (99%)
Wheaton College (IL) (90%)
Wheaton College (MA) (95%)
Williams College (94%)
Yale University (87%)

Medium Residential Schools (50-80% Living On Campus)

American University (55%)
Bard College (73%)
Boston University (77%)
Brandeis University (74%)
Brown University (79%)
Carnegie Mellon University (64%)
Case Western Reserve University (77%)
Clark University (71%)
College of the Atlantic (56%)
College of William and Mary (72%)
Colorado College (78%)
Cornell University (57%)
Emerson College (57%)
Emory University (67%)
Fordham University (56%)
George Washington University (68%)
Georgetown University (67%)
Georgia Institute of Technology (56%)
Gettysburg College (56%)
Illinois Institute of Technology (59%)
Ithaca College (69%)
Johns Hopkins University (54%)
Kalamazoo College (75%)
Lehigh University (69%)
Macalester College (62%)
Marquette University (54%)
New College of Florida (75%)
New York University (50%)
Northeastern University (55%)
Northwestern University (65%)

Pepperdine University (58%)
Pitzer College (74%)
Pratt Institute (52%)
Reed College (67%)
Rensselaer Polytechnic Institute (57%)
Rhodes College (71%)
Rice University (72%)
Rutgers University – New Brunswick (53%)
St. Johns College – Annapolis (70%)
Stony Brook University (53%)
Syracuse University (75%)
Tufts University (64%)
University of Chicago (60%)
University of Connecticut (72%)
University of Massachusetts – Amherst (61%)
University of New Hampshire (57%)
University of Pennsylvania (66%)
University of Vermont (50%)
Virginia Polytechnic Institute (51%)
Wake Forest University (68%)
Washington and Lee University (59%)
Washington University – St. Louis (79%)
Whitman College (67%)
Willamette University (68%)
Worcester Polytechnic Institute (50%)
Yeshiva University (69%)

Low Residential Schools (Fewer Than 50% Students Living On Campus)

Arizona State University (20%)
Brigham Young University (19%)
Clemson University (41%)
Colorado School of Mines (43%)
Cooper Union (20%)
Florida State University (20%)
Indiana University – Bloomington (38%)
Loyola University Chicago (41%)
Michigan State University (42%)
Ohio State University (25%)
Penn State University (36%)
Purdue University – West Lafayette (35%)
Shimer College (42%)
Southern Methodist University (32%)
Texas A&M University (22%)
Tulane University (44%)
University of California – Berkeley (26%)
University of California – San Diego (43%)
University of California – Davis (25%)
University of California – Irvine (38%)
University of California – Santa Barbara (37%)
University of California – Santa Cruz (48%)
University of California – Los Angeles (35%)
University of Maryland – Baltimore County (34%)
University of Colorado – Boulder (28%)
University of Delaware (44%)
University of Florida (24%)
University of Georgia (28%)
University of Illinois (37%)
University of Iowa (31%)
University of Maine (40%)
University of Maryland – College Park (47%)
University of Miami (39%)
University of Michigan (34%)
University of Minnesota – Twin Cities (21%)
University of New Mexico (8%)
University of North Carolina – Chapel Hill (46%)
University of Pittsburgh (44%)
University of Southern California (38%)
University of Texas – Austin (19%)
University of Virginia (42%)
University of Washington (13%)
University of Wisconsin – Madison (25%)

Chapter 10
Selectivity in Admissions

To attend any college within the United States, you will first need to apply and be accepted to a school. In the next section of this book, we will talk about what colleges are looking for in your application and what you can do to maximize your odds of gaining admission. For the purposes of this chapter, we will try to look at how you can figure out how selective different schools are so that you can tailor your college list accordingly.

Classifying selectivity in a way that will be useful for you is a difficult task because most colleges in the United States have a **holistic admissions process**. This means that instead of admitting students based on a simple quantitative metric, such as your grades or test scores, colleges evaluate students on a number of factors some quantitative and others qualitative.

In many countries, if you have certain grades or if you score to a certain level on a test, you know if you will get into a college or not. Or at least you'd have a pretty good idea. In many countries, college admissions is entirely or mostly based off of grades and test scores. In a holistic admissions process, quantitative data is only part of the equation.

Your extracurricular activities and personal characteristics are also very important components of your application. Are you an interesting person? Are you thoughtful? Do you work collaboratively? How will you contribute to the college community? Will you bring unique talents, an interesting perspective, and an inspiring attitude? Some students call these other components of their application "fluff" and spend all their time focused on getting the perfect test scores and grades. Yet time and again I see that the students who focus on these other facets do better in the admissions process.

For the purpose of this chapter, however, we need to have an easy way for you to get a sense of how selective a given school is and whether or not you would be a competitive applicant. Turning a complicated process into an easy chart is a very difficult task. Different schools value different things. For instance, Harvey Mudd College tends to pride itself on its math and science programs. While they too want students who excel in their extracurricular activities and leadership roles outside of math and science, it is important to them that most of their students stand out in math and science both in their grades and test scores. Thus, their average SAT math score is higher than say Dartmouth College's average SAT math score.

Dartmouth College, one of the Ivy League universities, is more oriented towards having a well-rounded student body in terms of both academic and extracurricular interests. So while the Dartmouth students coming in with an interest in science or math may score just as high or higher than the students getting into Harvey Mudd, many of the students are more focused on other areas where they have achieved outstanding levels of success by a different metric such as leadership roles, published writing, or national recognition in a sport. Looking at SAT scores alone, one might conclude that Harvey Mudd is more selective, but that is not necessarily the case. Actually, Dartmouth College only admits 9.8% of applicants while Harvey Mudd admits 19.2%.

But you cannot judge selectivity by admissions rate alone either. Dartmouth is a part of the Ivy League brand which is very powerful and because of that, it attracts a wide range of applicants many of whom are not qualified to attend. These additional applicants are part of the reason the college has such a low acceptance rate.

Harvey Mudd, on the other hand, has a higher acceptance rate than some of its peer schools because of its reputation and the rigorous nature of the curriculum. Every student coming into Harvey Mudd has to take a very challenging course load heavy in math and science. Students who are either not interested in these fields or who are not successful in these areas are much less likely to apply to Harvey Mudd. This makes it more likely that a higher percentage of applicants fit what the college wants, thus raising the rate of acceptance. Harvey Mudd is an example of a **self-selective school**, a school that attracts applicants from a niche applicant pool.

Harvey Mudd's lower acceptance rate does not reflect the quality of the entering class or the quality of the education offered at the school. As you can see from looking at its students' average test scores and grades, the students coming into Harvey Mudd are on an equal footing with students at some of the schools with the lowest acceptance rates in the country.

So hopefully you understand now why looking at scores or percent of students admitted or any of these other individual metrics can only show you a piece of a much more complex picture. But I need to give you a sense overall of where you can gain admission in an easily digestible way. I've developed six selectivity categories ranging from most selective (S-1) to least selective (S-6) and created a list of criteria for each one. Then, I used data collected from all of these schools to place each university featured in this book into its appropriate category.

Interestingly, many schools did not fit neatly into one category. Because of examples like the one I gave above about Harvey Mudd and Dartmouth, some schools had very high SAT averages but also pretty high acceptance rates and others had lower GPA averages than their SAT scores would indicate. The data reaffirmed that admissions is not a perfect science and that every school in this country has its own way of weighing the different factors involved in holistic evaluations.

Still, in most cases, I was able to find that schools fit best into one category. Perhaps not every piece of data matched the parameters of the category but generally most did, and if there was variation it matched the criteria in one of the adjacent categories. The result is a system that you can use to build your college list.

As we discussed at the beginning of the book, your ideal college list should contain somewhere between eight and twelve schools that you really like and can see yourself attending. Of these schools, you will want to make sure you have at least a few **safety schools** (schools where you think you will most likely be accepted), a handful of **best fit schools** (schools where you are in the average range for gaining acceptance), and several **reach schools** (schools that you're not sure if you are highly competitive for but that you think would make a good match for you otherwise).

My goal is that by the end of this chapter, you know which selectivity category fits with your good match schools. The next most selective category will be associated with your reach schools and the next less selective category will be associated with your safety schools. So, if you finish the chapter and figure out you mostly fit the profile of an S-3, you should select S-3 schools as your best fit schools, S-2 schools as your reach schools, and S-4 schools as your safety schools.

Just as colleges don't always fit perfectly into one of these categories, students don't always fit perfectly into a category. Perhaps your GPA fits into an S-1 or S-2 category but your SAT scores fit into the S-4 category. Or perhaps you got a 720 on the math SAT section but a 580 on the verbal section (i.e., there is a big difference on your performance in different subject areas). Neither of these scenarios is uncommon. For the purpose of finding your best fit category, pick the category that is in the middle.

In reality, if you have a strongly disjointed application in that you show to be much stronger in one subject over another or much better at taking tests than earning good grades or vice versa, different schools will have different reactions. Some technology institutes and engineering schools, while demanding proficiency on the verbal section of the SATs, will often take students with perfect math scores but verbal scores that may be 50-100 points lower. Similarly, if you prove to be a math genius who is great at computer programming and spent lots of time building your own programs at home, they may forgive a less than stellar GPA.

The Ivy League schools and their peers tend to be a bit less forgiving of huge gaps in performance. They like students who are pretty strong all-around. On the one hand, they may not have as high of a math SAT average among their student body, but they also will not be as forgiving of a lower verbal score. A difference of 100 points between an applicant's verbal and math score would be highly unusual. It would also be very unusual for these schools to admit someone with a mediocre or low GPA even with very high scores. The opposite situation, a high GPA with slightly lower scores than the average is a more likely admit at these sorts of schools, but given the competition these days for getting into the top schools, unimpressive test scores may still bring you down a tier unless you can make up for them in other types of accomplishments (awards, leadership experience, or personal qualities).

For your purposes now, make an honest assessment of yourself and pick the category that you feel overall fits the best with your profile. If you still have several years left before you graduate from school, keep in mind that your profile might change. You still have the opportunity to improve your grades, start new extracurricular activities, and win awards. Even if you have less than a year before you graduate, you may still improve your test scores or earn some type of honors before you submit your application. If something in your profile changes, you can revisit this chapter and adjust your college list accordingly. But for now, pick the category that you feel best fits who you are on track to become by the time you submit your application.

The reason I encourage you to include safety schools and reach schools in your college list as well as best fit schools is because making a holistic assessment of yourself is an imperfect science so by broadening your list, you mitigate risk. You want to make sure you come out of this process accepted to a couple of schools where you can be happy.

Metrics

We'll jump in to the categories in a moment, but first let's talk about the metrics I've included for consideration.

Admissions Rate

One of the first metrics you'll want to consider, and one that I've already mentioned, is the **admissions rate**. There is huge diversity in the percentage of students that different universities accept. The good news is that there are plenty of schools that accept the vast majority of applicants who apply. However, on the other side of the spectrum, the most selective schools may only accept 5% of the applicants (i.e., out of every 20 applicants, only one is going to be accepted).

Looking at a school's acceptance rate will give you some idea of the difficulty of getting in, but not all applicant pools are created equal. Some schools go to great lengths to inflate their applicant pools to bring down their admissions rate (that is, to make it look like they are as competitive as they can possibly look), and as I brought up with the example of Harvey Mudd, some schools are self-selective by nature because they attract a niche group of students. You should always look at multiple metrics in order to get a fuller picture of selectivity.

But as far as you making an assessment of what category you best fit into, the admissions rate is not useful. You should be more concerned with figuring out which selectivity category best matches you in terms of average scores, GPA, extracurricular involvement, quality of teacher recommendations, among other factors you can directly relate to yourself. The admissions rate is only relevant to you insofar as it gives you a sense of what to expect when you apply to a given school. I would not knock a school off your list purely because a college only accepts 8% of its applicant pool, but knowing this figure may help you round out the rest of your college list so that you make sure you include at least some schools with higher admissions rates.

Test Scores

A second metric I used to determine selectivity is the average SAT and ACT score or the middle 50% SAT and ACT range. The SAT and the ACT are standardized tests required for admission into most US colleges. There are a handful of colleges that do not require these tests (that list can be found on page 375). However, if you are considering applying to a US college, you are best advised to take one of these tests as early as possible (see Chapter 15 for how to prepare).

Historically, the SAT has been the most popular of the two tests, but today most colleges will accept the ACT as well, and both tests are offered to students internationally. Traditionally, the ACT was taken by students in the Midwest, and the SAT was used more on the coasts and internationally, but today things are starting to even out. You should check the websites for both tests to see if they are both offered in your country – some countries may just offer one or the other.

Colleges reporting their average SAT scores may report them by section or as a combined score. There are three sections to the test: critical reading, math, and writing. Each of these sections is graded on an 800-point scale so a perfect composite score would be 2400. The lowest possible score for each section would be 200. Of all test takers in 2012, the average composite score was approximately 1500, although most students at the schools profiled in this book scored higher than that average.

The alternative test, the ACT, is graded on a scale from 1-36. Although there are four different sections to the test (reading, English, math, and science) as well as an optional writing section, you will typically see ACT scores reported in composite form, so that there is only one number given to reflect performance on all four sections. The average national score last year was just under 21 although like with the SAT, most students gaining admission to the schools in this book scored higher than average.

Many colleges will only consider your highest score if you took the test multiple times so for the purpose of calculating your selectivity, use the highest score you achieved in one sitting of the test. Some colleges will even **superscore** the SAT (granting you credit for the highest score you received on each section of the test even if they were from different sittings), but you will need to check with each school's specific policy.

Grade Point Average

Another metric schools will usually publish is the **grade point average (GPA)** of admitted students. Colleges will typically only consider grades taken during high school (from 9th to 12th grade or your country's equivalent) to calculate this average. Different schools may have a different way of converting grades into a GPA, but the convention most colleges use is the 4.0 scale (also known as looking at **unweighted grades**). The 4.0 scale converts all the A's you've received into a "4", B's into a "3", C's into a "2", and so on. They then take the average of all of these numbers to calculate your GPA. If your school does not grade with A's and B's but on a 100-point scale or with an A+/A/A- system, you can find a conversion chart to an unweighted GPA on the College Board's website here:

www.collegeboard.com/html/academicTracker-howtoconvert.html

If you are on a completely different grading system in your country, there are international GPA calculators you can use to give you an idea of where you stand. This is the one I use:

www.foreigncredits.com/Resources/GPA-Calculator/

A lot of colleges will not actually go through the process of doing this conversion while making admissions decisions – they are familiar with the grading policies in different countries and will evaluate applicants directly based off of that. However, I think it is useful to do the conversion so you have at least a vague idea of where you stand.

One thing to keep in mind is that colleges know that certain countries and even certain schools grade differently. Some students are in more rigorous programs than others. GPA is therefore not a perfect metric because a student attending one school may have a higher GPA than student who attended a school with more rigorous grading but who learned just as much and performed just as well. This is why the GPA is just one of many factors schools use to make admissions decisions. Still, having some idea if you fall within the approximate range schools are looking for is useful.

More Subjective Factors

The GPA and test score averages for each school are simple to find and are the easiest metrics you can use to compare yourself to accepted applicants. However, as we discussed earlier, extracurricular activities and personal qualities also play a role in the admissions decisions at most US colleges. It can be hard to assess exactly how you will compare to the other applicants in these realms. However, you should use your best judgment based on the six different levels I've described corresponding to each of the categories.

With extracurricular activities, for example, you may participate in soccer and theater at school making you fit into the S-3 category ("Admitted students have participated in several extracurricular activities for a sustained period of time"). However, if you end up being asked to be captain this year and get a lead role in next semester's play, you may bump up to an S-2 ("Admitted students have participated in several extracurricular activities and have either demonstrated leadership positions or have won local recognition for these pursuits"). If then you go on to win the regional championship as captain of your soccer team, you might bump up to an S-1 ("Admitted students have received regional or national recognition for activities pursued outside of class or have demonstrated substantial leadership abilities").

For your personal assessment, think about the relationships you have with the teachers from whom you will ask for recommendations, and think about the degree to which you believe they can write a compelling and revealing essay about you. Figuring out which teachers are going to be able to offer the most helpful and thoughtful evaluation of your academic and personal qualities obviously requires a large degree of guessing and speculation, but I'd imagine you have a general sense of whether or not your teachers think very highly of you and if they would shower you with praise in a recommendation or if they'd be more neutral in their endorsement.

As for the personal essay, which most of the schools discussed in this book will also require of you, and which must be written for the Common Application, we'll talk a bit more about what colleges are looking for specifically in the next section. You may want to come back to this chapter after reading through Section II so you can feel more confident about the selectivity category you place yourself in for your College Match Profile.

Selectivity Categories

At the end of this chapter, I have applied the criteria I've used to designate selectivity ratings to the different schools covered in the book. As I mentioned at the beginning of this chapter, a number of schools do not fit into a selectivity category perfectly, but they are placed within the category where they fit best. If you want to get the specific information regarding average scores, GPA, acceptance rate, etc. for a given school, you can typically find it directly on a college's website (look for the "class stats").

Two other great resources you can use to look up most of this information are the *US News & World Report* college rankings and the *Princeton Review* (www.princetonreview.com). To get a more qualitative idea of what sorts of students are getting in as far as extracurricular activities and personal qualities, you can usually find some information directly on the college's website, but for the real details, spend some time scrolling through the online forums of the website College Confidential (www.collegeconfidential.com). This website has forums (some more active than others) for just about every school profiled in this book where high school students post their statistics and whether or not they were accepted. You can also use these forums to ask current students (a handful of whom lurk on the site) any questions you have about a specific school or their admissions experience.

Also of note is that all of the schools profiled in this book fit into categories S-1 through S-5. This means that they are all somewhat selective schools. There are many options throughout the country that would fall into the S-6 category (least selective) as well, but these schools are not the focus of this book. If you are interested in exploring some less selective options to add to your list, you can use the criteria I've outlined to evaluate whatever schools interest you. The websites I've mentioned above should give you all the information you need to evaluate any school based on the criteria below.

S-1 Schools

- Average SAT scores are in the 700s on all sections of the SAT (or above 32 on the ACT).
- Average GPA is above 3.8.
- Acceptance rate is under 16%.
- Admitted students have received regional, national, or international recognition for activities pursued outside of class or have demonstrated substantial leadership abilities.
- Both teacher recommendations use specific examples to demonstrate that the student is one of the best they've taught both personally and academically.
- Essay demonstrates clear writing, depth, and compelling personal qualities.

S-2 Schools

- SAT scores average in the mid-600s to low-700s by section (29-33 ACT).
- Average GPA is between 3.6-3.9.
- Acceptance rate is under 35%.
- Admitted students have participated in several extracurricular activities and have either demonstrated

leadership positions or have earned local recognition for these pursuits.
- Both teacher recommendations use specific examples to demonstrate that the student will contribute to the college both personally and academically.
- Essay demonstrates clear writing and compelling personal qualities.

S-3 Schools

- Average SAT scores average in the low- to mid-600s (28-32 SAT).
- Average GPA is between 3.4-3.8.
- Acceptance rate is under 50%.
- Admitted students have participated in several extracurricular activities for a sustained period of time (at least one year continuously).
- Both teacher recommendations endorse the applicant both personally and academically.
- Essay demonstrates clear writing and positive personal qualities.

S-4 Schools

- Average SAT scores are in the high-500s to mid-600s (25-30 ACT).
- Average GPA is between 3.2-3.6.
- Acceptance rate is under 70%.
- Some extracurricular activities are noted on the application but participation may or may not have been for a sustained amount of time.
- Both teacher recommendations are favorable.
- Essay demonstrates clear writing and fully answers the question being asked.

S-5 Schools

- Average SAT scores are in the mid-500s to low-600s (22-28 ACT).
- Average GPA is between 2.9-3.4.
- Acceptance rate is under 90%.
- Something is filled out on the extracurricular participation section of the application.
- Both teacher recommendations are neutral to favorable
- Essay demonstrates writing proficiency and fully answers the question being asked.

S-6 Schools

- Average SAT scores are in the mid-500s or below (below 24 ACT).
- Average GPA is below 3.0.
- Acceptance rate is between 90-100%.
- Little or no extracurricular participation is noted on the application.
- Teacher recommendations do not demonstrate illegal or highly disrespectful behavior and demonstrate that the student will not be a nuisance or liability for the college.
- Essay (if required) demonstrates some writing proficiency.

Make sure you look through these categories carefully and find the one that you think best fits with your profile. Most of you are going to be somewhere in the S-2 to S-4 category which is exactly where you want to be. Almost nobody should classify themselves as an S-1 for their best fit category. These schools are very competitive and for just about any kind of applicant, these are reach schools. Yes, of course many students do end up getting into these schools, but the admissions process for all the S-1 schools is extraordinarily competitive and unpredictable, and these schools should only comprise a handful of the schools on a college list for the majority of applicants. If you have won a medal at the Olympics (or have done anything on the list of truly extraordinary things below) and have perfect grades you might be the exception. If that is really the case, go ahead and only apply to S-1 and a couple of

S-2 schools, but just be careful because you don't want to be stuck without any options.

Truly Extraordinary Things That Would Maybe Make You an S-1

(You'll still need near perfect grades and solid scores)

- You won a medal at the Olympics.
- You've published an academic paper in a reputable, peer-reviewed journal.
- You've won international recognition for your achievements in a sport, the arts, or academics.
- You are a household name in your country because of your artistic career or business pursuits, or because you are the son/daughter of a major political leader or world figure.
- You have an unbelievable and awe-inspiring personal story such as having spent most of your life as a refugee and teaching yourself to read and do calculus without any formal schooling.

Don't worry if you are not any of these things. Lots of students get into S-1 schools without these sorts of crazy accomplishments, but for your sake, if you don't have these or equivalent truly standout accomplishments, just bump yourself down to S-2 and apply to those S-1 schools as reach schools with a couple of S-3 options in there for safeties. The worst thing would be to overestimate your category and end up without options, so especially at the top end of the selectivity categories where things are really competitive, I recommend being a bit conservative in your assessment of yourself. Remember, in total, most of you should apply to several schools from three different categories.

In general, I recommend the following breakdown:

Best Fit Schools: Pick at least 4 schools from your best fit category

Safety Schools: Pick 2-4 schools from one category less selective

Reach Schools: Pick 2-4 schools from one category more selective

Other Schools

Once you have your bases covered in these three categories, it is completely optional if you want to pick schools that don't fit into any of your three categories (i.e. you pick schools that are two or more categories away from your best fit selectivity category). If a college is two or more categories more selective than your best fit category, it is a long shot, and you should definitely make sure you have plenty of schools in your best fit, reach, and safety categories before adding it to your list as an extra.

If the college is two or more categories less selective than your best fit category, you can count it as a safety school if you think it would be a good fit for you for other reasons, but keep in mind that you may want to consider the social and academic implications of being at a school where your credentials are substantially higher than the majority of the student body. You may be able to get great scholarships at these kinds of schools, which might make them very attractive, but check to see if they have an honors program or equivalent that would keep you academically challenged and surrounded by like-minded peers.

How Extracurricular Activities Fit In

Before I give you the list of schools that fit into each category and you get busy looking through them, I want to make one note about extracurricular activities. I get a lot of questions about extracurricular activities from international students especially. In a lot of countries, these sorts of activities are not encouraged, so it is not uncommon for me to meet students who say, "I don't do anything else besides school!" Colleges will understand that there may not be as many options open to you as there are for a lot of American students where extracurricular involvement in the arts, sports, and community service are highly encouraged and offered by the schools directly. However, they will still usually expect you to have done something outside of class. And the really competitive schools will still demand some recognition or leadership unless you have truly earth-shattering academic accomplishments that will allow the admissions committee to overlook a deficit in extracurricular activities.

If it is still early enough, the best thing to do if you simply can't think of anything you've done that would fall into the "extracurricular" category would be to start doing something now. Even doing a little volunteer work over the next few weekends or taking an art or music class outside of school is something. It does make a big difference. And, really take the time to think about what you may have already done without realizing it. If you have ever volunteered for anything, helped organize an event at your school, played a musical instrument, held any kind of a job, worked on a political campaign, sung in a church choir, or attended a summer program (even summer school!), write that down. And after you've done that, think about your interests and hobbies. Even if you think colleges might not care, they actually might. If you like to bake frequently and do it on a regular basis, put that down. If you have been trying to learn Portuguese in your spare time, mark it down as well. If you help your little brother with his math skills, add it to the list.

After going through that exercise, I've met very few students who still can't think of anything to put down. By strict definition, an extracurricular activity is anything you do outside of class. Colleges want to see that you have other interests you might be able to use to contribute to your college community. If it really comes down to it, you could put down that you spend a lot of time watching YouTube videos of professional hip-hop dancers. If you pair that with a short essay about how you've always dreamed of doing hip-hop dancing, but the opportunities are not available at your school and you are excited about doing that in college (yes, most American colleges have hip-hop dance teams), you might just make a convincing case. I've never met anyone who doesn't fill their time with something other than their schoolwork, so dig down and figure out a way to make a pitch about why your unconventional extracurricular activities have been valuable ways to spend your time, if that is all you have. We'll talk about this topic a bit more in the admissions section.

For now, just try to get a sense of which tier is your best fit tier, reach tier, and safety tier. After you read through the admissions section, you may end up adjusting slightly but this will give you a good place to start.

College Match Profile: Selectivity

Go back to the list of selectivity categories above and figure out which category best fits your profile. Keep in mind that by the time you are ready to submit your application, things may have changed. Perhaps you'll win an award or get selected to be the captain of a sports team. Or maybe you will study very hard over the summer and increase your scores on the SAT. You can't predict everything that will happen but use your best judgment to determine which category you think will best describe you by the time you submit your college applications. You can always come back and readjust your categories once you get closer to your application submittal date.

Also, keep in mind that you don't have to fit perfectly into one group or another. Just choose the grouping that you think best describes you overall.

After looking through the categories one more time, identify that category (S-1 to S-6) that best fits you and fill it in here:

Best Fit Category (S-1, S-2, S-3, S-4, S-5, or S-6):

_____

Now, look at the category that is listed above your best fit category (one category more selective), and fill it in below. This is your reach school category.

Reach School Category (S-1, S-2, S-3, S-4, S-5, or S-6)

_____

Go back to your best fit category and look for the selectivity category below this option (one category less selective), and fill it in below. This is your safety school category.

Safety School Category (S-1, S-2, S-3, S-4, S-5, or S-6):

_____

Fill in all three selectivity ratings (for best fit, reach, and safety schools) and fill them in on the College Match Profile Chart in Chapter 17 (page 270) to reveal your College Match Profile.

S-1 Schools

Amherst College
Bowdoin College
Brown University
California Institute of Technology
Carleton College
Claremont McKenna College
Columbia University
Cornell University
Dartmouth College
Deep Springs College
Duke University
Harvard University
Harvey Mudd College
Massachusetts Institute of Technology

Olin College
Pomona College
Princeton University
Northwestern University
Rice University
Stanford University
Swarthmore College
University of Pennsylvania
Vanderbilt University
University of Chicago
Washington University – St. Louis
Williams College
Yale University

S-2 Schools

Barnard College
Bates College
Boston College
Brandeis University
Bryn Mawr College
Carnegie Mellon University
Case Western Reserve University
Colby College
Colgate College
College of William and Mary
Colorado College
Cooper Union
Davidson College
Emory University
Georgetown University
Grinnell College
Hamilton College
Haverford College
Johns Hopkins University

Kenyon College
Macalester College
Middlebury College
Mount Holyoke College
New York University
Oberlin College
Reed College
Scripps College
Smith College
Tufts University
University of California – Berkeley
University of Notre Dame
University of Southern California
University of Virginia
Vassar College
Washington and Lee University
Wellesley College
Wesleyan University

S-3 Schools

American University
Bard College
Bennington College
Boston University
Bucknell University
College of the Holy Cross
Colorado School of Mines
Connecticut College
Dickinson College
Denison University
Emerson College
Fordham University
Franklin and Marshall College
George Washington University
Georgia Institute of Technology
Gettysburg College
Lafayette College
Lehigh University
New College of Florida
Northeastern University
Occidental College
Pitzer College
Rensselaer Polytechnic Institute
Sarah Lawrence College
Skidmore College
St. John's College – Annapolis
St. John's College – Santa Fe
St. Olaf College

Thomas Aquinas College
Trinity College
Tulane University
University of California – Los Angeles
University of California – San Diego
Union College
University of Florida
University of Illinois
University of Maryland – College Park
University of Miami
University of Michigan
University of Minnesota – Twin Cities
University of North Carolina – Chapel Hill
University of Richmond
University of Rochester
University of Texas – Austin
University of Wisconsin – Madison
Wake Forest University
Wheaton College (IL)
Whitman College
Worcester Polytechnic Institute

S-4 Schools

Beloit College
Brigham Young University
Centre College
Clemson University
College of the Atlantic
DePauw University
Eugene Lang College at The New School
Florida State University
Furman University
Hampshire College
Hendrix College
Hobart and William Smith Colleges

Illinois Institute of Technology
Knox College
Lawrence University
Marquette University
Ohio State University
Penn State University
Pepperdine University
Pratt Institute
Rhodes College
Rutgers University – New Brunswick
Sewanee: The University of the South
Shimer College

S-4 Schools (cont.)

Soka University of America
Southern Methodist University
St. Lawrence University
Stony Brook University
Syracuse University
University of California – Davis
University of California – Santa Barbara
University of Connecticut

University of Delaware
University of Georgia
University of Massachusetts – Amherst
University of Pittsburgh
Virginia Polytechnic Institute
Wheaton College (MA)
Willamette University

S-5 Schools

Arizona State University
Clark University
Goucher College
Indiana University – Bloomington
Ithaca College
Kalamazoo College
Loyola University Chicago
Michigan State University
Ohio Wesleyan University
Purdue University – West Lafayette
St. Mary's College of Maryland
Texas A&M University

University of California – Irvine
University of California – Santa Cruz
University of Colorado – Boulder
University of Iowa
University of Maine
University of Maryland – Baltimore College
University of New Hampshire
University if New Mexico
University of Vermont
University of Washington
Wabash College
Yeshiva University

Chapter 11
Financial Aid for International Students

There are lots of benefits of attending a college within the United States, but one of the reasons many students do not consider studying in the US is cost. If you look up the tuition rates for various US colleges, they are some of the highest in the world. The exact amount can vary by school but in general, as of this writing, most public universities will estimate overall expenses (tuition, books, room and board) to be somewhere between $20,000-$35,000 and private schools typically between $50,000-$65,0000 annually. These are the advertised prices, and some students do pay these amounts. However, at most schools, at least half of students receive some sort of aid to reduce these costs.

Unfortunately for international students, aid is harder to obtain than for domestic students, but there are still options. If you are an American citizen (even if you have never lived here), you are eligible for the same aid as domestic students. You can fill out a government-issued form, the FAFSA, and receive aid in the form of grants and loans from the federal government. Also, you may receive additional aid directly from the college you choose.

If you are not a US citizen, in addition to your family's contribution, you will need to rely on a combination of school grants, outside aid, and loans. Before we get into the details of those options, let's discuss how the financial aid system works.

US Citizens

For a US citizen, the federal government provides a certain amount of aid (a combination or grants and loans) depending on a student's estimated need. Individual colleges rely on this government aid to help them fund the aid packages for domestic students. In addition to this aid, many colleges will also pitch in some of their own aid by giving students additional grants directly from the school.

A number of schools say that they are committed to meeting 100% of their students' demonstrated need (you can check on any college's website to see if a school has made this commitment). When a financial aid application comes in from a student who is a US citizen, the financial aid office at the college will assess the family's income, assets, and other financial metrics and make a determination on how much they believe the student's family can reasonably contribute to the student's education. They then deduct the amount that the federal government contributes through grants and loans and commit to funding the remaining amount through their own grants or loans.

One key thing to remember is that in these financial aid decisions, the college is the one determining what they think is a reasonable amount that a family might contribute. The student and family might agree with the school, and they might not. Different schools have different formulas. And some have dramatically different philosophies about how families should set their priorities.

The form in which financial aid is distributed also varies considerably from one school to the next, and this can make a huge difference in the obligations faced by the student in the years to come. A select number of schools, for example, will not ask their students to take out any loans that will have to be repaid after graduation, while others might use loans as a substantial percentage of their aid packages.

Non-US Citizens

Things start to get a bit more complicated if you are not a US citizen. For one thing, non-citizens are not eligible for federal aid (aid from the US government). Considering that federal aid makes up a large percentage of the aid colleges use to support their students, not having this aid available means that it costs the college a lot more to give the same aid to an international student as to a domestic one (since the domestic student's aid is subsidized by the government). As a result, many colleges within the United States, and about half of the colleges featured in this book, do not offer need-based financial aid (aid based on how much the student or student's family can pay) to international students.

However, just because a school does not offer need-based aid to international students doesn't mean they don't offer any aid to non-US citizens. The majority of colleges featured in this book that do not offer need-based aid to international students do offer merit scholarships which are either exclusively for or open to international students. In actual dollar amounts, many schools offering merit aid end up pouring in millions of dollars each year in supporting international students.

Merit Scholarships

Merit scholarships are grants given to students because of some personal quality that a college is trying to recruit in the student body. There is huge variation in the amount of money granted, but most schools have different scholarship types ranging from small annual grants to full tuition. Some merit scholarships are given to musicians who have demonstrated exceptional talent. Others are given to athletes who commit to playing a particular sport at the school. Some are given on the basis of exceptional academic achievement in a particular field or overall. There are also some scholarships that are restricted to students of particular ethnic origins. You need to check to make sure international students are eligible for these awards, but many are open to both domestic and international applicants.

Just a small sampling of scholarships open to international students to give you an idea include the following:

- Wesleyan University (Freeman Asian Scholars)
- University of Richmond (Science Scholars, Boatwright Scholars, Artists Scholars, Oldham Scholars)
- University of North Carolina – Chapel Hill (Johnston Scholarship)
- Washington and Lee University (Johnson Scholarship)

There are also some scholarships for international students specifically. Just a few examples of great merit scholarships for international students include Rice University's Allen International Scholarship, which awards full tuition to outstanding international students each year and Rice's Edgar Odell Lovett Scholarship that offers half tuition to international students as well. The University of Vermont offers four part tuition scholarships each year specifically earmarked for international students. In addition to having several merit scholarships open to both domestic and international students, Elon University chooses 20 International Fellows each year, 15 of whom are awarded a $3,500 grant during all four years of their studies as well as a one-time $1,500 grant that students can use to fund an internship or to conduct research. George Washington University offers a handful of merit-based scholarships for international students ranging from $10,000 to full tuition each year. You can check the financial aid page on each college's website to see if merit scholarships are available and find a list of what scholarships are offered.

Need-Based Aid

About half of the colleges featured in this book offer need-based aid to international students who are not US citizens. When I say need-based aid, I mean that the amount of aid that you are awarded is dependent on how much need the college assesses that you have. Some of these schools also offer merit scholarships that can make a stellar applicant's aid package exceed assessed need, whereas other schools will choose not to offer separate merit scholarships because they want to devote as much money as possible into need-based aid and help as many international students as they can. If you look at the actual amount of aid awarded to international students across all of the schools featured, there is wide variation between colleges in terms of how much money they offer, but there is little correlation between generosity to international students and the type of aid they offer (need-based vs. merit).

Colleges can be equally generous whether they offer need-based aid, merit-based aid, or both types of aid to international students. There are colleges with all of these variations that offer millions of dollars of aid to international students each year. However, looking at the types of aid available at each of the schools on your list may be useful in terms of figuring out your strategy as you apply. At some schools with merit-based aid, for instance, some of the scholarship deadlines will be due before the application deadline so you will want to plan for that well in advance. And if you are considering schools that offer need-based aid to international students, what I'm going to say next is very important.

Need Blind vs. Need Aware Admissions

The top schools in this country are often **need blind** for domestic students which means that your family's finances have nothing to do with your admissions decision. In an ideal world, your ability to pay to attend a particular school would not be a factor in a school's decision on whether or not to admit you. Many of the first tier colleges have implemented need blind systems for domestic students and even the second tier schools are aspiring to this ideal. They do not want your ability to pay for a school to affect your chances of getting admitted.

Yet as I mentioned before, offering need-based aid to international students can quickly add up to millions of dollars, since aid to international students is not subsidized by the government. If a college admits you without looking at your need and has made a commitment to giving need-based aid, they may then be stuck doling out huge amounts of money, which they may or may not be able to afford. As a result, the vast majority of colleges with need-based aid for international students are **need aware** – they will look at your ability to pay as a factor in the admissions process.

Just because a student needs aid, even substantial aid, doesn't mean they won't be admitted to a need-aware school. The school wouldn't be offering any need-based aid to international students if they didn't intend on granting aid to students who need it. However, they may have an annual cap of maybe $2,000,000 for international students so they have to admit their students very carefully. If they were to take all the applicants they would normally accept if aid weren't an issue, they might be at $4,000,000, so they need to cut that list of qualified students down to their budget. If you make that cut and are accepted, colleges committed to meeting 100% of demonstrated need will give you the full amount of aid they deem necessary – be it $5,000 or $50,000 annually. Once you're in, you will be treated just like a domestic student. The hard part, however, is getting in when you are subjected to more rigorous admissions standards than the domestic applicants. If you need substantial aid, colleges will often need to determine that you stand out from the average qualified student to justify the expense of admitting you.

If you are an international student who does not need financial aid, you will not be subject to any kind of different treatment than the domestic students. You will be admitted by the same standards as everyone else. But if you apply without asking for financial aid, most schools will say that you are not eligible for any financial aid during all four years. So if you decide not to apply for financial aid, make sure you know how you are going to finance your full education.

If you do need aid, you have a couple of choices. One is to go ahead and apply for it. Know that you may have a harder time getting accepted than the admissions statistics lead you to believe because your financial need will be a factor in a college's decision. Perhaps you want to apply to a few more schools from your safety category where you think you'll have the best shot of really standing out in the applicant pool. The other option is to look for other types of aid (we will discuss those options later in this chapter). If you find aid through other sources besides directly through the college, you may be able to apply without an application for financial aid and thereby get the same treatment domestic students are given in the admissions process.

I hope all of the information we just went through isn't too discouraging. The truth is that despite all of the obstacles, many schools offer millions of dollars each year to international students. Most schools value the diversity international students bring to the campus despite the financial limitations. Remember, every year hundreds of thousands of international students receive some sort of aid to study in this country. The key is to just make sure you understand the financial aid system at each school and apply to a solid college list so you can optimize your chances of getting the aid you need.

Need-Blind Colleges for International Students

There are six colleges that deserve tons of accolades because they are the only six college in the country that provide international students with the same treatment as domestic students regardless of their citizenship and financial status. These schools are both need-blind and committed to meeting 100% of demonstrated need for international students. This means that you are treated exactly the same as domestic students in the admissions process and will still be awarded the same amount of aid as a domestic student would. And even better, most of these schools are known to have a very favorable formula for calculating need.

Most of these need-blind schools are small or medium-sized and devote between $7 and $30 million dollars per year in aid to international students. If you like any of these schools and are a solid applicant for S-1/S-2 schools, you should make sure to include at least a couple of these on your college list:

- Harvard University
- Yale University
- Massachusetts Institute of Technology (MIT)
- Dartmouth College
- Amherst College

- Princeton University

In addition to these six, there are two colleges that are need-blind in the admissions process but will not necessarily commit to meeting 100% of demonstrated need for international students. These schools will not base your admissions decision on your ability to pay, but once you get in, you may not be given as generous of an aid package as a domestic student might receive.

- Cornell University
- Georgetown University

Finally, these three schools are free or highly discounted to all students (including international students):

- Cooper Union (full tuition)
- Deep Springs College (full tuition)
- Olin College (half tuition)

As you will note, the schools with the best aid for international students are also some of the most selective schools. This is not a coincidence. These are often institutions with large **endowments** because they are old and have had a lot of time to grow their resources or because they've recently received a large amount of funding. When you consider a school, checking to see the size of its endowment can be a way to get a sense of how good their financial aid is. It is not a perfect correlation, but in general if a school has a small endowment, it will have more trouble funding international students looking for need-based aid. In addition, *US News & World Report* collects data on the average financial aid awards to international students, which you can view if you join their premium service, College Compass.

Other Ways to Find Money

Besides getting money directly from a college, there are other ways to find money to finance your education. If you can take advantage of one (or more) of these other options, you may be able to attend a college you really like but that doesn't offer much aid for international students even if you need financial support.

Outside Scholarships

Besides aid offered directly through a particular college, there are many sources of outside aid to consider. Lots of organizations offer external scholarships where they will award you a certain amount of money in the form of a grant you can use no matter which college you choose. Google offers scholarships of $25,000 to $50,000 each year to students all over the world. The Ayn Rand Institute gives away $100,000 dollars annually to students who write compelling essays about Ayn Rand's books. And the Gulen Institute Youth Platform gives out 30 scholarships to students in the US and abroad based on essay responses to an annual theme related to solving a global challenge. These are just a few examples. You can find a list of online databases you can search to find outside scholarships on page 374.

Loans

In order to cover any shortfall in money, you may need to take out student loans. You may get lucky and not have to take out any. If you can find enough merit-based aid or if you are lucky enough to get a generous need-based package, loans might not be an issue. But the majority of even domestic students have to take out at least some loans.

The average student graduating from a college in the United States in 2013 graduated with approximately $35,000 in loans. Of course, this number takes into account students at all sorts of colleges across the country with varying tuition rates and aid options. Some students graduated with no debt at all and others with substantially more. I have met students with over

$70,000 in loans from their undergraduate educations. The amount that you decide is your limit is up to you. Do what makes you comfortable. You will be paying these loans off for a long time. Thankfully, you are usually not required to start paying loans off until after graduation so you don't need to worry about this while you are in school.

Once you have figured out how much to take out in loans, the next step is to get approved for a loan. Non-US citizens will need to get loans from a private lender. Unfortunately, since the financial crisis in 2008, the standards for getting approved for loans have become more stringent. Most lenders today will want an international student to have a domestic co-signer who will to agree to pay your loan if you default. The thinking is that it would be easy for you to return to your country after graduation and be hard to track you down if you were not making payments. If you have any family or friends in the United States who earn a stable income, these are the ideal people to ask. If not, take a look at the Global Student Loan Corporation (www.globalslc.com), one of the only companies that will offer student loans to international students with no US cosigner.

Another option is to get your loan in your home country. Some countries allow students to get loans to be used at foreign institutions, but others do not, so you will need to check local policies. Thankfully, the United States is considered to be a more stable place to invest educational dollars so you are better off asking for a loan to study here than in many other places.

Also, look into whether your home country has any government programs that support students looking to study in the United States. There are some countries that are trying to increase graduates from US institutions and will offer students money to help support them in doing so.

Finally, you can also try to put together a private loan by asking friends and relatives to pitch in to help fund your education. Even if you pay them back at a higher interest rate than they'd get in the bank, you will likely still be paying less than if you go through a private lending institution. It is not always an easy thing to ask, but if it works, it can be a lower hassle way to finance your education.

Additional Tips for Securing Financial Aid

You can find additional information and resources to help fund your education specifically for undergraduates on some of the websites listed on page 374. In addition, Education USA, a resource provided by the US Department of State (www.educationusa.info) has tips specifically for international students looking to finance their education in the United States and is also worth checking out.

Also make sure that you look through the financial aid sections on the website of each school you are applying to carefully. Don't be afraid to call up their financial aid office to ask questions about the process. Some schools are not particularly forthcoming about aid information on their websites. If this is the case, you may need to probe a bit. What other financing options have international students at their school pursued besides need-based aid? What merit-based scholarships do they recommend for an international student? What types of outside aid have other international students enrolled at their university used? If you can get someone on the phone to talk to you, they are usually pretty helpful.

Once you are admitted, you will be offered your financial aid package by the college. Hopefully you will be happy with it, but if you are not, keep in mind that students do negotiate these things. If you honestly don't think you will be able to attend that school because the package isn't high enough for you, call up the school's financial aid office and say that. I've known many students who have been able to get their package increased after an initial offering that was insufficient. Given that schools do have limited resources, please do this in good faith, but don't hesitate to at least ask if a better financial aid package would make the difference between enrolling or not enrolling.

College Match Profile: Financial Aid

The chart at the end of this chapter includes the overall assessment of whether schools offer the best, excellent, good, some, or no institutional aid to international students. These numbers are based on the number of international students offered aid and the total amount of aid granted to international students, adjusted for the size of the institution and tuition rate.

If you do not need aid or if you already have outside aid sources, this category may not be important to you, but if you do, this can be a very important category of your College Match Profile to consider.

Like with some of the other categories we've covered so far in earlier chapters, you don't need to necessarily pick one category for all of your schools to fit into. Obviously, if you need aid, the more aid a school offers, the better. But remember, if your first choice school is only on the "some" list, that doesn't mean you won't get a great financial aid package; you just may have to work a bit harder to get it. There may only be a few scholarships available at that school, so do as much research as you can about the source of the money being devoted to international students. Remember that someone is getting something even at schools with restricted aid for international students, so make sure to get the details and do everything you can to put yourself in a position to get it. And if you like a school that doesn't offer any aid, start researching outside options now.

The point of this category of your College Match Profile is to be aware of how different colleges fall in the aid spectrum. If you do need aid, try to make sure that your list includes at least a couple of schools with the best aid or excellent aid ratings. But don't be afraid to add in a few schools that match your profile for other reasons from the lower tiers as well – just make sure you take the time to thoroughly research their aid options so you get the best shot.

The Best Aid – These schools are the best of the best when it comes to giving aid to international students. Some of these schools are need-blind and committed to meeting 100% of demonstrated need, others guarantee scholarships to every student, including international students, and some just devote an unusually large pile of money to supporting international students compared to their peer institutions.

Excellent Aid – These are schools that fund a substantial number of international students each year and devote a significant percentage of their financial aid budgets to granting aid to international students.

Good Aid – These schools allocate regular funds to cover partial or full tuition scholarships to some of their international students.

Some Aid – These are schools that do have financial aid for international students, but the aid is limited or the exact aid numbers are unreported.

No Institutional Aid for International Students – These are schools that do not offer need-based or merit-based aid to non-US citizens.

Preferred Financial Aid Type (Best Aid, Excellent Aid, Good Aid, Some Aid, No Institutional Aid for International Students):

_____

Fill in your preference(s) for financial aid types from the options above on the College Match Profile Chart in Chapter 17 (page 270) to reveal your College Match Profile. If you are not sure which options to select, see the "Not Sure?" section on the next page to help you narrow down the options.

NOT SURE?

Not sure which financial aid characteristics you should consider? Consider the following questions to figure out which options you should include on your College Match Profile:

1) How much is your family willing to contribute to your education each year you are studying in the United States?

    a) Less than $10,000 USD
    b) Between $10,000 and $20,000 USD
    c) Between $20,000 and $40,000 USD
    d) Between $40,000 and $60,000 USD
    e) Money is not a factor in my college decision.

2) Are you comfortable taking out some student loans?

    a) No. I would rather give up my first choice college and settle for another school on my list if it were the difference between taking and not taking out loans.
    b) I don't know anyone in the United States that would co-sign for my loans, but if a lender would give me loans anyway I would consider taking out some loans.
    c) I have a friend or family member in the United States that might co-sign for me, but I would not feel comfortable taking out more than $10,000 USD per year in loans.
    d) I have a friend or family member in the United States that might co-sign for me, and I would consider taking out what I need to finance my education.
    e) I already know how I will get the funds to attend college so I will not need to consider loans.

3) How proactive are you willing to be with regards to finding alternative ways of funding your education (i.e. applying for outside scholarships, organizing a way to borrow money from family and friends, negotiating financial aid packages offered from various schools, etc.)?

    a) I don't have time to look for funding from multiple sources – I would like to choose a college that can offer me everything I need.

NOT SURE? (cont.)

b) I will make some effort to apply to outside scholarships and find ways to finance my education, but I would strongly prefer that I select a college that will be able to offer me the majority of funds I need to attend.

c) I will be creating a list of outside scholarships and other potential sources of funding and doing everything I can to get as much money as possible.

d) I am fairly confident I will be able to get funding to cover the majority of the funds I will need from sources other than my family or directly through the college.

e) I do not need to look for outside funding because I already have all of the funds I need.

If you selected two or more A's, you should look for a school with the **best aid**.

If you selected only A's and B's, look for a school that offers either the **best aid** or **excellent aid**.

If you selected, A's, B's, and C's, focus on schools that offer the **best aid**, **excellent aid**, or **good aid**.

If you selected at least one D or E option, you should keep schools with all of the financial aid categories – **best aid, excellent aid, good aid, some aid**, and **no institutional aid for international students**, on your list.

Fill in your Financial Aid Type preferences on the College Match Profile Chart in Chapter 17 (page 270) to reveal your College Match Profile.

Important Note

On the next few pages, you will see lists of the colleges that fit into each of the financial aid categories we discussed – best aid, excellent aid, good aid, some aid, and no institutional aid for international students. On these lists, you will see two numbers after the names of most of these colleges. The first number shows you the number of international students awarded aid last year. The second number (the one in parentheses) is the total amount of aid allocated to international students last year. This data were collected from information reported in *US News and World Report* and on Big Future by the College Board.

Schools with the Best Aid

Amherst College 146 ($7,655,287)
Bard College 196 ($7,617,880)
Bates College 84 ($4,081,959)
Bennington College 46 ($2,024,000)
Bryn Mawr College 157 ($6,179,834)
Colby College 82 ($3,957,995)
College of the Atlantic 52 ($2,164,213)
Cooper Union (full tuition to all students)
Dartmouth College 251 ($12,279,562)
Deep Springs College (full tuition all students)
DePauw University ($5,090,458)
Franklin and Marshall College 159 ($5,951,714)
Grinnell College 157 ($5,655,157)
Harvard University 530 ($27,866,340)
Illinois Institute of Technology 592 ($10,703,818)
Knox College ($2,976,408)
Macalester College 222 ($7,647,111)

Massachusetts Institute of Technology 374 ($16,854,797)
Middlebury College 129 ($6,313,628)
Mount Holyoke College 448 ($15,480,183)
Olin College – half scholarship guaranteed to all students 20 ($560,000)
Princeton University 409 ($16,397,219)
Sarah Lawrence College 73 ($2,592,487)
Smith College 168 ($7,339,206)
Soka University of America 164 ($5,308,880)
St. John's College – Annapolis 39 ($1,229,271)
St. Lawrence University 155 ($5,930,516)
Trinity College 146 ($7,446,464)
Wellesley College 114 ($5,417,075)
Williams College 80 ($4,373,650)
Worcester Polytechnic Institute 350 ($8,148,755)
Yale University 350 ($18,639,436)

Schools with Excellent Aid

Beloit College 111 ($2,143,031)
Brown University 207
($8,400,000)
California Institute of
Technology 26 ($1,124,845)
Carleton College 79 ($2,589,268)
Clark University 165 ($3,993,130)
Colgate College 114 ($5,360,736)
Colorado College 70 ($3,155,913)
Connecticut College 57
($2,747,848)
Denison University 153
($3,879,380)
Dickinson College 133
($4,429,897)
Hamilton College 66 ($2,975,464)
Kenyon College 58 ($2,304,722)
Hampshire College 87
($1,924,573)
Hendrix College ($1,687,347)
Lafayette College 103
($3,859,836)
Lawrence University 110
($2,222,784)
Oberlin College 146 ($4,343,742)

Ohio Wesleyan University 149
($3,368,998)
Reed College 45 ($2,080,424)
Skidmore College 80 ($4,281,849)
St. Olaf College ($5,309,947)
Stanford University 187
($9,088,919)
Swarthmore College 56
($2,604,476)
Union College 82 ($2,706,410)
University of Pennsylvania 332
($14,245,353)
University of Richmond 128
($5,628,674)
University of Rochester 328
($6,538,139)
Vassar College 92 ($4,445,049)
Wabash College 53 ($936,950)
Washington and Lee University
73 ($3,640,194)
Wesleyan University 83
($4,270,370)
Wheaton College (MA) 103
($2,344,486)
Yeshiva University 133
($3,209,689)

Schools with Good Aid

American University 114
($2,505,823)
Barnard College 13 ($546,265)
Boston University 119
($4,792,889)
Bowdoin College 28 ($1,134,934)
Bucknell University 26
($1,135,186)
Centre College 38 ($690,780)
Cornell University 73
($2,909,006)
Davidson College 48 ($1,689,552)
Duke University 134 ($6,484,394)
Eugene Lang College at The
New School 74 ($424,050)

Furman University 51
($1,607,743)
George Washington University
190 ($3,742,943)
Georgetown University 57
(1,740,210)
Gettysburg College 35
($1,297,308)
Goucher College 26 ($653,317)
Harvey Mudd College 11
($412,746)
Haverford College 12 ($548,575)
Hobart and William Smith
Colleges 89 ($2,210,772)
Ithaca College 98 ($2,499,092)

Schools with Good Aid (cont.)

Lehigh University 63 ($2,548,772)
Marquette University 201
($2,681,936)
Northeastern University 365
($5,145,175)
Occidental College 14 ($614,157)
Pepperdine University 68
($1,447,933)
Pomona College 37 ($1,457,826)
Pratt Institute 160 ($1,175,000)
Rhodes College 59 ($1,075,9=91)
Rice University 75 ($1,828,575)
Scripps College 18 ($580,522)
Southern Methodist University
189 ($5,068,739)
Texas A&M University 239
($4,597,643)
Thomas Aquinas College 10
($195,716)
Tufts University 90 ($3,901,600)
Tulane University 134
($2,521,166)
University of California – San
Diego 109 ($2,990,851)
University of California – Davis
140 ($2,157,642)

University of California – Irvine
117 ($1,623,896)
University of California – Los
Angeles 69 ($2,100,705)
University of Chicago 57
($3,215,600)
University of Illinois ($7,127,097)
University of Iowa 517
($2,787,664)
University of Maryland –
Baltimore County 82 ($1,432,420)
University of Miami 118
($3,318,202)
University of New Hampshire 52
($1,569,516)
University of Notre Dame 89
($2,770,314)
University of Southern California
221 ($4,254,635)
University of Vermont 93
($1,516,467)
Vanderbilt University 62
($2,869,569)
Washington University – St.
Louis ($4,308,928)
Whitman College 31 ($1,117,916)

Schools with Some Aid

Arizona State University 222
($2,086,688)
Brandeis University 20 ($560,000)
Brigham Young University 634
($2,574,040)
Case Western Reserve University
5 ($143,840)
Claremont McKenna College 6
($225,122)
Columbia University
(unreported)
Emerson College 5 (54,000)
Emory University 19 ($507,400)

Fordham University 46
($1,208,204)
Indiana University –
Bloomington 279 ($2,564,204)
Johns Hopkins University 32
($1,069,309)
Kalamazoo College (unreported)
Michigan State University 169
($1,193,653)
New College of Florida 2
($19,000)
Northwestern University 38
($1,580.078)

Schools with Some Aid (cont.)

Ohio State University 426 ($2,499,338)
Pitzer College 3 ($182,217)
Purdue University – West Lafayette 224 ($369,665)
Rutgers University – New Brunswick 4 ($3,750)
Sewanee: The University of the South 7 ($289,789)
Shimer College 1 ($10,000)
St. Johns College – Santa Fe (unreported)
St. Mary's College of Maryland 21 ($115,696)
Stony Brook University 108 ($1,323,350)
Syracuse University 31 ($404,450)
University of California – Santa Barbara 33 ($972,015)

University of California – Santa Cruz 6 ($112,104)
University of Colorado – Boulder 51 ($587,927)
University of Maine 24 ($112,728)
University of Minnesota – Twin Cities (unreported)
University of New Mexico (unreported)
University of Texas – Austin (unreported)
Wake Forest University (unreported)
Wheaton College (IL) 103 ($195,752)
Willamette University 9 ($104,000)

Schools with No Institutional Aid for International Students

Boston College
Carnegie Mellon University
Clemson University
College of the Holy Cross
College of William and Mary
Colorado School of Mines
Florida State University
Georgia Institute of Technology
Loyola University Chicago
New York University
Penn State University
Rensselaer Polytechnic Institute
University of California–Berkeley
University of Connecticut
University of Delaware

University of Florida
University of Georgia
University of Maryland – College Park
University of Massachusetts – Amherst
University of Michigan
University of North Carolina – Chapel Hill
University of Pittsburgh
University of Virginia
University of Washington
University of Wisconsin
Virginia Polytechnic Institute

Chapter 12
Prestige

Prestige factors into the equation for many students as they choose a college. What do I mean by prestige? Prestige is hard to quantify and people have different perceptions. But in general, I would define a prestigious school as one that the general public recognizes and thinks of highly in terms of providing an outstanding education and/or attracting excellent students.

Prestigious schools have a "name brand," and many of the students I work with feel that choosing a name brand school is an important consideration in their college search. I understand that mentality, and I don't blame anyone who considers prestige a factor. There are advantages to attending a school that has a good reputation. Going to a school with a name brand means that some people will consider you to have a certain amount of credibility just because you went to that particular school. It may also make your resume stand out. Plus, there is often some truth behind prestige in terms of academic quality, institutional resources, and the overall college experience (though this is not to say that one cannot get an equally fantastic education at a school with lesser prestige).

Yet, I would caution any student to choose a college for this reason alone. I knew a lot of people in college that chose to come to Harvard because it was Harvard and couldn't give any other explanation as to why they were there. And though Harvard is a wonderful school for many reasons, it isn't the right school for everyone. Some of these students spent four years complaining that they wished there were more engineering options, that they wanted to go to a school with a bigger sports culture, or that they hated the snow. Other students said it was too big, too intense, filled with too many ambitious students, and too liberal. Personally, I loved my experience at Harvard. I wouldn't have had it any other way looking back. It was one of the best experiences I ever had. I met some of my best friends there. I started a business, discovered my passion for entrepreneurship and writing, studied abroad, and learned a new language. I felt inspired by the environment of constant activity and innovation.

Going to Harvard also meant I gained some of the benefits associated with attending a highly prestigious school. In fact, at my last job, the Human Resources Manager told me that one day before I was hired, the Vice President of the company walked into her office and said, "We need more Harvard people!" So, the HR Manager did a search through the database of resumes for the word "Harvard," and I appeared at the top of the list of over 10,000 resumes in their database. The preference for Harvard people alone did not get me the job, nor did it assure that I kept that job, of course, but it did get me an interview that eventually led to the job. In this instance and in many others, I have been given a chance in part because of going to a name brand college.

For me, this has all been a great surprise. I wasn't naïve in high school. I knew that people considered some schools to be more prestigious than others, but I did not build my college list around prestige. There were lots of highly prestigious schools I did not seriously consider because of some of the factors we discussed in this book. If I wasn't comfortable with the size, location, curriculum, housing system, etc. at a college, it wasn't on my list. I didn't care if it was ranked in the top 25 in *US News & World Report*.

So one thing to consider is that you might not be happy at every prestigious school. But another thing to consider is that some schools that might not be as prestigious might also be worth your time. Certain large public universities, for example, may not be the most prestigious, but many of them offer honors programs and other types of special tracks that may give you an education equal or maybe even better than what you'd find at the "elite" universities. Furthermore, many small liberal arts colleges are completely shortchanged when you look at the public's perception. Because small liberal arts colleges are designed with the intention of educating undergraduates, they are not constantly producing research that makes the news. The research universities are constantly making newsworthy discoveries and their name is perpetually floating around. There are fewer reasons you would hear about smaller liberal art colleges in the media, but this in no way reflects upon the quality of education these schools offer. In fact, small liberal arts colleges are the ones that hire professors based on their ability to teach and are the schools that have nobody else to worry about besides undergraduates, so they can often make for the best undergraduate experiences.

So in general I'd say it is fine to think about prestige and use it as one factor in your decision-making process, but your search should not put prestige above everything else.

What Makes a College Prestigious?

The next question is how do you accurately assess prestige? Prestige is a somewhat subjective category. Most people have their own personal biases perhaps influenced by other people they've known who have gone to certain schools. But in addition to that, a lot of people turn to the popular lists of college rankings to make a determination. There are actually many different rankings and many of them yield very different results.

One thing to keep in mind is that rankings are a big business. *Us News and World Report,* one of the most well-known ranking magazines in the United States, was a failing publication until they started the annual college and university ranking issue, which revived the magazine's reputation.

It always amazes me that every year I run into students who say, "Well of course I chose X school because it was ranked higher than Y school." And I ask them where, and they say "in *US New & World Report*" or sometimes "in *Forbes*" or in one of the other popular rankings. Then I ask them why they selected that ranking system and not another one. And they have no idea. That was just the ranking system they saw first. I can almost always pull out another list where the schools were ranked in the opposite order.

Every ranking system follows a different methodology, and some of the categories considered in the methodology may or may not have relevance to your life. For instance, one of the well-known ranking systems places a huge emphasis on what percentage of students at each school are involved with public service. Maybe this is something you care about, but maybe it isn't. But either way, realize this factor is a subjective thing to value, and you just as well could factor in the percentage of students who live on campus or the percentage of students who participate in the arts, or sports, or whatever it is you might value but someone else doesn't.

Another ranking system puts a big emphasis on acceptance rate, based on an assumption that the lower the chances of an individual application being accepted, the higher the school's competitiveness and desirability. As a result of this metric many colleges have started offering incentives to get more students to apply such as eliminating application fees and allowing students to submit applications without their traditional supplement. By making it very easy for students to apply, they increase the number of applications. The catch is, some of these additional applications come from students who have little interest in the school and are not as well qualified as it previous pool of applicants. As a result, the acceptance rate decreases, but the quality of the accepted students does not change – nor is it really any harder than ever for a well-qualified applicant to be accepted. Schools that play these games well will increase their rank without making any material changes to the experience of attending them.

But as much as I think you should approach all rankings with some degree of skepticism, I think that having these lists out there does affect the public's perception of "prestige" of various schools. The most respected rankings domestically are *US News and World Report* and *Forbes*. Princeton Review's annual rankings of *The Best 378 Colleges* is also very popular but ranks schools into very specific categories like "Happiest Students" and "Best College Dorms" rather than creating a master list of best overall schools. *Times Higher Education* is not as widely known in the United States, but it is a UK-based publication with an international following that assesses institutions internationally based on surveys of the public's perception of universities' reputations, so it is useful in determining what the public thinks of different institutions.

I don't think any of these lists are anywhere near perfect or the universal standard of determining which schools are the most prestigious, but I've categorized schools as "most prestigious" if they are ranked in the top 25 overall in *Forbes'* college and university rankings, in the *Times Higher Education* world reputation ratings, or in *US News & World Report* university rankings (or top 10 in the *US News & World Report* liberal arts college category).

I have ranked schools as "prestigious" if they are in the top 50 in *Forbes*, in *Times Higher Education*, or in the university category in *US News & World Report* (or in the top 25 in the liberal arts category). If they do not appear in these placements on any of these lists, they do not have a prestige ranking. If I haven't given a school a prestige ranking, it doesn't necessarily mean that the school doesn't garner prestige in some circles.

A school like St. Johns College, for instance, the tiny great books school, based in Santa Fe, NM and Annapolis, MD does not appear on any of these lists because they ask to be excluded from the ranking system. It is a very quirky school that cannot be easily compared. It is not a household name and keeps a low profile. However, within certain academic circles, philosophy and classics departments and law schools, it has a very strong reputation.

There are many other schools that do not have a prestige ranking on this list that are very well known in certain circles or that offer a select group of departments or specialty programs that are widely recognized (e.g. honors programs, music department, journalism school, etc.). For example, the

University of Iowa is widely recognized for its writing program and Indiana University – Bloomington's music department is one of the best even though neither of these schools has the same kind of overall reputation as some of the other schools on this list. If you enroll in the University of Iowa for Writing or the Indiana University for music, most educated writers and musicians respectively will know what that means. The list at the end of this chapter, however, reflects the institutions that are most widely recognized and respected by a general audience around the country and the world.

The Down Sides to Prestige

It may seem obvious to you that any rational person would pick a highly prestigious college over a less prestigious one if given the choice of two schools they like equally well. Sure, you might think that if one school seemed like a better overall fit for its academic offerings and campus culture, and if it were less prestigious, it might make sense to choose it over a more prestigious option. But if two colleges were equally good fits, would there ever be a reason to choose the less prestigious school?

I have seen several students come across this kind of a decision and choose the less prestigious school. There can be several reasons why someone may want to choose a less prestigious school over a similar school with higher recognition. Some of these reasons are more legitimate than others.

One reason I sometimes hear is that students think a prestigious school would be more expensive and that they'd get a better deal picking a less prestigious option. While in some cases less prestigious options will offer outstanding scholarships to top students, it is not true that highly prestigious schools do not offer good financial aid. In fact, because the most prestigious schools often tend to have large endowments, they frequently offer some of the best aid. Therefore, financial aid should not be a major factor in your decision about what type of prestige you'd like your college to have. That being said, there are several very good reasons you might decide a less prestigious school might be for you.

For one, prestigious schools often attract some students that choose to enroll because of prestige in and of itself. As I mentioned before, Harvard did have its share of people that were prestige snobs (though they were in the minority). What I mean by that is these were people that chose Harvard primarily because it was prestigious (rather than for more meaningful and substantive reasons) and who tended to pursue academic, extracurricular, and social opportunities based on their perception of what would make them seem the most impressive regardless of their true interests and passions. Again, these people were in the minority, but some people would prefer not to have to be at a school where they would encounter people like that. At a school without a prestige rating, most students choose to attend their school for other reasons besides prestige (i.e. like they really just liked the place) which means you may find that the students at schools with less prestige as a whole are happier with their college experiences.

Additionally, a lot of students feel that it would be easier to earn better grades and stand out more on a campus that is slightly less prestigious. A student once told me that she was interested in being a Rhodes Scholar, one of the most prestigious scholarships granted to college students each year (which funds their graduate studies in England) and said that the prestige-hungry students that attend the most prestigious schools would all want to apply for the scholarship making it more difficult for her to secure her school's nomination than if she were at a less prestigious school where presumably fewer students would be applying. At a less prestigious school, it is easier to feel like you are a "big fish in a small pond" rather than a "small fish in a big pond" like you might feel at the highly prestigious options.

Overall, while there will always be students that want to go to the most prestigious school possible, not everyone feels that way. Some students prefer just the opposite and would rather stand out at an institution that might be less recognized by the public but is a good fit for them personally. And there are also students that prefer to take a more middle-of-the-line approach and choose schools that will give them some benefits of prestige (like name recognition from employers and graduate schools) without some of the downsides they might find at one of the most prestigious institutions.

College Match Profile: Prestige Rating

Some students come to college in the United States because they want to attend a name brand school that everyone back home will have heard of and that will impress their future employers. If this is you, you will want to look for schools that fit into the most prestigious or prestigious category.

If you feel that you would actually be happier at a school where prestige wasn't a huge draw because you feel it would attract other students for better reasons or because you think you would be able to stand out in that environment, then perhaps you want to look at schools without a prestige rating.

Just as a reminder, here are the different prestige ratings you could put into your College Match Profile and what they mean:

Most Prestigious – Schools ranked in the top 25 overall in *Forbes'* college and university rankings, the *Times Higher Education* world reputation ratings, or *US News & World Report* university rankings (or top 10 in the *US News & World Report* liberal arts college category).

Prestigious – Schools ranked in the top 50 in *Forbes, Times Higher Education,* or in the university category in *US News & World Report* (or top 25 in the liberal arts category).

No Prestige Rating – All of the schools that do not meet the criteria for most prestigious or prestigious as outlined above.

After considering these different categories, you may feel that prestige just isn't something that should have a significant impact on your college search. You might think that while going to a school that is prestigious would be nice, if you were to find a school that isn't prestigious but that you prefer for other reasons, that would be fine too. If you are somewhat ambivalent about narrowing down your list by prestige, you can select all of these options (most prestigious, prestigious, and no prestige rating) into your College Match Profile so that you don't narrow down your college list based on prestige.

Preferred Prestige Rating (most prestigious, prestigious, no prestige rating?):

_____

At this time, you should flip to the College Match Profile Chart in Chapter 17 (page 270), and fill in your preference(s) for a prestige rating. Write down which of these categories you would consider, and if you do not consider prestige to be a major factor in your college selection, just write in all three. Or, if you still aren't sure, see the "Not Sure?" box on the next page to help you figure out which category to select.

NOT SURE?

If you are not sure how important prestige is to you, consider the following questions:

1) What is your primary motivation for coming to school in the United States? (Pick the option you feel most strongly about.)

   a) I want to return to my country and be able to have a competitive edge in securing top jobs and prestigious positions.
   b) I believe I will have a superior academic experience in the United States.
   c) I want to be able to stay in the United States after graduating either to work or attend graduate school.
   d) I prefer the university experience in the United States (liberal arts philosophy, residential campus, active extracurricular life) to the experience of going to school in my country.

2) Which of the following ideas most appeals to you?

   a) I am fine going to a school where I am average if I am surrounded by incredibly impressive, ambitious, and inspiring people.
   b) I would not like to feel like I am at the top of my class – I want to be challenged by my peers in my extracurricular and academic pursuits – but I would be disappointed if I felt average or below average.
   c) I want to be a leader in my campus community either by gaining distinction in my studies or by leading a campus group or organization.
   d) I believe you have something to learn from everyone no matter where you are. My primary concern is that I want to go to a school where I will be able to get a solid education and have the kind of experience I'm looking for.

3) When I come home from college during my school vacations, I want everyone:

   a) To be impressed by me because of where I go to school. It would be best if people – my family, friends, and of course job recruiters and graduate admissions committees – have heard of my school and respect the kind of education I'm pursuing.

NOT SURE? (cont.)

b) I don't really care about everyone's opinion. If I'm happy that is basically what matters, but it would be great if when I applied for summer internships or jobs out of college, the recruiters would know a bit about the school I attended so I would perhaps stand out a bit in the pool.

c) As far as I'm concerned, if the school is a legitimate four-year college in the United States, and I do well in my classes and earn a degree, people in my country will respect my education. And if I had to pick, I would rather impress people with the really great grades I earned than with the name of the school I attend.

d) It is most important that I pick a school where I like the school's academic programs, offerings, and culture regardless of everyone else's opinion.

If you selected mostly A choices, a college from the **most prestigious** list might be very important to you.

If you selected mostly B choices, a college from the **prestigious** list, where you gain the benefits of name recognition from the people that matter but also are able to earn recognition more easily than at a school on the most prestigious list, might be your best bet.

If you selected mostly C choices, you may actually prefer a school with **no prestige rating** because it may be a less competitive place to get good grades and give you the opportunity to stand out more.

If you selected mostly D choices, prestige is probably not a very important factor in your decision to select a school so you may want to put keep all three prestige categories into your College Match Profile.

Fill in your preferences for Prestige Rating on the College Match Profile Chart in Chapter 17 (page 270) to reveal your College Match Profile.

Most Prestigious Schools

Amherst College
Bowdoin College
Brown University
California Institute of Technology
Carleton College
Carnegie Mellon University
Claremont McKenna College
Columbia University
Cornell University
Dartmouth College
Davidson College
Duke University
Emory University
Georgetown University
Harvard University
Haverford College
Johns Hopkins University
Massachusetts Institute of Technology
Middlebury College
Northwestern University
Pomona College
Princeton University

Rice University
Stanford University
Swarthmore College
Tufts University
University of California – Berkeley
University of California – Los Angeles
University of Chicago
University of Illinois
University of Michigan
University of Notre Dame
University of Pennsylvania
University of Southern California
University of Virginia
Vanderbilt University
Wake Forest University
Washington and Lee University
Washington University – St. Louis
Wellesley College
Williams College
Yale University

Prestigious Schools

Bates College
Boston College
Boston University
Brandeis University
Bryn Mawr College
Case Western Reserve University
Colby College
Colgate College
College of the Holy Cross
College of William and Mary
Georgia Institute of Technology
Grinnell College
Hamilton College
Harvey Mudd College
Lafayette College
Lehigh University
Macalester College
New York University

Northeastern University
Oberlin College
Penn State University
Rensselaer Polytechnic Institute
Scripps College
Smith College
University of California – San Diego
University of California – Davis
University of California – Irvine
University of California – Santa Barbara
University of Florida
University of Massachusetts – Amherst
University of Miami
University of North Carolina – Chapel Hill

Prestigious Schools (cont.)

University of Richmond
University of Rochester
University of Texas – Austin
University of Washington

University of Wisconsin –
Madison
Vassar College
Wesleyan University
Yeshiva University

Schools with No Prestige Rating

American University
Arizona State University
Bard College
Barnard College
Beloit College
Bennington College
Brigham Young University
Bucknell University
Centre College
Clark University
Clemson University
College of the Atlantic
Colorado College
Colorado School of Mines
Connecticut College
Cooper Union
Deep Springs College
Denison University
DePauw University
Dickinson College
Emerson College
Eugene Lang College at The
New School
Florida State University
Fordham University
Franklin and Marshall College
Furman University
George Washington University
Gettysburg College
Goucher College
Hampshire College
Hendrix College
Hobart and William Smith
Colleges
Illinois Institute of Technology

Indiana University –
Bloomington
Ithaca College
Kalamazoo College
Kenyon College
Knox College
Lawrence University
Loyola University Chicago
Marquette University
Michigan State University
Mount Holyoke College
New College of Florida
Occidental College
Ohio State University
Ohio Wesleyan University
Olin College
Pepperdine University
Pitzer College
Pratt Institute
Purdue University – West
Lafayette College
Reed College
Rhodes College
Rutgers University – New
Brunswick
Sarah Lawrence College
Sewanee: The University of the
South
Shimer College
Skidmore College
Soka University of America
Southern Methodist University
St. John's College – Annapolis
St. John's College – Santa Fe
St. Lawrence University
St. Mary's College of Maryland

Schools with No Prestige Rating (cont.)

St. Olaf College
Stony Brook University
Syracuse University
Texas A&M University
Thomas Aquinas College
Trinity College
Tulane University
University of California – Santa Cruz
Union College
University of Colorado – Boulder
University of Connecticut
University of Delaware
University of Georgia
University of Iowa
University of Maine

University of Maryland – Baltimore County
University of Maryland – College Park
University of Minnesota – Twin Cities
University of New Hampshire
University of New Mexico
University of Pittsburgh
University of Vermont
Virginia Polytechnic Institute
Wabash College
Wheaton College (IL)
Wheaton College (MA)
Whitman College
Willamette University
Worcester Polytechnic Institute

Chapter 13
How to Differentiate Good Match Colleges

Up until this point in the book, we've explored some fundamental differences between colleges in the United States. Hopefully, you've had a chance to write down your preferences in each category and fill them in on the College Match Profile Chart in Chapter 17 (page 270). Perhaps you have looked through the list of colleges in the back of the book and found some schools that meet some or all of your preferences. It is likely that you've identified at least a handful of schools that keep appearing in your preference categories and that look like they could be good options. Now what? How do you distinguish one school that meets your basic parameters from another?

As we've discussed before, different campuses have different vibes, and the best way to get a sense of a particular school's vibe is to visit that school. But when that is not a possibility, you need another option. In this section, I have identified various **designations** that may apply to various schools. These are schools that stand out for a particular reason beyond their peers.

When I've given a school a designation for say, theater, it is not to say that other schools do not have strong theater offerings. The intention is to show you that certain schools shine particularly brightly in certain ways. Hopefully, the earlier chapters of this book have helped you understand the qualities you are looking for in a school. Once you know those, these designations will help you get a better sense of the culture at each of your match schools so you can better rank the schools on your list.

Below, you will find an explanation of all of the designations that have been considered along with the schools that have been designated with this particular marker. At the end of this book, under the list of schools with their profiles, these designations are also noted.

Sports Designation

These are schools where attending sporting events is a large part of student culture, and the campus social life, and a significant portion of students, can often be found as spectators at these events. At many schools, the biggest sport is intercollegiate football, but at some, hockey, basketball, or other athletic pursuits are also popular. Students are generally aware of their athletic teams' performance and organize large social events in celebration of wins.

Schools with a Sports Designation

Arizona State University
Boston College
Brigham Young University
Bucknell University
Clemson University
Duke University
Florida State University
Georgetown University
Lehigh University
Ohio State University
Penn State University
Purdue University – West Lafayette
Rutgers University – New Brunswick
Southern Methodist University
Syracuse University
Texas A&M University
University of California – Los Angeles
University of Colorado – Boulder
University of Connecticut
University of Delaware
University of Florida
University of Georgia
University of Illinois
University of Iowa
University of Maine
University of Maryland – College Park
University of Miami
University of Michigan
University of Minnesota–Twin Cities
University of New Mexico
University of North Carolina – Chapel Hill
University of Notre Dame
University of Pittsburgh
University of Southern California
University of Texas – Austin
University of Virginia
University of Washington
University of Wisconsin
Virginia Tech
Wabash College

Athletic Designation

An athletic designation reflects a high percentage of students who are involved with athletic pursuits either by playing on varsity teams (most competitive), club teams (moderately competitive), or in intramural sports (casual). It does not necessarily mean that attending sporting events is a large part of student culture (see sports designation), but it means that the majority of students participate in athletics in some way.

Schools with an Athletic Designation

Brigham Young University
Clemson University
Colorado College
Dartmouth College
Florida State University
Georgetown University
Lehigh University
Ohio State University
Penn State University
Sewanee: The University of the South
St. Lawrence University
St. Mary's College of Maryland
Stanford University
Syracuse University
University of California – Los Angeles

University of Colorado – Boulder
University of Connecticut
University of Delaware
University of Florida
University of Georgia
University of Illinois
University of Miami
University of New Hampshire
University of Notre Dame
University of Texas – Austin
Wabash College
Wake Forest University
Wheaton College (IL)
Wheaton College (MA)
Whitman College
Willamette University
Williams College

Outdoors Designation

These are schools where a large percentage of students enjoy participating in outdoor activities such as hiking, skiing, biking, rafting, sailing, and camping. These campuses are usually in close proximity to forest preserves, lakes, or rivers, and many students spend weekends and school vacations participating in these sorts of activities.

Schools with an Outdoors Designation

Bennington College
Brigham Young University
Carleton College
Colby College
Colgate College
College of the Atlantic
Colorado College
Colorado School of Mines
Cornell University
Dartmouth College
Deep Springs College
Hampshire College
Middlebury College
Pomona College

Sewanee: The University of the South
Soka University of America
St. John's College – Santa Fe
St, Lawrence University
St. Mary's College of America
University of California – Santa Cruz
University of Colorado – Boulder
University of Maine
University of New Hampshire
University of Vermont
Whitman College
Willamette University
Williams College

Artistic Designation

These are schools with a strong appreciation for the arts, including theater, dance, music, and visual art. These campuses have devoted significant resources to building artistic facilities and art-related academic offerings, and many students enjoy attending music, theater, and/or other artistic events socially even if they themselves do not participate.

Schools with an Artistic Designation

Bard College
Bennington College
Carleton College
Colorado College
Cooper Union
Emerson College
Eugene Lang College at The New School
New York University
Pratt Institute

Sarah Lawrence College
Skidmore College
Swarthmore College
University of Maryland – Baltimore County
Vassar College
Wesleyan University
Wheaton College (MA)
Yale University

Social Activism and Community Service Designation

These are campuses where students care a lot about specific social causes and where a large percentage of students volunteer in the local community. Students concerned with social activism and community service are pervasive at just about every American college, but these schools stand out particularly strongly in their efforts. At these schools, a substantial percentage of students join organizations promoting particular social causes by raising awareness or reaching out to politicians. Other students spend their afternoons, weekends, and school vacations involved in community service efforts in fields as diverse as housing, healthcare, education, international development, and environmental protection.

Schools with a Social Activism and Community Service Designation

Boston College
Brandeis University
Brown University
Bryn Mawr College
Connecticut College
Dartmouth College
Grinnell College
Harvard University
Loyola University Chicago
New College of Florida
Oberlin College

Ohio Wesleyan University
Pitzer College
Princeton University
Rhodes College
Soka University of America
Swarthmore College
University of California –
Berkeley
Vassar College
Wesleyan University
Yale University

Government and Politics Designation

These are campuses where a large number of students are interested in government, political science, or international relations. At these schools, many students spend their summers working at NGOs, assisting politicians and ambassadors in Washington DC, or getting public policy internships. Many of these colleges also have a large percentage of students who are involved in student government associations and who volunteer for local and national political campaigns.

Schools with a Government and Politics Designation

American University
Bowdoin College
Brandeis University
Brown University
Claremont McKenna
College of William and Mary
Cornell University
Dartmouth College
Davidson College
Dickinson College
Florida State University
George Washington University
Georgetown University
Gettysburg College

Harvard University
Johns Hopkins University
Kalamazoo College
Lafayette College
Macalester College
Ohio Wesleyan University
Princeton University
Reed College
Rice University
Tufts University
University of Maryland –
College Park
University of Virginia
Wellesley College

Serious Academic Designation

This designation reflects schools where a substantial percentage of the student body takes their studies very seriously. There are students at all schools that take academics seriously, but these are schools that attract a large percentage of students who want to go into academia. Many students at these schools are interested in going into masters and PhD programs directly out of college.

Schools with a Serious Academic Designation

Bowdoin College
Bryn Mawr College
California Institute of
Technology
Carleton College
Colorado College
Colorado School of Mines
Columbia University
Cooper Union
Davidson College
Deep Springs College
Grinnell College
Harvard University
Harvey Mudd College
Haverford College
Illinois Institute of Technology
Johns Hopkins University

Mount Holyoke College
Princeton University
Rice University
Sarah Lawrence College
Smith College
St. Johns College – Annapolis
St. Johns College – Santa Fe
Stanford University
Swarthmore College
University of California –
Berkeley
University of Chicago
Wellesley College
Whitman College
Williams College
Yale University

School Spirit Designation

These are colleges and universities where students are very proud of their school. Students tend to walk around with clothing bearing the name or mascot of their school. Many of these institutions are also known for their devoted alumni who remain very active with their schools well after graduation.

Schools with a School Spirit Designation

Clemson University
College of the Holy Cross
Georgia Institute of Technology
Marquette University
Ohio State University
Penn State University
Purdue University – West Lafayette
Rutgers University – New Brunswick
Southern Methodist University
Syracuse University
Tulane University
University of California – Davis
University of California – Los Angeles
University of Texas – Austin
University of Florida
University of Iowa
University of Maryland – College Park
University of Miami
University of Michigan
University of North Carolina – Chapel Hill
University of Notre Dame
University of Wisconsin
Virginia Polytechnic Institute
Wake Forest University

Religious Designation

These are schools that are officially associated with a religious organization. This is not to say that every student at these schools belongs to the associated faith (in fact, all of these schools have some degree of religious diversity), but a substantial percentage of students are a part of the affiliated religious organization. These schools represent a variety of faiths.

Schools with a Religious Designation

Boston College
Brigham Young University
Centre College
College of the Holy Cross
Davidson College
Fordham University
Georgetown University
Hendrix College
Loyola University Chicago
Marquette University
Ohio Wesleyan University

Pepperdine University
Rhodes College
Sewanee: The University of the South
Southern Methodist University
St. Olaf College
Thomas Aquinas College
University of Notre Dame
Wheaton College (IL)
Willamette University
Yeshiva University

Entrepreneurship Designation

These are schools where a large percentage of students are interested in starting their own businesses. Many of these schools have classes related to entrepreneurship or active clubs devoting to helping students launch their business by hosting lectures, offering funding, and organizing networking events.

Schools with an Entrepreneurship Designation

Brown University
California Institute of Technology
Dartmouth College
Harvard University
Harvey Mudd College
Illinois Institute of Technology
Indiana University – Bloomington
Loyola University – Chicago
Massachusetts Institute of Technology
Northwestern University
Olin College
Princeton University
Stanford University
Syracuse University
Tufts University

University of California – Berkeley
University of California – San Diego
University of Texas – Austin
University of Maryland – College Park
University of North Carolina – Chapel Hill
University of Pennsylvania
University of Southern California
University of Washington
University of Wisconsin – Madison
Washington University – St. Louis
Worcester Polytechnic Institute
Yale University

Techie Designation

These are schools where students are very interested in technology. Usually, they have a large percentage of students interested in computer science whether or not it is their major. Outside of class, techie students may build robots, design video games, and/or watch science fiction movies, among other technology-related pursuits.

Schools with a Techie Designation

California Institute of Technology
Carnegie Mellon University
Cornell University
Georgia Institute of Technology
Harvey Mudd College
Illinois Institute of Technology
Massachusetts Institute of Technology
Olin College
Princeton University
Purdue University – West Lafayette
Rensselaer Polytechnic Institute
Rice University
Stanford University
University of California – Berkeley
University of California – San Diego
University of Illinois
University of Michigan
University of Southern California
University of Texas – Austin
University of Washington
University of Wisconsin
Virginia Polytechnic Institute
Worcester Polytechnic Institute

Music Designation

These are schools where a large percentage of students are involved in music. In many cases, these schools have well-regarded music departments where students can major or minor in music. In addition, these schools have a number of musical student groups including orchestras, bands, jazz ensembles, choirs, a cappella groups, and/or chamber music.

Schools with a Music Designation

Bard College
Boston University
Carnegie Mellon University
Cornell University
Indiana University –
Bloomington
Ithaca College
Lawrence University
New York University
Northwestern University
Oberlin College
Ohio Wesleyan University

Rice University
St. Olaf College
University of Maryland –
Baltimore County
University of Miami
University of Michigan
University of Rochester
University of Southern California
Vanderbilt University
Wheaton College (IL)
Yale University
Yeshiva University

Theater Designation

These are campuses where there are a large number of theatrical productions produced each year relative to the size of the student body. Some of these schools offer theater as a major and others do not. All of these campuses allow students not majoring in theater to participate in theater in some capacity.

Schools with a Theater Designation

Bennington College
Carnegie Mellon University
Emerson College
Fordham University
Hendrix College
Indiana University –
Bloomington
Ithaca College
Kenyon College

Northwestern University
New York University
Oberlin College
Sarah Lawrence College
Skidmore College
University of Chicago
Vassar College
Wellesley College
Yale University

Journalism Designation

These are campuses known for either their journalism schools or their campus newspapers and other publications, which give journalistic opportunities to undergraduates.

Schools with a Journalism Designation

American University
Arizona State University
Boston University
Emerson College
George Washington University
Harvard University
Illinois Institute of Technology
Indiana University –
Bloomington
Ithaca University
Kenyon College
New York University
Northwestern University
Penn State University
Pepperdine University
Stony Brook University

Syracuse University
University of Florida
University of Georgia
University of Iowa
University of Maryland –
College Park
University of Minnesota –Twin
Cities
University of North Carolina –
Chapel Hill
University of Southern California
University of Texas – Austin
University of Wisconsin –
Madison
Yale University

Quirky Designation

These are schools where there is a strong cultural appreciation for creativity, uniqueness, and individuality. Some people might call the students at these schools "weird," but these students see it differently. In general, there are a number of students at these schools that dress creatively (or non-conventionally), often within a subgenre like Steampunk, hipster, grunge, or gothic. And many of these students pursue somewhat fringe hobbies like anime, fantasy and sci-fi novels, indie music, etc. These students would probably be insulted that I just labeled them the way that I did. They would claim they are unique and not a part of a wider genre.

Schools with a Quirky Designation

Bard College
Beloit College
Bennington College
Brown University
Carleton College
College of the Atlantic
Emerson College
Eugene Lang College at The
New School
Grinnell College
Hampshire College

Harvey Mudd College
Kalamazoo College
Knox College
Massachusetts Institute of
Technology
New College of Florida
Oberlin College
Reed College
Sarah Lawrence College
Shimer College
St. Johns College – Annapolis

Schools with a Quirky Designations (cont.)

St. Johns College – Santa Fe   Wesleyan University
University of Chicago

Economics Designation

These are schools known for the quality of their economics departments. They are also schools where economics is one of the most popular majors. At many of these schools, students are very interested in participating in economics-related activities outside of class, such as participating in finance and investing clubs and during summers, working in micro-finance and getting consulting/investment banking internships.

Schools with an Economics Designation

Boston University
Brown University
California Institute of
Technology
Carnegie Mellon University
Claremont McKenna College
Columbia University
Cornell University
Denison University
Duke University
Harvard University
Johns Hopkins University
Massachusetts Institute of
Technology
Northwestern University
New York University
Occidental College
Princeton University
Stanford University
University of California –
Berkeley
University of California – San
Diego

University of California – Los
Angeles
University of Chicago
University of Maryland –
College Park
University of Massachusetts –
Amherst
University of Michigan
University of Minnesota – Twin
Cities
University of Pennsylvania
University of Rochester
University of Wisconsin –
Madison
Yale University

Business Designation

These are schools where a substantial percentage of students are interested in learning about business, and the school devotes significant resources to educating and providing opportunities to students in this field. Some of these schools offer business majors. Others encourage their students to major in different fields but then devote substantial resources to encouraging students to learn about basic accounting, finance, and/or economics and then helping them get jobs in the private sector after college. Schools with a business designation have a campus culture where many of the students are interested in having business careers and approach college from that lens, seeking out summer internships, attending networking events, and building a large network amongst their fellow students.

Schools with a Business Designation

American University
Arizona State University
Brigham Young University
Carnegie Mellon University
Clemson University
Cornell University
Dickinson College
Emory College
Fordham University
Georgetown University
Indiana University – Bloomington
Lehigh University
Marquette University
Massachusetts Institute of Technology
New York University
Northwestern University
Ohio State University
Penn State University
Pepperdine University
Southern Methodist University
Texas A&M University

University of California – Berkeley
University of Illinois
University of Iowa
University of Maryland – College Park
University of Michigan
University of Minnesota – Twin Cities
University of New Mexico
University of North Carolina – Chapel Hill
University of Pennsylvania
University of Richmond
University of Rochester
University of Southern California
University of Texas – Austin
University of Virginia
University of Wisconsin – Madison
University of Notre Dame
Washington and Lee University
Washington University – St. Louis

Humanities Designation

These are schools where a high percentage of students take advantage of opportunities in the humanities, courses that are usually thought to include English, philosophy, classics, history, and art history. These schools offer a wide range of courses in these areas and have a culture where students and professors consider humanities courses to be the cornerstone, or at least a key part, of any student's education. In addition to encouraging students to take humanities courses within the classroom, these colleges maintain art collections and historical archives that students can use to enhance their educations outside of class.

Schools with a Humanities Designation

Amherst College
Bard College
Columbia University
Hampshire College
Harvard University
Hendrix College
Kenyon College
Middlebury College
Mount Holyoke College
New College of Florida
Pitzer College
Reed College
Sarah Lawrence College
Scripps College

Shimer College
Smith College
St. Johns College – Annapolis
St. Johns College – Santa Fe
St. Olaf College
Swarthmore College
Thomas Aquinas College
University of Chicago
Wabash College
Wellesley College
Wesleyan University
Williams College
Yale University

Engineering Designation

These are colleges that are known for the quality of their engineering programs. They have the facilities to offer students the opportunity to specialize in a wide variety of subfields of engineering.

Schools with an Engineering Designation

Arizona State University
California Institute of Technology
Carnegie Mellon University
Case Western Reserve University
Clemson University
Colorado School of Mines
Columbia University
Cooper Union Cornell University
Duke University
Georgia Institute of Technology
Harvey Mudd College
Illinois Institute of Technology
Johns Hopkins University
Lafayette College
Lehigh University
Massachusetts Institute of Technology
Northwestern University
Olin College
Penn State University
Princeton University
Purdue University – West Lafayette
Northwestern University
Rensselaer Polytechnic Institute
Rice University

Smith College
Stanford University
Stony Brook University
Swarthmore College
Texas A&M University
Tufts University
University of California – Berkeley
University of California – Los Angeles
Union College
University of Florida
University of Illinois
University of Massachusetts – Amherst
University of Michigan
University of Minnesota – Twin Cities
University of New Mexico
University of Pennsylvania
University of Pittsburgh
University of Texas – Austin
University of Wisconsin – Madison
Virginia Polytechnic Institute
Worcester Polytechnic Institute

Hard Sciences Designation

These are schools that have a large percentage of students who are interested in biology, physics and chemistry and pride themselves in these fields. In addition, these schools have a strong reputation and have a number of resources devoted to the study of these fields. These schools excel in offering their students with the opportunity to participate in research during the school year or devote substantial resources to helping students find research placements during the summer.

Schools with a Hard Sciences Designation

Bowdoin College
California Institute of Technology
Carnegie Mellon University
Case Western Reserve University
Columbia University
Cornell University
Georgia Institute of Technology
Harvard University
Harvey Mudd College
Illinois Institute of Technology
Johns Hopkins University
Massachusetts Institute of Technology
Ohio State University
Penn State University
Princeton University
Purdue University – West Lafayette
Rensselaer Polytechnic Institute
Rice University
Stanford University
Stony Brook University
Texas A&M University
University of California – Berkeley
University of California – San Diego
University of California – Irvine
University of California – Santa Barbara
University of California – Los Angeles
University of Maryland – Baltimore County
Union College
University of Chicago
University of Colorado – Boulder
University of Illinois
University of Maryland – College Park
University of Massachusetts – Amherst
University of Michigan
University of Minnesota – Twin Cities
University of North Carolina – Chapel Hill
University of Pennsylvania
University of Rochester
University of Texas – Austin
University of Washington
University of Wisconsin – Madison
Wabash College
Wellesley College
Yale University

Environmental Awareness and Activism Designation

These are schools where there has been a strong effort to promote environmental sustainability. A school with this designation has probably implemented policies to cut down on energy consumption on campus, and many students choose to be involved in environmental activism and research by working on student-run farms, taking research positions studying environmental science and environmental public policy issues, and interning over the summer for environmentally-focused non-profits.

Schools with an Environmental Designation

Carleton College
Colby College
College of the Atlantic
Goucher College
Hampshire College
Illinois Institute of Technology
Middlebury College
Pitzer College

Soka University of America
St. Mary's College of America
Stanford University
University of California – Davis
University of Colorado – Boulder
University of Iowa
University of Pittsburgh
University of Vermont

Pre-Med Designation

These are schools where a high percentage of students are interested in attending medical school. All of these schools also have a high medical school acceptance rate. While many of these schools do not necessarily have a major called "pre-med," all of them have substantial resources put in place to help students interested in medical school become prepared. A few of these colleges also offer specialized programs where students graduate with both a bachelor's degree and a medical school degree in six to eight years.

Schools with a Pre-Med Designation

Boston University
Bowdoin College
Brown University
Case Western Reserve University
Clark University
Franklin and Marshall College
George Washington University
Georgetown University
Harvard University
Hendrix College
Johns Hopkins University
Loyola University Chicago
Mount Holyoke College
Northwestern University
Oberlin College
Ohio Wesleyan University
Pomona College
Rhodes College
Rice University
Smith College
Stanford University

Stony Brook University
University of California – San Diego
University of California – Irvine
University of California – Los Angeles
University of Maryland – Baltimore County
Union College
University of Texas – Austin
University of Florida
University of Georgia
University of Illinois
University of Miami
University of Michigan
University of Minnesota – Twin Cities
University of New Mexico
University of North Carolina – Chapel Hill
University of Pennsylvania

Schools with a Pre-Med Designation (cont.)

University of Rochester
University of Virginia
University of Washington
University of Wisconsin –
Madison
Vanderbilt University

Washington University – St.
Louis
Wellesley College
Yale University
Yeshiva University

Architecture Designation

These are schools known for their undergraduate academic programs in architecture.

Schools with an Architecture Designation

Cooper Union
Cornell University
Georgia Institute of Technology
Illinois Institute of Technology
Pratt Institute
Rensselaer Polytechnic Institute
Rice University

Syracuse University
University of California –
Berkeley
University of Southern California
University of Texas – Austin
University of Virginia
Virginia Polytechnic Institute

International Student Body Designation

These are schools where the student body is more than 9% international.

Schools with an International Student Body Designation

Beloit College
Boston University
Brandeis University
Brown University
California Institute of
Technology
Carnegie Mellon University
Clark University
College of the Atlantic
Columbia University
Cooper Union
Cornell University
Emory University

Eugene Lang College at The
New School
Georgetown University
Georgia Institute of Technology
Harvard University
Illinois Institute of Technology
Indiana University –
Bloomington
Johns Hopkins University
Macalester College
Massachusetts Institute of
Technology
Michigan State University

Schools with an International Student Body Designation (cont.)

Middlebury College
Mount Holyoke College
New York University
Northeastern University
Princeton University
Purdue University – West Lafayette
Rensselaer Polytechnic Institute
Rice University
Soka University of America
Stony Brook University
University of California – Berkeley
University of California – San Diego
University of California – Los Angeles
University of Chicago
University of Colorado – Boulder
University of Illinois
University of Iowa
University of Miami
University of Pennsylvania
University of Washington
University of Southern California
Worcester Polytechnic Institute
Yale University

Greek Life Designation

These are schools where Greek Life is the dominating social force. At these schools, over 25% of the student body is involved in a fraternity or a sorority and even students not involved in a fraternity or sorority often attend events hosted by fraternities and sororities.

Schools with a Greek Life Designation

Arizona State University
Bucknell University
Case Western Reserve University
Centre College
College of William and Mary
Cornell University
Dartmouth College
Davidson College
Denison University
DePauw University
Dickinson College
Emory University
Florida State University
Franklin and Marshall College
Furman University
Gettysburg College
Hamilton College
Lafayette College
Lehigh University
Northwestern University
Ohio Wesleyan University
Penn State University
Rhodes College
Sewanee: The University of the South
Southern Methodist University
Syracuse University
Trinity College
University of California – Santa Barbara
Union College
Union College
University of Connecticut
University of Delaware
University of Florida
University of Georgia

Schools with a Greek Life Designation (cont.)

University of Illinois
University of Maryland –
College Park
University of Michigan
University of New Hampshire
University of Southern California
University of Richmond

University of Virginia
Vanderbilt University
Virginia Polytechnic Institute
Wabash College
Wake Forest University
Washington and Lee University
Whitman College

College Town Designation

These are schools that are known to be located within close proximity of a particularly vibrant and active college community. All of these schools are within close proximity to shops, restaurants, coffee shops, and arts venues.

Schools with a College Town Designation

Barnard College
Boston University
Columbia University
Cooper Union
Cornell University
Emerson College
Eugene Lang College at The
New School
Fordham University
Georgetown University
Harvard University
Illinois Institute of Technology
Loyola University Chicago
Massachusetts Institute of
Technology
Northeastern University
Northwestern University
Penn State University

Pratt Institute
Shimer College
Smith College
Tulane University
University of California –
Berkeley
University of California – Santa
Cruz
University of Texas – Austin
University of Colorado – Boulder
University of Georgia
University of Michigan
University of Vermont
University of Washington
University of Wisconsin –
Madison
Vanderbilt University

Housing Designation

These are schools that not only have the capacity to offer housing to the majority of students who want to live on campus but also are schools that offer high quality housing that students are generally pleased with. Instead of just traditional dorm building, these schools stand out because they offer students suite living, communal amenities within the dorms, townhouse-style apartments, full houses, or rooms with unusual character and charm. This list includes a number of schools with community housing systems where colleges divide their dorms into communities that represent a diverse microcosm of the greater school as well as specialty housing schools where there are many types of housing available including dorms separated by interest, co-ops, houses, and traditional dorms.

Schools with a Housing Designation

Bates College
Bryn Mawr College
Gettysburg College
Harvard University
Massachusetts Institute of
Technology
Middlebury College
Mount Holyoke College
Pepperdine University
Pomona College

Princeton University
Rice University
Scripps College
Smith College
University of Chicago
Vanderbilt University
Wellesley College
Williams College
Yale University

Single Sex Designation

These are colleges that enroll students of a single gender (either all-male or all-female). All of the schools on this list are all-female with the exception of Wabash College, which is an all-male school. Some students really want to be at a single sex school because they are known to create class camaraderie. All of these schools are known for their devoted alumni who feel strongly connected to their colleges for their entire lives.

One common misconception about single sex colleges is that they are single sex for moral or religious reasons. In the case of most of the schools on the list below, that is absolutely not the case. These are mostly schools that had a historical legacy and decided to remain single sex because they felt that if they were to become co-educational, they would lose a fundamental aspect of their student culture. Many women at all-female schools have commented that there was something freeing about being in a classroom where everyone else was female. Some have said that it allowed them to speak in situations where they otherwise would have felt more timid or allowed them to feel empowered in a class that at other schools might be dominated by men (for example, at other colleges computer science classes can be 70-80% male so some students find it really liberating to be in a computer science class of all women).

Additionally, the campuses at single sex schools are usually as active and vibrant as at their co-educational peers. Some of these schools have a very strong lesbian/gay/queer/trans scene, but there are of course many straight students too who really appreciate the sisterhood/brotherhood aspect of being a part of a single sex community. Regardless of your sexual orientation, single sex schools typically instill a deep sense of pride and belonging to the students who attend.

If you are unsure about whether or not you could be happy at a single sex school, keep in mind that many single sex schools are in consortium arrangements or are in close proximity to co-ed schools, so students who choose these schools can easily interact with students of the opposite sex. For example, students at Barnard College take many of their classes at Columbia University (which is right across the street). Wellesley College students can take classes at MIT (there is a college-operated bus that runs between the campuses multiple times each day). And Smith and Mount Holyoke Colleges are part of the Five College Consortium where they can take classes at Hampshire, Amherst, and the University of Massachusetts – Amherst (all of which are located with a short bus ride on a college-operated bus) any time they want.

If you notice that a school has a single sex designation as you create your college list, make sure you check to make sure it is an all-female school if you are female or an all-male school if you are male. Even if your profile matches the school in all other ways, if a school is single sex, and you are of the opposite sex, you will need to take it off your college list.

Schools with a Single Sex Designation

Barnard College
Bryn Mawr College
Mount Holyoke College
Scripps College

Smith College
Wabash College
Wellesley College

Writing Designation

These are schools that stand out in their offerings in creative writing. Some of these schools may offer creative writing majors, but others are also recognized because they have a wide range of course offerings in fiction writing, creative nonfiction, playwriting, etc. and allow students from across the college and university – regardless of their major – to participate.

Schools with a Writing Designation

Bard College
Beloit College
Colorado College
Columbia University
Emory University
Eugene Lang College at The New School
Florida State University
Hamilton College
Kenyon College

Knox College
Massachusetts Institute of Technology
New York University
Sarah Lawrence College
University of Iowa
University of Michigan
Washington University – St. Louis
Yale University

Section II
Admissions

For a lot of students, one of the scariest things about the idea of coming to college in the United States is the idea of getting through the admissions process. Take a deep breath. It is not as scary as you've been told. You just need to understand the basics of what American colleges are looking for and the requirements for submitting an application, and you will make it through. Yes, it will take some work, but if you are reading this with at least a few months before the deadline (the last possible deadline for most schools is in January of the year you would like to enroll), you should be able to make it through.

In this section, we are going to talk about the philosophy behind the American admissions system and how you will be evaluated. Then, we will talk about each of the components of a completed application and what you can do to impress the admissions officers in each of these components.

Finally, we'll answer some of the common questions international students have about getting all of this done in an easy, efficient, and effective way. This section might not sound as fun as the last one where you were evaluating schools rather than thinking about them evaluating you, but by the end of this section, you will at least know exactly what you are getting into and that should empower you to take control of your own college application and admissions process.

Chapter 14
Getting In

As we discussed in some of the previous chapters, most American colleges follow a holistic admissions process. There are three pillars to this process: academics, extracurricular activities, and your personality.

Grades and test scores are certainly a major factor in the evaluation of your application, but these other components are worth no less. What you participate in outside of class, or your extracurricular activities, matter. What did you participate in? Did you hold any positions of leadership? How did you spend your time over the summers? Your application is also evaluated in terms of personal characteristics. What kind of person are you? How do you stand out? What will you bring to this community? There are other factors that you may have less control over. Colleges care about building a class. They want diversity – they want students to come from a wide variety of places, represent a wide variety of ethnic backgrounds, and have a wide variety of skills and life experiences.

You cannot control every aspect of this process. There is a degree of randomness to it all. This is a key point: the college admissions process is not a fair game. Success depends upon recognizing this reality and then playing this game intelligently. This is the reason I recommend applying to eight to twelve schools. If you could just look at your academic profile and make a determination of whether or not you qualify, there would be no need to waste your time on so many applications. You fill out multiple applications because nobody can control all of the factors involved. You can learn about the evaluation process and take steps to maximize your chances, but nobody can guarantee acceptance. It doesn't matter if you have perfect grades and perfect scores; **there is no guarantee** in college admissions.

Because of the elusiveness of this process, especially at elite universities, there are probably more books and websites on this subject than on any other topic relating to American universities. I have recommended some of these resources to you on page 371. However, I hope this chapter will give you some perspective on how this process works and at the very least provide a good starting point when it comes to planning your applications.

Pillar I: Academics

You are going to college to get an education. Making sure you can handle the coursework and that you will take advantage of the resources that the college offers is of prime importance to colleges while reviewing your application. Different schools will have different considerations that weigh more heavily in their particular value system, but in general, most schools will consider the following academic factors:

- Grades
- Class rank or percentile (if available)
- Test Scores (SAT, ACT, TOEFL, Subject Tests, and/or AP Scores)
- Challenge of your secondary school course load
- Achievement within the context of the school
- Well-roundedness of secondary school course load
- Academic awards and distinctions
- Academic interests

Grades

Colleges want to see that you performed well in the classes offered at your school. Different schools will have different grading systems. In the United States, the most common grading system is the letter grade system, i.e., A's, B's, C's, etc.). However, some schools grade in further gradients (B+,B, B-, etc.), and others grade on a 100-point scale. Additionally, some schools have a system of **weighting grades**, which means that when they convert grades into a Grade Point Average (GPA), they increase the value of certain classes (usually harder classes) in the formula. So, for instance, if at a school an A is usually equal to a 4.0, some schools will change the weighting of a difficult class like calculus to a 5.0 for the purpose of calculating GPA.

In some countries, these systems may not make any sense at all. If you want to get a very rough sense of how your grades compare to the American students being admitted for the purpose of assessing the selectivity of a school, you can always use a GPA calculator online. These are not perfect and cannot take into account the difficulty of your individual school, but they should give you some sort of idea if you have no clue where you stand compared to American applicants. That said, most colleges have a more nuanced system to evaluate your application.

Colleges want to see that you did well at your school regardless of what grading system the school used. When you apply, colleges will ask your guidance counselor to send along a school profile that explains to them your high school's grading system and how to interpret it. They will use this report either to evaluate your grades directly or, less frequently, to decide how best to convert them into their own standardized evaluation system.

If available, another metric schools will use to inform their evaluation of your grades is your class rank or percentile. Not all high schools will release this information. If your school does not release this data, you are not at a disadvantage. However, if your school says you are ranked 36 of 200 or in the top 15% of your graduating class, the admissions committee will take this into account. If your school grades particularly harshly, having an idea of how you rank compared to the rest of your class can be an asset to your application since it could show that relative to your classmates your performance was exceptional despite perhaps a couple of grades that were not perfect.

Test Scores

In addition to your grades, your test scores will be used to determine how you stand academically. At the majority of schools, you will need to submit scores from either the SAT or ACT (most schools will accept either one).

In addition, some schools require you take several SAT subject tests (also known as the SAT II). These tests are offered in a number of subjects (math, world history, various foreign languages, physics, biology, etc.), and you can usually choose whichever subjects you prefer. Like each of the three components of the regular SAT, each of the SAT II subject tests is also graded on an 800-point scale.

If English is not your first language or if you attend a high school that is primarily conducted in a different language, you will also likely need to submit your TOEFL score to show proficiency in English. Finally, if your school offers Advanced Placement (AP) courses, you can submit the scores from your AP tests (though this is usually optional).

Context in the Evaluation Process

One thing that is important to understand is that when you apply to a particular college, you are not being compared apples to apples with everyone else. You are being assessed for your ability to do the best you could do given the circumstances you had. In general, a student who takes the hardest courses at an average school and took advantage of all of the opportunities open to him or her will be looked upon more favorably than a student who went to a better school, who took objectively harder courses but did not take advantage of as many of the opportunities that school offered, even if this second student has higher test scores.

If your school does not offer as many hard courses as other schools, this should not be held against you. On that same class profile that your guidance counselor will submit, it will list the most challenging courses your high school offers so colleges can assess appropriately. They key is that the colleges want to see that, for the most part, you signed up for at least some of these courses. Of course, if your school offers tons of hard classes you may be best advised not to take all of them. The best advice is to take at least some of these advanced courses and to approach course selection in general with the intention of challenging and enriching yourself. If it looks like you only signed up for courses because they were easier and you thought you could get a good grade, you will not be viewed as favorably as a student who signed up for a more challenging load.

Besides choosing hard courses, choosing a well-rounded group of classes is also important. Colleges view high school as a time to develop fundamental academic skills regardless of whatever field you end up working in for your career. If you avoided math altogether in high school, for example, you will be at a disadvantage. Make sure your high school schedule contains all of the core academic subjects. Math, science, social studies (particularly history and government), and English (or literature/writing courses in your native language) are essentials, and you should try to take at least one course in all four of these areas for all four years if this is an option at your school. Other courses colleges like to see are at least some foreign language study (if English is your second language, that will count) and some exposure to the arts (visual arts, music, dance, or drama). Electives in other subjects are fine too, but just make sure you don't skimp on the core fields.

Your achievement in your classes and the quality of your course load will depend upon your school, and what they offer. If the education at your school did not prepare you well for the SAT or ACT, you may not have done as well on these tests. For instance, if English is not your first language, you are at an inherent disadvantage on the verbal section of your SAT and ACT.

The good news is that the evaluation process is all about context. Again, colleges will not compare your grades and scores next to the student who went to the best boarding school in the continent and is the son of two English professors if you went to a public school in Bulgaria and took all of your classes in Bulgarian. They will look at your application and consider: Did this student take a challenging course load at his or her school? Did this student try to choose courses in the core areas? Did he or she perform to a high level in these courses? Did he or she perform well on tests considering his or her background? Keep in mind, however, that considering a student's particular context only goes so far. You will still need to perform well enough objectively that they believe you can handle the workload at their college. This means that while your verbal SAT score might be able to be lower than the student at the prestigious boarding school and get the same weight, it will still need to be high enough that a college believes you will be a competent student at their school.

Awards and Honors

Several other factors that could affect a college's assessment of you academically are the awards and distinctions you have won. While not essential to the viability of your application, external recognition can be a great way to make your application stand out. There is a space on the application for you to list your academic awards and distinctions.

There are lots of ways to earn academic recognition. Some high schools will give out awards for stellar papers, science fair projects, or for general achievement in a particular subject. If your school has recognized you in any way, make sure you put this into your application.

If you have ever entered an essay contest, been admitted to a conference or summer program based on your academic achievements, had any of your work published anywhere, or won an academic scholarship, these are all perfect things to put down. Winning a scholarship is probably one of the best ways to get academic recognition. Firstly, you get money that can help you pay for college. Then you can use the recognition from the scholarship as an academic accomplishment. Scholarships thus serve a double purpose.

There are also academic recognitions you can apply for locally that are not attached to a scholarship program. Large universities, especially the most prestigious ones, have alumni associations all over the world. These alumni associations often offer awards to local high school students based on their accomplishments. You can check the local branch of the alumni association in your city to see what they offer. Some colleges, like Princeton, Middlebury, Brown, Yale, Bryn Mawr, Wellesley, and others award "Book Awards" to outstanding high school students all over the world through local branches of their alumni associations. In some cases, your high school will need to sign up with the alumni association to make you eligible to win the award, but this is usually a simple process of filling out a couple of forms which you can help facilitate.

Academic Interests

The academic interests you select on your application can also play a role in your academic evaluation. Most schools will ask you if you know what you want to major in or at the very least to explain your academic interests. While many schools will be fine if you say that you are "undecided" especially if you can give good reasons why you want to use the first couple of years of college as a time for academic exploration, if you do specify an interest, make sure it makes sense. If you say you want to study biology but did the worst in all of your science classes, your expressed academic interest may not make the most sense. Or if you say you want to study history but only took one history course during the past four years, that also may raise questions.

If you do specify a specific academic interest, make sure that it reflects the courses you've taken, your performance, and ideally the awards and recognition you've received. And remember, just because you specify an interest on your application doesn't mean you can't change it later on. The majority of college students in the United States change their major from the one they specified on their application.

Pillar II: Extracurricular Activities

The next big category that colleges will consider along with your academics is what you did outside of class. Colleges are interested in the following:

- Breadth and depth of activities participated in outside of class
- Leadership positions
- Awards and recognitions within activities
- Contribution that your various skills and interests may make to the university community
- Summer activities
- Student jobs

There is value in participating in a lot of activities. There is more value in participating in at least a few activities in a significant way. Ideally, you've gained both depth and breadth in your extracurricular pursuits. Perhaps you've done something artistic, something athletic, and something related to service or political activism. In the best case scenario, you have at least one area that has been your focus and where you've received some recognition.

The trick to having an all-star college application is to appear well-rounded but also to have something that makes you stand out. Usually, whatever you decide makes you stand out is referred to as a "hook" because it makes you memorable. You might be the applicant the admissions officers remember as the great student who is also a regionally recognized gymnast (athletic hook), or you might be the well-rounded student who also won a national art competition (art hook). Your hook could come from a particular activity where you've gained distinction, held positions of leadership, or just did something interesting and memorable. The whole point is that you don't just want to come across as the "good and talented student," but you want to come across as the "good and talented student who particularly stands out in X way." If you can stand out at something, you are less forgettable, and when your admissions officer has dozens of applications to get through each day, that is important.

Keep this in your mind: The key to admissions success is to be well-rounded but also have a compelling hook

You want to appear competent at a lot of things but to get into the most competitive colleges, you want to be really spectacular at something. You might be thinking that you are not spectacular at anything. Maybe you are, and you don't even realize it. Think about these questions:

- Have you ever held a position of leadership? Have you organized an event? Been an officer (President, Vice-President, etc.) for a club? Been the captain of a team? Have you started an organization? Planned a trip? Put together a fundraiser? Started a petition to promote a particular cause? These things all count as leadership experience.
- Have you won any awards or other types of recognition? Have you been cast as a lead in a play? Have you gone on to be on an all-star (e.g., all district or regional) sports team? Have you been given a distinction for your performance in music? Has your art been selected to be displayed in a gallery? Have you published a story or an article you wrote about something that interests you? These are all distinctions colleges will recognize.
- What did you do over the summer? Did you practice your musical instrument? Play a sport? Attend a special program to develop skills in art, theater, a particular academic subject, or anything else? Did you tutor younger students? Volunteer on a service project? When you choose to devote yourself to something over the summer, your passion for something stands out.

Every school needs a certain number of athletes, a certain number of musicians, and a certain number of students who will work in research labs in their free time. Every school also needs a certain number of students who will be in their plays, participate in the student government, and volunteer for local organizations. If you can fit into one of these categories, that is fantastic. Use your extracurricular activities to prove that you can really make a contribution to a campus in one of these ways.

Perhaps your interests are a bit less conventional. That is fine too and can also work to your benefit. Let me give you a few examples.

I once knew a student who had an interest in bird watching. You might say that this may not be a particularly useful interest in terms of getting into college. He was a good student and he got good grades, but in his free time he liked to scout out and identify various types of birds.

There were no clubs related to bird watching at his school, so he couldn't participate in an organized group or gain a leadership role and then write that down on his application (perhaps he could have started a club, but apparently there wasn't much interest from other students). Still, he did spend many hours each week going out and looking at birds. Even if informally watching birds was all he did, he may have still written his habits down on his college application.

He could have written a nice essay along with it about his love of looking at birds and how it inspired him to become a conservationist. An admissions officer could potentially read this essay and think "Here is a really interesting, creative, and self-directed kid with a really unique passion." Then he might think "I don't think I've seen any other application about someone with an interest in bird watching. This guy is unique and could really contribute to the diversity on this campus."

Executed correctly with a good essay, this student may have been able to get into a lot of schools just with that. However, he took it one step further. He found out about an international bird-watching contest, and he placed in it. Now he had international bird-watching recognition and a hook that made him really stand out. He ended up going to Yale.

Last year, I worked with another student who had an unconventional hook. In this case, he didn't even realize it until we started talking. He was applying from an international school in Japan. When I started talking to him, he told me he was either interested in studying music or biology. He said he had experience in both but wasn't sure which he wanted to pursue in college. After school, he took violin lessons. He had also won recognition for his violin-playing locally. In addition, he had a research position at a biology lab at a university in Tokyo.

I told him working at a college lab while in high school in and of itself could be a hook as could his violin experience. Once I probed deeper though, I found out that one of these hooks made more sense than the other and that he actually had the potential to really stand out. When I asked him what he was working on at the university in Tokyo, he said he was studying fungi. I asked him why he was so interested in fungi. He said that he loved wandering through the woods in Japan. To this day, he spends a lot of his free time walking around the woods observing nature. One time, when he was in elementary school he found a particularly interesting fungus while on one of his walks in the woods. He picked it up, and later found out that he had identified a fungus that had never before been found in Japan. He was flown to Germany to receive an award.

Now instead of just saying that he worked in a "biology lab" he said he worked at a "fungus lab." He wrote an essay about how he developed his passion for fungus while taking long walks in the woods of Japan. He still included all of the violin stuff – the lessons and awards – in the extracurricular list. He ended up coming across as both well rounded, and a real standout. How many other students are applying with a passion for fungus? He is now a student at the University of California – Berkeley.

Really think about what makes you stand out. Consider what you've done and the areas in which you've gained recognition. You may go to a school that doesn't offer many conventional extracurricular activities, but even so, you must have filled your spare time somehow. It is best if you've attained some position of leadership or gained recognition, but even if you haven't, the way you've spent your spare time may still be worth writing down. Whether you write poetry, teach yourself languages, read science fiction, or build castles out of sugar cubes (I once worked with an aspiring architecture student who did this for fun, and he considered sending a picture with his application) – these things reflect you, your passions, and the kind of person you are. If you have unstructured activities like these, put them down. And if you want to make them really work for you, pair them with an essay explaining how these things have made you who you are, defined your interests and ambitions, and make it clear how you will use what you've gained from these activities to contribute to your college community and beyond. By explaining their value to you, you explain the value to the college and turn what perhaps you consider just a hobby into an asset to your application.

Finally, if you've ever held a job, that is also something to write down. A job is not always going to reflect your interests, but it may be a financial necessity – and, even if it's a job you hate, it can help shape who you are and how you see the world. If you have spent time working, you should definitely make note of it. Working shows a level of maturity and responsibility that is also valuable.

I know a student who worked at a convenience store for 20 hours per week. He did this to help support his family. And he originally didn't want to put it on his application because he thought that was embarrassing. He did do a few extracurricular activities. He had volunteered part-time at a hospital over the summer, and he did some tutoring after school for students who were struggling in English and math. However, he had not been able to achieve high levels of distinction in these areas because his time was so restricted by his job. What he failed to realize is that the personal qualities required to hold a 20 hour/week job while in school and still be able to graduate at the top of his class (he was the valedictorian) are extremely impressive. The improbable success that he had despite his family's circumstances made him stand out and gave him a hook. Today, he is at Harvard.

Pillar III: Personal Qualities

When colleges talk about evaluating your personal qualities, they are usually talking about the following factors, any of which could potentially impact how you as a person might enhance or contribute to life in the classroom and on the campus in general:

- Likeability
- Ambition and motivation
- Interesting background or story
- Overcoming obstacles/transcending one's background
- Ethnic/racial identification
- Legacy status (a parent or relative attended the college)
- First-generation status (neither parent attended college)
- Financial status (if need-aware)

Over the years, I've noticed that many applicants devote little time to considering how their personal qualities are reflected on their application, but many of the top schools consider this element of the application just as important as academics and extracurricular activities. That is why I can't stress enough how important it is to consider how to make sure you make this part of your application just as strong. Your personal qualities are evaluated through your essays, your teacher and guidance counselor recommendations, and for some schools, a personal interview. The personality traits colleges will be looking for can vary but include strength of character (resilience), the ability to overcome challenges, self-motivation, leadership potential, confidence, kindness, assertiveness, drive, ambition, focus, intellectual curiosity, and a sense of humor, among others.

Admissions officers will show concern if your own statements or those of your recommenders reveal that you are overly aggressive, unable to motivate or take care of yourself, irresponsible, scattered, disorganized, or worst of all, potentially going to put their reputation at risk for cheating or illegal behavior (drugs, alcohol, etc.).

Like it or not, your likeability matters. The method in which an admissions committee evaluates your application varies school to school, but in general it usually goes something like this: When your application arrives at the admissions office, it will usually be assigned a first reader. Readers are typically experts in a particular geographic area. A school will, for instance, have a reader for all applications from Western Europe or all the applications coming from China. These readers have a good sense of the grading systems in their regions, the extracurricular activities that are available, and have a more nuanced sense as to how to evaluate the application.

This first reader will read your application start to finish. He or she will look over your biographical information, your essays, your teacher recommendations, your extracurricular activities, you grades, test scores, and if you have one, your interview report. At many schools, the first reader will also make a note if you represent an underrepresented minority (many colleges would like to make sure they admit students from a wide variety of ethnic backgrounds and cultures), if one of your parents or relatives went to the college (these students will sometimes get a slight advantage), or if you are a first-generation college student (students who are the first in their families to attend college also are looked upon favorably). Additionally, you may receive a special designation if you are being recruited to the school for a sport. And if a school is need aware for international students, your status as a non-citizen will likely be noted if you are applying for need-based aid. After reading through pages and pages of material, the first reader is going to make a judgment: Are you a good candidate? Different schools will have different rating systems, but the basic idea is that they will either recommend that you are an outright deny, a possible admit, or a likely admit.

Regardless of the first reader's opinion, in most cases, schools will require that a second reader review the application as well. The second reader is often assigned randomly (they are not a geographic expert), and they read the application start to finish and form their own independent evaluation. If both readers independently agree that the application should be outright denied, usually that is the decision, and the process ends there.

If both readers select "possible admit" or "likely admit," the application will typically move on to the next stage of the process: the committee. If one of the readers recommends a deny and the other one recommends a possible admit or a likely admit, the application usually goes on to a third reader to determine if the application will move on to the committee stage to be put to a final vote.

Once you get into the committee stage, your personality really matters. If your grades are fantastic, you have great test scores, and have won high levels of distinction in your extracurricular activities, it would be unlikely that you would be dismissed outright. However, if there is something that you say in your essays that rubs an admissions officer the wrong way or if your teacher put something into your recommendation that might come across as questionable, it could be held against you.

At the committee stage, your fate is largely dependent on the opinion of your first reader. If your first reader likes you, they become your strongest advocate. They will get up in front of the committee and summarize your application to "make a case" for your admission.

Here is an example of the kind of summary you would want:

> *John is a fantastic applicant. He has a 3.9 GPA and is ranked fifth in his class of 452 students. He scored a 2150 on his SATs (690W, 720CR, 740M) and has taken a challenging course load including 5 AP classes out of the 7 offered at his school. He has a deep passion for music. He has played the violin since he was five years old and was the first chair in a local youth orchestra. He was selected as one of five students out of a pool of 1,000 students who*

auditioned to play with the professional orchestra at a special concert in his city. In his spare time, he has composed several jazz pieces, some of which have been performed by his school jazz band. He has also been very involved in the community outside of music. He has tutored peers in math 5 hours/week for the past four years, and he played soccer on a local traveling team during his freshman and sophomore years. In college, he says he would like to study composition and play in the orchestra. His music teacher said "John plays the violin with great emotional depth, more than I've ever seen from someone his age. He has an intuitive understanding of every piece I've given to him, and I've never seen that quality in any of my other music students in my 30 years of teaching." His math teacher said that though he has "never seen John have any trouble grasping the concepts he introduces almost immediately, John always makes an effort to help his struggling classmates deconstruct problems so that they arrive at answers."

John obviously had to be a stand out applicant in order to get this kind of summary from his first reader. He earned good grades and solid test scores, and showed both depth and breadth in his extracurricular activities. Plus, his teachers drew attention to his unique intuitive abilities. However, more importantly, the admissions officer reading the application also liked John. After reading an application containing probably 20-30 pages, she selected certain items to share with the committee. She chose compelling lines from the recommendations sent in and presented John in such a way where it seemed like she truly believed he would make a contribution to the music scene at the university and be a great peer to his fellow classmates.

Now let's say that John wrote an essay in which he said that he believed that he was academically superior to other people. Now that same first reader might present a very different report on him as follows:

John is clearly an academically accomplished kid. He has pretty good grades and is ranked within the top 5% of his class. His scores are solid (2150 on the SAT), and he took a pretty challenging course load at his school. He plays the violin, and he's been in the local youth orchestra and played with the local symphony. He has also written a few jazz compositions. He played soccer for a bit and did some math tutoring. His teachers think he has an intuitive understanding in both math and music. He seems like a smart kid. But he also seems a bit wrapped up in himself. He wrote his essay about how he only helps other students in his math class because, and I quote, "It sounds arrogant to say, but I've never met anyone as smart as me. I'm just being honest. I just get things. I tutor students and sometimes help out students in my math class because it is pitiful to see how slow they are at solving the most basic problems. I need to go to a college where people are at my level." He seems smart, but that sounds a little extreme. His scores are good and so are his grades, but they are not exceptional compared to some of the other stuff we see. And that ego is a bit much. What do you guys think?

In the first summary and this one, John is the same person. He has exactly the same grades and the same accomplishments. His teachers even said equally glowing things about him in both examples. The difference is that in the second example, something about the application rubbed the first reader the wrong way. His academic and extracurricular record was good enough to get him through to the committee stage despite the reader's feelings about his personality. And to be fair, she still shared the positive aspects of John's application in her report (which is her job), but she clearly didn't *like* John, and accordingly shared some of the less savory parts of his application as well. John's essay made her believe that he was arrogant and would not necessarily be a positive force in the college community. What this reader perceived as an out-of-proportion ego made her see his grades and test scores in a new light. *Well they are good, but not necessarily good enough to warrant that huge ego.* In the holistic admissions process, it is perfectly acceptable to consider these more subjective qualities. Likability counts.

None of this is to say that you should try to portray yourself as someone different than who you are. However, read over your essay carefully to make sure make sure it reflects a version of yourself that you yourself actually like. What kind of tone are you using? Are you putting other people down? Are you blaming your failures on others? What qualities does this essay show that you have? Read your essays from the eyes of a stranger, and think "What kind of person do I think this is?" "Would I want to meet this person?" "Would I want to help this person?" In the end, admissions officers are human beings, and, like all human beings, they can't help being influenced by their emotions, at least to some extent.

Recommendations are another way readers will try to get a sense of your personality. Firstly, make sure that the teacher you pick actually knows you. Don't just pick someone because you got a good grade in his or her class. "Alex did well in my class and got an A" is not a good recommendation. If that is all your recommendation says, it actually makes you look worse because a reader can't help but wonder what is not being said. Did you really not leave any other impression on this teacher? Or is the teacher only stating the objective truth to avoid saying what they really think? Instead of picking a teacher who gave you a good grade but doesn't know anything about you as a person, pick a teacher who is able to describe not merely your academic strengths but your personal qualities as well. How do you feel about learning? How do you interact with your peers? What kind of personality traits do you exhibit within the classroom – or, perhaps, outside it as well? If you have distinguished yourself in class by interrupting students and showing that you are smarter than everyone else, you may want to choose a different teacher for a recommendation.

Chapter 15
The College Application

In the past, every college had their own application and their own application requirements. In recent years, in part because of the Internet, the application process has become more consistent between schools. Although a few schools continue to use their own applications, most of those featured in this book will now accept the **Common Application** (www.commonapp.org), which can be used to apply to 517 schools, or its competitor, the **Universal College Application** (www.universalcollegeapp.com), which can be used to apply to 32 schools. These are applications you can access and complete online.

When you log into either of these sites, you will be able to complete a main application that you will submit to every school to which you apply. This application typically consists of the following.

- Biographical section asking for your full name, address, nationality, racial/ethnic designation (you don't have to disclose this if you don't want to), first language and all languages in which you are proficient, and the occupation and level of education attained by your parents
- GPA and class rank (if calculated by your school)
- Course selection during your senior year
- Awards and honors you have received
- Test scores for the SAT or ACT, SAT Subject Tests (required by some schools), AP scores (usually optional to report), and TOEFL scores (if English is not your first language)

- A list of all of your extracurricular activities, years of participation, and positions of leadership
- Personal statement of no more than 650 words (there are several prompt options available)

In addition, many schools will ask you complete a supplement (which you can access directly through the Common Application or Universal College Application website) that is specific to the school. Typically supplements ask you to complete short-answer or additional essay questions relating to topics of a school's choosing. It may also ask you to select your preferred major and the names of several extracurricular activities in which you'd like to be involved during your undergraduate years. Many schools will also give you the opportunity to write in any information you feel is missing from the rest of your application. This is a great opportunity for you to explain a grade you feel needs explanation, elaborate on a particular extracurricular activity or award (especially if it is something unusual an admissions officer might not recognize), or include anything else you think might be important to get across.

Personal Statement and Essays

Once you register online to fill out the application, the process is pretty self-explanatory. You can fill most of it out within a few hours. The part of the online application and supplement that will take you the most time will be the personal statement and any supplementary essays.

For many students, this is the part of the application process they are the most worried about. The first thing to understand about the essay is that its primary purpose is not to assess your writing ability. If your essay is written extremely poorly that may end up being considered, but the main reason colleges ask you to write essays is to get a better sense of who you are. The essay is the most critical part of the personality component of your evaluation process, and it can also help inform admissions officers of your academic and extracurricular interests.

Generally, you will have a lot of latitude in terms of the subject matter of the essay. The personal statement in the Common Application gives you six different topics including "Topic of Your Choice" where you can write about anything you want. You can write about your relationship with your little sister or how you were obsessed with toothpicks as a child. Anything goes. The key is to use this essay as an opportunity to reveal something interesting about yourself. You want to show the admissions officers that you have one or several of these things:

- A thoughtful or unique perspective of the world
- Deep interests in a particular field (this can be academic, extracurricular, philosophical, or anything)
- Interesting life experiences
- Capacity to contribute to the university community in a valuable way

If you can do one or several of these things well, you will have an effective essay. In a moment, I will give you some advice about how to tackle the large number of essays you may be required to write in a time efficient matter, but first I wanted to say just one more time that the essay is not a test of your writing ability.

Over the years, the majority of students I've worked with have handed me the first draft of their essays filled with words they would never actually use in everyday life. These are words like "plethora" and "myriad" that they saw in their SAT preparation book and felt were important to use to show that they had a big vocabulary. Unless these words are genuinely a part of your everyday speech, I would advise you to leave them out. They tend to sound stilted and make your writing sound unnatural if they aren't part of your natural voice. You want your essay to read like you are speaking to the admissions officer directly so that you come across as honest and authentic.

Now, how do you write your essays most efficiently? A lot of students ask me, "How am I going to write 16-24 essays?" If you apply to 8-12 schools and each school requires two essays (generally the average), that is a lot of writing!

But here's the thing: although there will always be some unusual questions hidden throughout certain supplements, most questions tend to be pretty open-ended. Some schools just give you an very general essay prompt and basically say "write whatever you want," but even when the question doesn't appear to be quite that open, there is usually room for overlap between one essay and the next. Let me give you an example:

Question 1: Tell us about something that is important to you.
Question 2: Who has influenced you the most and why?

On the surface, these are two separate essays. But if you stop and think about it, they could potentially be related. Let's say that you love making pastries so you decide to write your first essay about how you discovered your love of pastry while spending the summer working at a hotel restaurant and how ever since then you have continued to develop your pastry making skills, even opening your own pastry business.

This concept has promise because it demonstrates a unique skill and interest that you have, shows that you have a strong work ethic, and reflects an entrepreneurial spirit. All of these things can help build your case for why you could be a good fit for a university.

Now let's consider Question 2. To answer this one, you still want to show these same qualities you demonstrated when answering Question 1 so let's stick with a similar theme. But, don't forget this question is about the person who most influenced you and why. Well, remember that when you worked at the hotel that one summer there was a pastry chef, Mr. Smith, that taught you all of the techniques that you use today? Remember how he encouraged you to start a business, and helped put you into contact with some of your biggest clients? Well, take your answer to Question 1 and *modify* it so that now the first sentence reads, "I took a summer job at The Four Seasons because I wanted to earn some extra cash, but when on my first day I took one bite out of a chocolate almond tart, made by Mr. Smith, the hotel's head pastry chef, my world changed. By the end of the summer, Mr. Smith had taught me to make the tart (and a dozen others) myself, and instilled a passion in me that inspired me to spend the next two years running my own pastry operation." The remainder of the essay can remain 85-90% the same as in the original version. You may want to bring Mr. Smith back into it in a few places and circle back around to him again at the end. But at the end of the day, all you need to do is reshape the essay, not rewrite it.

You do need to make sure you actually answer the question being asked (read it through thoroughly once you finish editing to make sure), but once you start applying this reshaping method, you will actually find lots of questions are related.

When I've suggested this before, some students have said things like, "But Mr. Smith is not the most important person to me – my mom is."

Okay, well if 98% of the people answering this question were to think of it so literally, they would also pick their mothers. And while a few of those essays might be interesting if written well enough, most of them would be pretty boring, non-specific, and frankly, repetitive. Most of us had mothers who taught us how to walk, talk, bathe, and what have you. Obviously those things are pretty important. Probably more important than knowing how to make a chocolate almond tart, but that is beside the point. Most of the time, recounting the story of your mom helping you learn to tie your shoe is not going to help your application.

Your mission should be to communicate whatever you are not able to communicate in the rest of your application that you think is important to convey to the admissions committee. Of course, if you can write a compelling essay about why some more unique feature of your mother (for example, her Latin American heritage, or her devotion to tae kwon do, or her passion for museums) influenced you in a way that is relevant to your future and your education, by all means use that for a personal essay.

I always have my students make a list of important things they want to come across in their essays – things that have bearing on what colleges *really* want to know, which amounts to who are you and why do you belong at that particular school. You don't have to, and, usually, shouldn't, answer these questions directly, but keep a list of important things you want to communicate in the back of your mind as you plan your essay. There are no right answers, but you need to think about what needs to be elaborated from the rest of your application, experiences you think are important to share, or personal qualities that are unique and not communicated elsewhere. I would make this list before you even look at the essay topics.

Here is an example of such a list that could have been written by the student who wrote the pastry essay:

- Ambitious
- Hard worker
- Overcame struggle freshman year
- Spent time working job over the summer
- Passionate about pastry and developed that passion
- Entrepreneurial
- Multicultural (complex identity)

The pastry essay would cover most of those topics. The part about overcoming struggle freshman year and the multicultural background might be different enough thematically that they are probably best incorporated into a second completely different essay (remember most schools ask for at least two anyway), but remember you can recycle that one too.

All in all, with this recycling/reshaping method, most students I work with applying to eight to twelve schools end up writing a total of about three to four completely different essays, not sixteen or more. I do have them edit all sixteen or more versions carefully because with all of the modifying this method requires, there is a lot of room for typos and sentences being pieced together in the wrong order. Still, I firmly believe that this method is not only a huge time saver overall, but it also helps you stay on track and write about the things you need to convey, not just parrot back some easy answer to the question. You need to make every essay count, and you do that by making it do what you need it to do to make the best case possible for your admission to a particular school.

Additional Components of the Application

Along with the submission of this written application, the following should be sent to colleges separately:

- An official high school transcript sent directly from your school
- A letter of recommendation from either your counselor or principal
- Your teacher recommendations (ideally from two teachers who have taught you an academic subject in the last two years of high school and who are likely to write something specific and positive about you as a learner and/or a human being)
- Official score reports from your tests (you should be able to order these reports on the College Board's website for SAT and AP score reports, the ACT website for the ACT, and the ETS website for the TOEFL)
- Interview report sent directly from your interviewer (if applicable)
- Any additional materials you want to send in directly (e.g., professional recordings of you performing music; a portfolio of artwork; a copy of a published or prizewinning story, essay, or musical composition; a couple of newspaper clippings about your community service; or anything else that you think would be valuable to supporting your application. Keep in mind, though, that if these additions don't reflect truly extraordinary achievement, relate to your genuine interests, or tell something relevant about you that the admissions committee doesn't already know, supplemental materials are apt to be annoying rather than enlightening.)

Common application questions

Should I take the ACT or the SAT?

The SAT and the ACT are competitors. Most colleges will accept either one, and you should choose whichever test you prefer. Some students find the style of one to be easier than the other. The SAT advertises itself as a reasoning test and the ACT as a content-based test. At the end of the day though, the most significant difference between the tests is the style in which questions are asked.

Figuring out what the SAT questions are asking you to do is part of the test. The questions themselves are worded in such a way that you need to spend a few seconds understanding what the question is about. ACT questions tend to be much more straightforward. Students who are less familiar with English sometimes prefer the ACT style. However, the ACT does have slightly harder math than the SAT, and there is a science section that is completely different than anything on the SAT and so requires more preparation. You can take practice tests of both online and see which one you prefer. Also, check online to see if they are both offered in your country because some countries will only offer one or the other.

How do I sign up for the SAT or ACT?

You can sign up for the SAT on the College Board's website:

sat.collegeboard.com/register

You can sign up for the ACT online at their registration website:

www.actstudent.org/regist/

How can I best prepare for taking the required tests?

Neither of these tests requires extensive preparation. The knowledge tested is all material you have learned in school.

The most important thing to do is familiarize yourself with the test before you sit down to take it. You can learn about the different types of questions for the SAT on their website (sat.collegeboard.org/practice/) and for the ACT on their website (actstudent.org/testprep). You can take a practice test free on those websites as well. There are many books available with additional practice tests if you want more practice. Several private companies make replica tests for practice, but the best books are the "Official" books that publish actual exams that have been used in prior years (check the back of the book to make sure that it says the tests are "real"). I recommend you try to do a couple of practice tests within the time constraints of an actual test. Set a timer and go through each section without interruptions just like you would on testing day. Mimicking actual testing conditions will give you the best sense of where you currently are and how much preparation you need to do.

After you are done, go through the test and review all of the questions you got wrong. You will find that variants of the same questions come up time and time again. After a careful review of every question, it is likely your score will improve the next time you take the test (unless you start off with an extremely high score on your first try).

If you are still having trouble reaching your desired score, there are many resources available to you. Nowadays, there are test prep companies all around the world that cater to SAT and ACT preparation. These companies will help troubleshoot your problem questions and administer additional practice tests under realistic testing conditions. In addition, there are several online courses you may want to look into.

A lot of the value of these courses is that they force you to set time aside to work on your test preparation. Because most preparation has to do with familiarizing yourself with the types of questions being asked and reviewing things you learned years ago in school, classes will not focus on new material. If you have the discipline to take some practice tests and go through them carefully on your own, you will likely have the same kind of results as someone going through a class, but some students like having the structure a teacher provides.

The exception to this is that if English is your second language and you have not taken extensive courses in writing in English, a course focusing on the Verbal and Writing sections may introduce you to new concepts that were not a part of your high school education.

When should I take the SAT or ACT?

Most US students take the SAT or ACT during the spring of 11th grade (that is, about 6-9 months before the application deadline), which is what I would recommend. If you take these tests too early, you risk not doing as well and having to still show those scores to certain schools. If you take them too late, you may not have the opportunity to try again if you decide you want to try to improve your score. If you take the test in the spring before applications are due, and you are unhappy with your results, you can study over the summer and take it again at the beginning of your final year of high school (12th grade in the USA). The last possible testing date most colleges will accept is usually the January test during your year of application (again, 12th grade, or senior year, in American high schools).

Do I need to take the SAT II/SAT Subject Tests?

The SAT Subject Tests (also known as the SAT II) are separate exams from the regular SAT, and you must take them on a separate testing date. These tests are hour-long exams on specific topics. Many colleges do not require that you take these tests or submit scores from them, but a handful of the elite colleges do require scores from 2-3 of these tests. So, if you're considering applying to any of these schools (which include Ivy League Schools and many of the most prestigious small liberal arts schools), consider taking these tests when you feel prepared for them academically. Because these tests are related to content you learn in school, it is usually easiest to take these tests as soon as you finish taking the relevant course material in school.

I often recommend taking the subject tests in May or June of your junior year (11th grade) in subjects related to what you are studying that semester. You can take the test right after you've finished studying for your final exam in that subject at school so you do not have to study the same material at two separate times. If you are starting to prepare early, I've known some students who take these tests at the end of their sophomore year, and, in exceptional cases, freshman year, just to lighten their load later on. As with the regular SAT, the last possible testing date most colleges will accept is usually the January test during your final year of high school, the year you are applying to that college. However, please note that you cannot take the regular SAT and the subject tests at the same sitting, so you will need to schedule these tests on different dates.

Which SAT Subject Tests should I choose?

There are 20 different SAT Subject Tests offered in a variety of subjects from physics to Japanese to world history. Typically, you can choose to take whichever you'd like (although there are a few schools that require a particular test). Unlike the standard SAT or ACT, the subject tests do require some specialized knowledge, so it is best to pick areas where you already are skilled.

If you've studied French at school for eight years, for example, that could be the perfect test. If you just finished taking biology, the biology exam may be a good choice. Taking an SAT Subject Test in your native language, however, is not looked upon favorably, so I would typically advise against it. You can find practice exams online so you can look through them and figure out which tests you prefer. There are also a number of preparation books available most of which include additional practice tests.

Do I have to take a test to go to an American college?

The majority of 4-year colleges will require that you take either the SAT or ACT to gain acceptance to the school. There are a select group of schools, including some top-notch institutions that are testing optional and will not require you to take an entrance exam. These schools are listed on page 375.

Do I need to take the TOEFL?

Many colleges will require you to submit a TOEFL score if your high school experience was not in English. Even if you went to an international school where everything was in English, some schools will require that if you reside outside of the US and report that English is not your first language, you still must submit TOEFL scores. I recommend that all international students from non-English-speaking countries who are not American citizens take this exam just in case. You don't need to get a perfect score on the TOEFL, but proving proficiency in English helps schools know that the language of instruction will not be an issue for you.

Can I take the admissions tests more than once?

Yes. You can take the SAT, ACT, and any of the other tests as many times as you'd like. The tests are long, and costly, and most students wouldn't call taking them a fun experience, however, many students find that their scores improve on a second or third try. If you are happy with your scores on the first go, however, there is no need to put yourself through a second attempt.

Will colleges see my scores each time I took the test?

The majority of schools have implemented score choice, which means that you only need to submit the scores that you want the college to see. If you took the SAT three times, for example, you could choose just to send in your scores from the third attempt. You cannot pick and choose by section, though, so if you scored highest on the verbal section the second time and highest on the math during the third test, you must submit all of the scores from both of those sittings if you want colleges to see both of those scores.

There are some colleges that will not accept score choice. These colleges request that you submit scores from every sitting. This is not to say that if you took both the ACT and the SAT that you would need to submit both, but rather if you took the ACT twice and decided to send in those scores, these schools would want to see the scores from both attempts of that particular test. If you chose not to send in your SAT scores at all, that would be fine.

Regardless of whether a school has score choice or not, you can also check whether a school "superscores." Some schools will only consider the highest scores from each section if you've sent them test results from multiple sittings. In other words, they will mix and match scores that you achieved on different dates in a way that gives you the highest possible score, and they will use that highest score to evaluate your application.

Who should I ask for my teacher recommendations?

Most schools will ask for at least two academic recommendations. In most cases, it is best to choose teachers from 11th or 12th grade (i.e., your final two years of high school), although if you had a teacher in 9th or 10th grade with whom you've maintained an active relationship, that can be okay as well. Pick someone that you know personally and who has more to say about you than the fact that you got a good grade in their class. But just as important as your relationship, pick a teacher that you think will write about you in a lively way. You don't want your teacher to just recite facts about you, especially facts that are probably clear from other parts of your application. (e.g., "Maria is the editor of the newspaper and gets good grades on all of her writing assignments."). You want someone who will talk about your passions, interests, and personal qualities (e.g., "Maria always goes the extra mile to research her new articles. I've rarely met a student so thorough. She applies this meticulous nature to every assignment she's turned in during class. She has a great appreciation and love for details.").

If English is not your teacher's first language, and if you believe this will affect the quality of the writing, consider having that teacher write the recommendation for you in his or her native language and offer to hire a translator to translate the recommendation to English after its written. Also, although some admission officers insist this doesn't matter to them because they care about personal qualities the most, try to pick teachers from different subject areas. Instead of picking two science teachers, choose one science teacher and one history teacher. Or pick a math teacher and a literature teacher. Unless you are applying to an art school or music conservatory, it is best to have both of your recommendations come from a teacher that taught you a core academic subject (math, science, social sciences, English/literature). If you have an art, music, physical education, or other teacher that you think would write a stellar recommendation, you can always ask them to submit you a third recommendation as a supplementary material.

Do I need an interview?

Most colleges will not require an interview, but many will offer optional interviews. Interviews are not always available to international students – it depends on the number of interviewers in your country. If you are not offered an interview, it usually does not mean anything with regards to the status of your application. It usually just means there wasn't someone available to interview you. If you are offered an interview, it is best to take it. It shows your interest in the school and is a great opportunity for you to learn more about where you are applying.

Who will interview me?

The majority of interviewers are alumni who volunteer to do interviews for their schools. Unless you decide to do an on-campus interview (which very few students opt to do because it requires traveling to the campus), your interviewer will most likely not be employed by the admissions office, and they will not have access to the rest of your application.

What happens during an interview?

The interview is not a technical interview: it is a personal interview. The interviewer's job is to get a sense of who you are, what you are interested in, and why you are interested in attending their university.

Here are some of the most common questions you'll encounter:

- Tell me about yourself.
- What courses are you currently taking?

- What is your favorite and least favorite course? Why?
- What extracurricular activities do you participate in?
- What do you do in your free time?
- How have you spent your summers?
- What was the last book you read?
- Who has influenced you most?
- What is the biggest challenge you've faced?
- What do you consider to be your greatest strength and greatest weakness?
- Why do you want to go to college?
- What attracts you to a university in the United States?
- What are your biggest concerns about college?
- Why do you want to study at _____ University?
- What do want to study?
- Do you plan on continuing to participate in the same extracurricular activities in college?
- What questions do you have for me?

That last question is the most important to think about. What questions will you ask your interviewer? Half the reason schools offer interviews is because they want to give you the opportunity to learn about the school. Remember that the interviewers are most often alumni interviewers who volunteer in large part because they loved their college experience and want to share that with others. If you give them a chance to talk about their lives in college, they will like you more. Try to ask them as many questions as they ask you, and don't be afraid to ask them questions interspersed with them asking you questions. The best interviews are conversations.

Here are some examples of great questions to ask:

- Why did you choose _____ University?
- Looking back on your experience, what did you like most about your college experience?
- What did you study?
- What extracurricular activities did you participate in?
- Did you have any professors who changed your life?

- Did you feel your peers enjoyed their experiences at your college as much as you did?
- Did you live on-campus all four years?
- Did you study abroad?
- What did you like least about your college experience?
- How has your education influenced the rest of your life?

Should I send in additional materials?

Many students get accepted into even the best colleges without sending in any materials beyond the requirements. However, if there is something that you feel is missing from your application that you need to communicate another way, supplementary materials are always an option. The most common supplementary materials sent in are CDs with recordings of instrumental or vocal performances. If you are a musician with a high level of skill, sending in a recording may help support your application. Musical CDs are usually sent directly to the music department by the admissions office where they are evaluated by a music professor. If they are outstanding, the music department will alert the admissions office, which could help your application. Plenty of musicians do not send in supplementary CDs, but if you have a good recording, it could help your application. Art portfolios are also commonly sent in and reviewed in a similar fashion.

Other common supplementary materials include newspaper clippings you were featured in, short pieces of writing you perhaps had published, or supplementary recommendations (in addition to the two required). Be careful not to send too many of these things, and be careful that these things really give new insights about you that may have bearing on their admissions decision. Although admissions officers will guarantee they'll read every page you send, if you send them 50 newspaper clippings, they won't be so happy with you. Keep it to one or two pages of supplementary reading material if possible – and make sure that this material is necessary to give the admissions office new, relevant, and, of course, positive information about you. Admissions officers are swamped reading and evaluating thousands of applications, and the last thing you want to do is add to their workload by sending them unnecessary, unhelpful material.

Chapter 16
Application Timeline

You should begin working on your application during August of your senior, or final, year of high school or secondary school, exactly one year before you plan on enrolling in college. Colleges typically release their applications during the first week of August, so you can begin filling everything out directly then. How much time you have to complete your application will depend on whether you are applying during the regular or early round.

Most colleges set their application deadline for regular decision sometime between December 31st and January 15th. There are a few select schools (like the University of California campuses and many music conservatories) that set their deadlines earlier (e.g., mid-November or early December), but they are the exception. Once you submit your application, you will likely need to wait several months before you receive your decision. You may receive word as early as February, but most decisions for the colleges in this book will come in towards the end of March. All decisions will be available before the first week of April.

Many colleges also offer students the opportunity to submit their applications early (usually between October 15th and November 1st) and receive a decision early (usually mid-December). Different schools have very different policies regarding their early admissions programs. Make sure you read the early admissions policies for the schools you are looking at very carefully before applying. Here are the most common early options:

Early Decision – You can only apply to one school early under an early decision plan. You will need to make sure it is your first choice school. The decision is **binding** which means that if you are accepted, you will be required to matriculate. If you are not accepted, you are free to apply to other schools during the regular round of admissions. Students who are **deferred** (told to wait until the regular round of admissions for their decision) are also able to apply to other schools during the regular round. Early decision is great if you are completely positive about your first choice school. If you get in, you won't have to apply anywhere else. Plus, the acceptance rate at early decision programs is usually higher than during the regular pool because colleges want to "lock in" a certain number of students into their class, so you may gain an admissions advantage.

Early Action – If you want to know about how you fare in the admissions process early, early action programs are a great way to go. You can apply to as many schools early as you want as long as they also have an early action plan. You will find out whether you are accepted, deferred, or denied by mid-December, but regardless of the decision, you are free to apply elsewhere during the regular admissions round.

Single Choice Early Action – Like early decision, you can only apply to one school under a single choice early action plan. However, unlike early decision, your decision is non-binding. If you are accepted into the college early, you will not be required to matriculate. You are still free to apply to additional colleges during the regular decision round and select from all of your acceptances in April after you've heard back from everyone.

Rolling Admissions – Instead of offering regular and early admissions rounds, a few schools will have a **rolling admissions process**. These schools do not have a fixed application deadline and response date; schools with a rolling process say you can apply anytime between this date and that date. Once your application has been received, they will review it, make a decision, and typically send you an answer within a matter of weeks. They will not wait until they have received all of the applications before they begin the reviewing process. If you are looking at a school with a rolling process, you are at an advantage if you apply earlier in the process when there are still many spots open.

After all of your decisions have come in, you will typically have until May 1st to make your final decision about where you'd like to enroll and submit your deposit (with the exception of early decision schools, which you are expected to attend if they admit you in December). Between April 1st and May 1st, many colleges will host a visiting students day for all admitted students. These are several-day events, specifically for recently admitted students, where new admits are invited to stay with current students on campus in a dorm, sit in on classes, attend extracurricular fairs, see student performances, and experience campus life. If you are able to travel out to one of these events, they are a great opportunity to meet other new admits, talk to current students and professors, and get a sense of the campus culture. Plus, colleges go out of their way to make these events really fun (lots of free food, concerts, and lectures), which some could say paints a slightly unrealistic picture of day-to-day life, but at the very least these events give you an opportunity to see many different facets of the college community in just a couple of days.

Section III
Finalizing Your List

Now that we've gone through the logistical details of the application process, it is time to get back to the fun part. You know what you are looking for in your college experience and you know what you need to do to complete your applications and get acceptance to an American college, so now it is time to set your sights on a specific list of colleges.

In this section, we'll revisit your College Match Profile preferences, and you'll be able to identify the schools that fit the criteria that you care about most. The process of matching your preferences to the 176 schools profiled is going to require a bit of work, but at the end you will have a list of eight to twelve schools that you should be excited about, and it will make your efforts worth it.

Armed with a list of target schools, you're going to want to learn more about each school on the list. You'll want to learn about their specific academic and extracurricular programs, hear what current students say about their experience, see pictures of the campus, read the admissions statistics, and familiarize yourself with their specific application deadlines and requirements. Later in this section, I've created a list of resources you can use to get all of this information without having to set foot on the campus.

Finally, I've included several other useful lists for you including a list of resources for researching financial aid and a list of schools that are testing optional (for those of you who hate taking tests).

You still have a long journey ahead before you step foot in the place where you'll spend four of the best and most exciting years of your life, but you are well on your way to getting to that day ready and fully prepared for everything that lies ahead.

Chapter 17
Building Your College List

Now is the time where we take all of the preferences you determined in Section I and translate them into a specific list of colleges where you can apply. Hopefully, you filled your preferences into the chart on the next page as you went through each chapter in Section I. If you have not done so, now might be the time to review some of the chapters in Section I and identify the categories and preferences you felt were the best fits for you.

College Match Profile Chart

To fill out the College Match Profile Chart, go through each of the eleven categories we discussed in Section I, and determine which characteristics you would want in a school. For example, if you are sure you want to attend a college and not a university, select "college" but not "university" in the "school type" category. If you are flexible about attending a college in a "small city" or "city," but do not want to be in anything smaller, select both "small city" and "city" for the "surrounding area" category. Write down the characteristics you prefer for each category in the third column labeled "College Match Profile". If you need to review the definitions and pros/cons of any of the characteristics, you can revisit the chapters on each of these categories on the pages listed for each one.

If you do not feel strongly about a particular category, write down all of the characteristics for that category in the "College Match Profile" column. For instance, if you decide you are fine with any prestige ranking, write down "most prestigious," "prestigious," and "no prestige ranking," in the third column.

College Match Profile Chart

Category	Characteristics	College Match Profile Write in the characteristics (listed in the middle column) that you prefer for each category.
School Type Chapter 3 (pg. 23)	College University	
School Funding Chapter 4 (pg. 35)	Public Private	
Campus Structure Chapter 5 (pg. 53)	Island Street-side Integrated	
Surrounding Area Chapter 5 (pg. 53)	Rural Town Suburb Small City City	
Region Chapter 6 (pg. 71)	New England Mid-Atlantic South Pacific Coast West Midwest	
Size Chapter 7 (pg. 103)	Very Small Small Medium Large	
Curriculum Type Chapter 8 (pg. 113)	Open Distribution Requirements Loose Core Core	

Residential Type Chapter 9 (pg. 133)	High Residential Medium Residential Low Residential	
Selectivity Chapter 10 (pg. 147)	S-1 S-2 S-3 S-4 S-5 S-6	**Best Fit Category** (the category that best matches you): **Safety Category** (one category less selective than where you best fit): **Reach Category** (one category more selective than where you best fit):
Financial Aid Chapter 11 (pg. 169)	The Best Aid Excellent Aid Good Aid Some Aid No Institutional Aid for International Students	
Prestige Chapter 12 (pg. 189)	Most Prestigious Prestigious No Prestige Rating	

Using Your College Match Profile to Determine a Perfect Match

Now that you have filled out the entire chart, you should have your College Match Profile (the third column on the chart). Let's review for a moment exactly what this means. Your College Match Profile represents the characteristics you are looking for in your ideal school. You may have several characteristics for each of the eleven categories that you might be equally happy with and that is fine. For instance, you might be okay with a school with an "open curriculum" or a system of "distribution requirements," and include both of those categories in your College Match Profile. Or you might have a specific preference for one particular characteristic in a given category such as deciding you have a strong preference for schools with a "high residential" campus rather than any of the other residential characteristics.

The purpose of creating this profile is to give you a comprehensive list of characteristics you consider desirable in a school. You will be using your College Match Profile to compare your ideal characteristics to the characteristics of the 176 schools profiled in this book. When you come across a school that has a characteristic that matches one of the options you selected on your College Match Profile for all eleven categories, you have found a perfect match school.

For example, your College Match Profile could look like this:

School Type: **University**
School Funding: **Private**
Campus Structure: **Integrated** or **Island**
Surrounding Area: **Small City**, **City**, or **Town**
Region: **New England**, **Mid-Atlantic**, **Pacific Northwest**
Size: **Small** or **Medium**
Curriculum Type: **Distribution Requirements** or **Loose Core Curriculum**
Residential Type: **High Residential**
Selectivity: **S-1**, **S-2**, **S-3**
Financial Aid: **The Best Aid** or **Excellent Aid** or **Good Aid**

Prestige: **Most Prestigious** or **Prestigious** or **No Prestige Ranking**

A matching school might look like this:

School Type: **University**
School Funding: **Private**
Campus Structure: **Integrated**
Surrounding Area: **Small City**
Region: **New England**
Size: **Medium**
Curriculum Type: **Distribution Requirements**
Residential Type: **High Residential**
Selectivity: **S-3**
Financial Aid: **Good Aid**
Prestige: **Prestigious**

Or it could look like this:

School Type: **University**
School Funding: **Private**
Campus Structure: **Island**
Surrounding Area: **Town**
Region: **Mid-Atlantic**
Size: **Medium**
Curriculum Type: **Loose Core**
Residential Type: **High Residential**
Selectivity: **S-1**
Financial Aid: **Best Aid**
Prestige: **Most Prestigious**

Both of these schools have different characteristics, but they both are perfect matches to your College Match Profile. There are a number of other variations that would also be a perfect match as you can see. In a moment, you are going to through the list of 176 colleges and their characteristics so you can identify these perfect match schools.

As you do this, you are going to start to notice a few things. While you are going through the list of colleges, you are going to start to see some schools that almost match your profile. Perhaps you think it is a perfect match, but then you notice that there is one category where a characteristic does not match an option you selected in your College Match Profile. For instance, let's say everything matched except in the "Region" category, the school is listed as being in the Midwest, and you only selected New England and the Mid-Atlantic in your College Match Profile.

If you come across a scenario like this, you are going to have to use your judgment. Would I be okay with a school in the Midwest? Is that a deal breaker item? There are going to be some things you are willing to compromise on and other things you won't compromise on. You might decide you are okay considering schools in the Midwest even though that wasn't on your original College Match Profile, but you would absolutely rule out any college with, for instance, an open curriculum for the "Curriculum Type" category even if it matched all of your match characteristics in the other ten categories. Ultimately, where you draw the line is up to you. You are entitled to decide that some factors are more important than others and that there are areas where you might not be willing to make any exceptions.

In my experience, colleges that may not match in one, two, and occasionally even three categories can still be good matches, however, you will need to make a judgment on a case by case basis to determine if the non-matching characteristics are things you can live with. There are plenty of schools on this list so if the non-matching characteristics just don't sit well with you, just leave that school off your college list.

Finding Your Match Schools

It is time to start building your college list. In a moment, you are going to see a long alphabetical list of 176 colleges. Below each college, you are going to see the location of the college (for your reference) as well as eleven characteristics of that school (one for each of the eleven categories). Below those characteristics, you will see a list of designations for each school, which you can ignore for now.

The alphabetical list of colleges is long, and it will take you a while to get through. The time you put into doing this carefully will pay off in the end so take your time and go slow.

The first thing I recommend you do is to get a separate piece of paper and write down your College Match Profile; doing so will make this process a lot easier than having to flip back to the College Match Profile Chart (pg. 270) multiple times. Simply write out the eleven categories like this:

School Type:

School Funding:

Campus Structure:

Surrounding Area:

Region:

Size:

Curriculum Type:

Residential Type:

Selectivity:

Financial Aid:

Prestige:

Then, fill in the characteristics you selected in the third column of the chart, and you will be able to reference your College Match Profile easily as you work your way through the long list of schools.

On the other side of that same piece of paper, write down "College List" and leave plenty of space to start filling in the names of the schools that you determine are a match.

Now here is what you should do:

1) **Review College List**

   Start at the top of the alphabetical list of colleges on page 281 and begin reading through the list of eleven characteristics for each school (ignoring the designations for now).

2) **Find Perfect Match Schools**

   Compare the characteristics listed for each school to the characteristics you've written down on your College Match Profile. If the college has a matching characteristic for each of the eleven categories, write the name of the school down on your "College List". This is a perfect match school. Next to the name of the school, also write down which selectivity category the school falls into (such as S-1, S-2, S-3, etc.).

3) **Add Near Perfect Matches**

   If a school has three or more characteristics that do not match your profile, skip over it; it is probably not a good match school for you. If a college has a matching characteristic in every category except for one, two, or possibly even three categories, read through the non-matching characteristics and decide if they are things you don't feel strongly about. If you think these schools could still be good options, you can add them to your college list. But if something just doesn't feel right about the combination of non-matching characteristics, just skip over those schools – there will be plenty of other options.

4) **Sort for Selectivity**

   When you have gone through the entire list of schools, you will likely have more than eight to twelve schools written down on your college list. Now is the time to start narrowing things down. The first step is to divide the schools you wrote down by selectivity ranking so you can determine which are best fit, safety, and reach schools. Take each school on your list, and put them into the chart below (or create a similar chart on your piece of paper). Remember, your "Best Fit" schools are the schools that are in the selectivity category that best fits you. The "Reach Schools" are one selectivity category more selective and the "Safety Schools" are the schools one selectivity category less selective. If you have a couple of schools in selectivity categories that are several categories off from your best fit category, you can include several of those as well in your reach or safety categories.

Selectivity Chart

Safety Schools	Best Fit Schools	Reach Schools

Remember that you want to make sure that you apply to at least two safety schools, at least four best fit schools, and at least two reach schools. Make sure you have at least that many options in each of the categories on the Selectivity Chart. If not, you may need to reconsider some of the schools you skipped over to make sure you have a sufficient number of options in each category. Chances are, however, that you will have more schools than you need in each category. Now is the time to narrow down your options a bit more.

5) Narrowing Down Your Options

You are going to start looking at the designations for each of the schools on your Selectivity Chart. You have already determined that these schools have the base characteristics you are looking for in a college, but do they fit you in other ways? You need to make sure that the culture at the schools on your list will be a good match for you. This is where the designations come in.

Go back to the alphabetical list of colleges and look up each of the schools you've put into the Selectivity Chart. Read through the designations for each of the schools listed and ask yourself, "Do these qualities sound desirable?" If a school has a theater and a quirky designation, and you think both of those things sound great, keep it on your list. On the other hand, if the school has a religious designation, and you definitely don't want a religious school, cross the school out.

As you go through the designations for each school on your list, ask yourself both of the following questions. Does this school sound like a place where I could fit in? Do I feel inspired to do more research about this school? If the answer is yes, keep it on your list. If not, cross it out. Just make sure that you keep a minimum of two safety schools, two reach schools, and four best fit schools on your chart. If you have more schools left on there for some of the categories, that is fine.

6) Create Your College List

The remaining schools on the Selectivity Chart (i.e. those you have not crossed out) make up your final college list. Write down the names of those schools on the My College List chart below.

My College List

Write down the colleges left on your Selectivity Chart
1.
2.
3.
4.
5.
6.
7.
8.
9.
10.
11.
12.

Your college list should have a minimum of eight schools. You will likely have more and that is okay as well. I recommend applying to anywhere from eight to twelve schools. You can apply to more schools if you'd like, but because it takes a lot of work to apply to each school, you might find that if you apply to too many schools, you won't be able to devote as much time as you'd want to each application. Plus, eight to twelve schools, selected the right way, should still give you at least several good options to choose from once you receive your admissions decisions so there is no need to spend the extra time and money on more.

If you have more than twelve schools, you may want to narrow down the list further. You can read through the alphabetical list of colleges and eliminate schools you don't feel are as well suited to your profile as others, but you can also do more extensive research on each of the schools to decide which ones offer specific programs you are excited about, have the most exciting extracurricular and residential offerings, and so on. In the next chapter, I have included additional resources you can use to begin this process.

176 College and Their Profiles

American University
Washington DC

Category	Characteristics
School Type	University
School Funding	Private
Campus Structure	Island
Surrounding Area	City
Region	Mid-Atlantic
Size	Medium Size (7,299)
Curriculum Type	Loose Core
Residential Type	Medium Residential (55%)
Selectivity	S-3 Selectivity
Financial Aid	Good Aid 114 ($2,505,923)
Prestige	No Prestige Rating
Designations	Government and Politics; Journalism; Business

Amherst College
Northampton, Massachusetts

Category	Characteristics
School Type	College
School Funding	Private
Campus Structure	Integrated
Surrounding Area	Town
Region	New England
Size	Small Size (1,817)
Curriculum Type	Open
Residential Type	High Residential (97%)
Selectivity	S-1 Selectivity
Financial Aid	Best Aid 146 ($7,655,287)
Prestige	Most Prestigious
Designations	Humanities

Arizona State University
Phoenix, Arizona

Category	Characteristics
School Type	University
School Funding	Public
Campus Structure	Integrated
Surrounding Area	City
Region	West
Size	Large Size (59,382)
Curriculum Type	Loose Core
Residential Type	Low Residential (20%)
Selectivity	S-5 Selectivity
Financial Aid	Some Aid 222 ($2,086,688)
Prestige	No Prestige Rating
Designations	Sports; Journalism; Business; Engineering; Greek Life

Bard College
Annandale-on-Hudson, New York

Category	Characteristics
School Type	College
School Funding	Private
Campus Structure	Island
Surrounding Area	Rural
Region	Mid-Atlantic
Size	Small Size (2,051)
Curriculum Type	Loose Core
Residential Type	Medium Residential (55%)
Selectivity	S-3 Selectivity
Financial Aid	Best Aid 196 ($7,617,880)
Prestige	No Prestige Rating
Designations	Artistic; Music; Quirky; Humanities; Writing

Barnard College
New York, New York

Category	Characteristics
School Type	College
School Funding	Private
Campus Structure	Street-Side
Surrounding Area	City
Region	Mid-Atlantic
Size	Small Size (2,504)
Curriculum Type	Loose Core
Residential Type	High Residential (91%)
Selectivity	S-2 Selectivity
Financial Aid	Good Aid 13 ($546,265)
Prestige	No Prestige Rating
Designations	College Town; Single Sex (all-female)

Bates College
Lewiston, Maine

Category	Characteristics
School Type	College
School Funding	Private
Campus Structure	Island
Surrounding Area	Small City
Region	New England
Size	Small Size (1,753)
Curriculum Type	Loose Core
Residential Type	High Residential (92%)
Selectivity	S-2 Selectivity
Financial Aid	Best Aid 84 ($4,081,959)
Prestige	Prestigious
Designations	Housing

Beloit College
Beloit, Wisconsin

Category	Characteristics
School Type	College
School Funding	Private
Campus Structure	Island
Surrounding Area	Town
Region	Midwest
Size	Small Size (1,359)
Curriculum Type	Distribution Requirements
Residential Type	High Residential (94%)
Selectivity	S-4 Selectivity
Financial Aid	Excellent Aid 111 ($2,143,031)
Prestige	No Prestige Rating
Designations	Quirky; International Student Body; Writing

Bennington College
Bennington, Vermont

Category	Characteristics
School Type	College
School Funding	Private
Campus Structure	Island
Surrounding Area	Rural
Region	New England
Size	Very Small Size (688)
Curriculum Type	Open
Residential Type	High Residential (95%)
Selectivity	S-3 Selectivity
Financial Aid	Best Aid 46 ($2,024,000)
Prestige	No Prestige Rating
Designations	Outdoors; Artistic; Theater; Quirky; International Student Body

Boston College
Chestnut Hill, Massachusetts

Category	Characteristics
School Type	University
School Funding	Private
Campus Structure	Island
Surrounding Area	Suburb
Region	New England
Size	Medium (9,110)
Curriculum Type	Loose Core
Residential Type	High Residential (85%)
Selectivity	S-2 Selectivity
Financial Aid	No Institutional Aid for International Students
Prestige	Prestigious
Designations	Sports; Social Activism and Community Service; Religious

Boston University
Boston, Massachusetts

Category	Characteristics
School Type	University
School Funding	Private
Campus Structure	Street-Side
Surrounding Area	City
Region	New England
Size	Large Size (18,306)
Curriculum Type	Distribution Requirements
Residential Type	Medium Residential (77%)
Selectivity	S-3 Selectivity
Financial Aid	Good Aid 119 (4,792,889)
Prestige	Prestigious
Designations	Music; Journalism; Economics; Pre-Med; International Student Body; College Town

Bowdoin College
Brunswick, Maine

Category	Characteristics
School Type	College
School Funding	Private
Campus Structure	Integrated
Surrounding Area	Town
Region	New England
Size	Small Size (1,839)
Curriculum Type	Distribution Requirements
Residential Type	High Residential (92%)
Selectivity	S-1 Selectivity
Financial Aid	Good Aid 28 ($1,134,934)
Prestige	Most Prestigious
Designations	Government and Politics; Serious Academics; Hard Sciences; Pre-Med

Brandeis University
Waltham, Massachusetts

Category	Characteristics
School Type	University
School Funding	Private
Campus Structure	Island
Surrounding Area	Suburb
Region	New England
Size	Small Size (3,588)
Curriculum Type	Loose Core
Residential Type	Medium Residential (74%)
Selectivity	S-2 Selectivity
Financial Aid	Some Aid 20 ($560,000)
Prestige	Prestigious
Designations	Social Activism and Community Service; Government and Politics; International Student Body

Brigham Young University
Provo, Utah

Category	Characteristics
School Type	University
School Funding	Private
Campus Structure	Integrated
Surrounding Area	City
Region	West
Size	Large Size (31,060)
Curriculum Type	Core
Residential Type	Low Residential (19%)
Selectivity	S-4 Selectivity
Financial Aid	Some Aid 634 ($2,574,040)
Prestige	No Prestige Rating
Designations	Sports; Athletic; Outdoors; Religious; Business

Brown University
Providence, Rhode Island

Category	Characteristics
School Type	University
School Funding	Private
Campus Structure	Integrated
Surrounding Area	City
Region	New England
Size	Medium Size (6,435)
Curriculum Type	Open
Residential Type	Medium Residential (79%)
Selectivity	S-1 Selectivity
Financial Aid	Excellent Aid 207 ($8,400,000)
Prestige	Most Prestigious
Designations	Social Activism and Community Service; Government and Politics; Entrepreneurship; Quirky; Economics; Pre-Med; International Student Body

Bryn Mawr College
Bryn Mawr, Pennsylvania

Category	Characteristics
School Type	College
School Funding	Private
Campus Structure	Island
Surrounding Area	Suburb
Region	Mid-Atlantic
Size	Small Size (1,322)
Curriculum Type	Distribution Requirements
Residential Type	High Residential (94%)
Selectivity	S-2 Selectivity
Financial Aid	Best Aid 157 ($6,179,834)
Prestige	Prestigious
Designations	Social Activism and Community Service; Serious Academic; Housing; Single Sex (all-female)

Bucknell University
Lewisburg, Pennsylvania

Category	Characteristics
School Type	College
School Funding	Private
Campus Structure	Island
Surrounding Area	Town
Region	Mid-Atlantic
Size	Small Size (3,536)
Curriculum Type	Loose Core
Residential Type	High Residential (86%)
Selectivity	S-2 Selectivity
Financial Aid	Good Aid 26 ($1,135,186)
Prestige	No Prestige Rating
Designations	Sports; Greek Life

California Institute of Technology (Caltech)
Pasadena, California

Category	Characteristics
School Type	University
School Funding	Private
Campus Structure	Integrated
Surrounding Area	Suburb
Region	Pacific Coast
Size	Very Small (997)
Curriculum Type	Core
Residential Type	High Residential (85%)
Selectivity	S-1 Selectivity
Financial Aid	Excellent Aid 26 ($1,124,845)
Prestige	Most Prestigious
Designations	Serious Academic; Entrepreneurship; Techie; Economics; Engineering; Hard Sciences; International Student Body

Carleton College
Northfield, Minnesota

Category	Characteristics
School Type	College
School Funding	Private
Campus Structure	Integrated
Surrounding Area	Town
Region	Midwest
Size	Small Size (2,055)
Curriculum Type	Loose Core
Residential Type	High Residential (94%)
Selectivity	S-1 Selectivity
Financial Aid	Excellent Aid 26 ($2,589,268)
Prestige	Most Prestigious
Designations	Outdoors; Artistic; Serious Academic; Quirky; Environmental Awareness and Activism

Carnegie Mellon University
Pittsburgh, Pennsylvania

Category	Characteristics
School Type	University
School Funding	Private
Campus Structure	Integrated
Surrounding Area	City
Region	Mid-Atlantic
Size	Medium Size (6,279)
Curriculum Type	Open (some departments have requirements but none are university-wide)
Residential Type	Medium Residential (64%)
Selectivity	S-2 Selectivity
Financial Aid	No Institutional Aid for International Students
Prestige	Most Prestigious
Designations	Techie; Music; Theater; Economics; Business; Engineering; Hard Sciences; International Student Body

Case Western Reserve University
Cleveland, Ohio

Category	Characteristics
School Type	University
School Funding	Private
Campus Structure	Integrated
Surrounding Area	City
Region	Midwest
Size	Medium Size (4,386)
Curriculum Type	Loose Core
Residential Type	Medium Residential (77%)
Selectivity	S-2 Selectivity
Financial Aid	Some Aid 5 ($143,840)
Prestige	Prestigious
Designations	Engineering, Hard Sciences, Pre-Med, Greek Life

Centre College
Danville, Kentucky

Category	Characteristics
School Type	College
School Funding	Private
Campus Structure	Island
Surrounding Area	Town
Region	South
Size	Small Size (1,344)
Curriculum Type	Loose Core
Residential Type	High Residential (98%)
Selectivity	S-4 Selectivity
Financial Aid	Good Aid 38 ($690,780)
Prestige	No Prestige Rating
Designations	Government and Politics; Religious; Greek Life

Claremont Mckenna College
Claremont, California

Category	Characteristics
School Type	College
School Funding	Private
Campus Structure	Island
Surrounding Area	Town
Region	Pacific Coast
Size	Small Size (1,264)
Curriculum Type	Loose Core
Residential Type	High Residential (94%)
Selectivity	S-1 Selectivity
Financial Aid	Some Aid 6 ($225,122)
Prestige	Most Prestigious
Designations	Government and Politics; Pre-Med; Economics

Clark University
Worcester, Massachusetts

Category	Characteristics
School Type	University
School Funding	Private
Campus Structure	Integrated
Surrounding Area	City
Region	New England
Size	Small Size (2,352)
Curriculum Type	Loose Core
Residential Type	Medium Residential (71%)
Selectivity	S-5 Selectivity
Financial Aid	Excellent Aid 165 ($3,993,130)
Prestige	No Prestige Rating
Designations	Pre-Med; International Student Body

Clemson University
Clemson, South Carolina

Category	Characteristics
School Type	University
School Funding	Public
Campus Structure	Island
Surrounding Area	Small City
Region	South
Size	Large Size (16,562)
Curriculum Type	Loose Core
Residential Type	Low Residential (41%)
Selectivity	S-4 Selectivity
Financial Aid	No Institutional Aid for International Students
Prestige	No Prestige Rating
Designations	Sports; Athletic; School Spirit; Business; Engineering

Colby College
Waterville, Maine

Category	Characteristics
School Type	College
School Funding	Private
Campus Structure	Island
Surrounding Area	Rural
Region	New England
Size	Small Size (1,843)
Curriculum Type	Distribution Requirements
Residential Type	High Residential (93%)
Selectivity	S-2 Selectivity
Financial Aid	Best Aid 82 ($3,957,995)
Prestige	Prestigious
Designations	Outdoors; Environmental Awareness and Activism

Colgate College
Hamilton, New York

Category	Characteristics
School Type	College
School Funding	Private
Campus Structure	Island
Surrounding Area	Town
Region	Mid-Atlantic
Size	Small Size (2,871)
Curriculum Type	Loose Core
Residential Type	High Residential (91%)
Selectivity	S-2 Selectivity
Financial Aid	Excellent Aid 114 ($5,360,736)
Prestige	Prestigious
Designations	Outdoors

College of the Atlantic
Bar Harbor, Maine

Category	Characteristics
School Type	College
School Funding	Private
Campus Structure	Island
Surrounding Area	Town
Region	New England
Size	Very Small Size (330)
Curriculum Type	Core
Residential Type	Medium Residential (56%)
Selectivity	S-4 Selectivity
Financial Aid	Best Aid 52 ($2,164,213)
Prestige	No Prestige Rating
Designations	Outdoors, Quirky, Environmental Awareness and Activism, International Student Body

College of the Holy Cross
Worcester, Massachusetts

Category	Characteristics
School Type	College
School Funding	Private
Campus Structure	Island
Surrounding Area	Suburb
Region	New England
Size	Small Size (2,926)
Curriculum Type	Distribution Requirements
Residential Type	High Residential (91%)
Selectivity	S-3 Selectivity
Financial Aid	No Institutional Aid for International Students
Prestige	Prestige Rating
Designations	School Spirit; Religious

Colorado College
Colorado Springs, Colorado

Category	Characteristics
School Type	College
School Funding	Private
Campus Structure	Island
Surrounding Area	City
Region	West
Size	Small Size (2,008)
Curriculum Type	Distribution Requirements
Residential Type	Medium Residential (78%)
Selectivity	S-2 Selectivity
Financial Aid	Excellent Aid 70 ($3,155,913)
Prestige	No Prestige Rating
Designations	Athletic; Outdoors; Artistic; Serious Academic; Writing

Colorado School of Mines
Golden, Colorado

Category	Characteristics
School Type	University
School Funding	Public
Campus Structure	Integrated
Surrounding Area	Suburb
Region	West
Size	Medium Size (4,169)
Curriculum Type	Core
Residential Type	Low Residential (43%)
Selectivity	S-3 Selectivity
Financial Aid	No Institutional Aid for International Students
Prestige	No Prestige Rating
Designations	Outdoors; Serious Academic; Engineering

College of William and Mary
Williamsburg, Virginia

Category	Characteristics
School Type	University
School Funding	Public
Campus Structure	Integrated
Surrounding Area	Town
Region	South
Size	Medium Size (6,171)
Curriculum Type	Distribution Requirements
Residential Type	Medium Residential (72%)
Selectivity	S-2 Selectivity
Financial Aid	No Institutional Aid Available for international Students
Prestige	Prestigious
Designations	Government and Politics; Greek Life

Columbia University
New York, New York

Category	Characteristics
School Type	University
School Funding	Private
Campus Structure	Integrated
Surrounding Area	City
Region	Mid-Atlantic
Size	Medium Size (6,068)
Curriculum Type	Core
Residential Type	High Residential (94%)
Selectivity	S-1 Selectivity
Financial Aid	Some Aid (unreported)
Prestige	Most Prestigious
Designations	Serious Academic; Economics; Humanities; Engineering; Hard Sciences; Pre-Med; International Student Body; College Town; Writing

Connecticut College
New London, Connecticut

Category	Characteristics
School Type	College
School Funding	Private
Campus Structure	Island
Surrounding Area	Small City
Region	New England
Size	Small Size (1,926)
Curriculum Type	Loose Core
Residential Type	High Residential (99%)
Selectivity	S-3 Selectivity
Financial Aid	Excellent Aid 57 ($2,747,848)
Prestige	No Prestige Rating
Designations	Social Activism and Community Service

Cooper Union
New York, New York

Category	Characteristics
School Type	College
School Funding	Private
Campus Structure	Street-Side
Surrounding Area	City
Region	Mid-Atlantic
Size	Very Small Size (880)
Curriculum Type	Core
Residential Type	Low Residential (20%)
Selectivity	S-2 Selectivity
Financial Aid	Best Aid (Full tuition for everyone)
Prestige	No Prestige Rating
Designations	Artistic; Serious Academic; Engineering; Architecture; International Student Body; College Town

Cornell University
Ithaca, New York

Category	Characteristics
School Type	University
School Funding	Private
Campus Structure	Island
Surrounding Area	Small City
Region	Mid-Atlantic
Size	Large Size (14,261)
Curriculum Type	Distribution Requirements
Residential Type	Medium Residential (57%)
Selectivity	S-1 Selectivity
Financial Aid	Good Aid 73 ($2,909,006)
Prestige	Most Prestigious
Designations	Outdoors; Government and Politics; Techie; Economics; Business; Engineering; Hard Sciences; Pre-Med; Architecture; International Student Body

Dartmouth College
Hanover, New Hampshire

Category	Characteristics
School Type	University
School Funding	Private
Campus Structure	Integrated
Surrounding Area	Town
Region	New England
Size	Medium Size (4,193)
Curriculum Type	Loose Core
Residential Type	High Residential (92%)
Selectivity	S-1 Selectivity
Financial Aid	Best Aid 251 ($12,279,562)
Prestige	Most Prestigious
Designations	Athletic; Outdoors; Social Activism and Community Service; Government and Politics; Entrepreneurship; Pre-Med; Greek Life

Davidson College
Davidson, North Carolina

Category	Characteristics
School Type	College
School Funding	Private
Campus Structure	Integrated
Surrounding Area	Town
Region	South
Size	Small Size (1,790)
Curriculum Type	Loose Core
Residential Type	High Residential (92%)
Selectivity	S-2 Selectivity
Financial Aid	Good Aid 48 ($1,689,552)
Prestige	Most Prestigious
Designations	Government and Politics; Serious Academic; Religious; Pre-Med; Greek Life

Deep Springs College
Big Pine, California

Category	Characteristics
School Type	College
School Funding	Private
Campus Structure	Island
Surrounding Area	Rural
Region	Pacific Coast
Size	Very Small Size (26)
Curriculum Type	Core
Residential Type	High Residential (100%)
Selectivity	S-1 Selectivity
Financial Aid	Best Aid (full tuition to all students)
Prestige	No Prestige Rating
Designations	Outdoors; Serious Academic

Denison University
Granville, Ohio

Category	Characteristics
School Type	College
School Funding	Private
Campus Structure	Island
Surrounding Area	Rural
Region	Midwest
Size	Small Size (2,336)
Curriculum Type	Loose Core
Residential Type	High Residential (99%)
Selectivity	S-3 Selectivity
Financial Aid	Excellent Aid 153 ($3,879,380)
Prestige	No Prestige Rating
Designations	Athletic; Economics; Pre-Med; Greek Life

DePauw University
Greencastle, Ohio

Category	Characteristics
School Type	College
School Funding	Private
Campus Structure	Island
Surrounding Area	Rural
Region	Midwest
Size	Small Size (2,336)
Curriculum Type	Distribution Requirements
Residential Type	High Residential (95%)
Selectivity	S-4 Selectivity
Financial Aid	Best Aid 70 ($5,090,458)
Prestige	No Prestige Rating
Designations	Music; Greek Life

Dickinson College
Carlisle, Pennsylvania

Category	Characteristics
School Type	College
School Funding	Private
Campus Structure	Integrated
Surrounding Area	Town
Region	Mid-Atlantic
Size	Small Size (2,386)
Curriculum Type	Distribution Requirements
Residential Type	High Residential (95%)
Selectivity	S-3 Selectivity
Financial Aid	Excellent Aid 133 ($4,429,897)
Prestige	No Prestige Rating
Designations	Government and Politics; Business; Greek Life

Duke University
Durham, North Carolina

Category	Characteristics
School Type	University
School Funding	Private
Campus Structure	Integrated
Surrounding Area	City
Region	South
Size	Medium Size (6,655)
Curriculum Type	Loose Core
Residential Type	High Residential (85%)
Selectivity	S-1 Selectivity
Financial Aid	Good Aid 134 ($6,484,394)
Prestige	Most Prestigious
Designations	Sports; Economics; Engineering; Pre-Med; International Student Body; Greek Life

Emerson College
Boston, Massachusetts

Category	Characteristics
School Type	University
School Funding	Private
Campus Structure	Street-Side
Surrounding Area	City
Region	New England
Size	Small Size (3,675)
Curriculum Type	Core
Residential Type	Medium Residential (57%)
Selectivity	S-3 Selectivity
Financial Aid	Some Aid 5 ($4,000)
Prestige	No Prestige Rating
Designations	Artistic; Theater; Journalism; Quirky; College Town

Emory University
Atlanta, Georgia

Category	Characteristics
School Type	University
School Funding	Private
Campus Structure	Island
Surrounding Area	City
Region	South
Size	Medium Size (7,656)
Curriculum Type	Loose Core
Residential Type	Medium Residential (67%)
Selectivity	S-2 Selectivity
Financial Aid	Some Aid 19 ($507,400)
Prestige	Most Prestigious
Designations	Business; Pre-Med; International Student Body; Greek Life; Writing

Eugene Lang College at The New School
New York, New York

Category	Characteristics
School Type	University
School Funding	Private
Campus Structure	Street-Side
Surrounding Area	City
Region	Mid-Atlantic
Size	Small Size (1,511)
Curriculum Type	Loose Core
Residential Type	Low Residential (27%)
Selectivity	S-4 Selectivity
Financial Aid	Good Aid 74 ($424,050)
Prestige	No Prestige Rating
Designations	Artistic; Quirky; International Student Body; College Town; Writing

Florida State University
Tallahassee, Florida

Category	Characteristics
School Type	University
School Funding	Public
Campus Structure	Integrated
Surrounding Area	City
Region	South
Size	Large Size (32,171)
Curriculum Type	Distribution Requirements
Residential Type	Low Residential (20%)
Selectivity	S-4 Selectivity
Financial Aid	No Institutional Aid for International Students
Prestige	No Prestige Rating
Designations	Sports; Athletic; Government and Politics; Greek Life; Writing

Fordham University
Bronx, New York

Category	Characteristics
School Type	University
School Funding	Private
Campus Structure	Island
Surrounding Area	City
Region	Mid-Atlantic
Size	Medium Size (8,325)
Curriculum Type	Core
Residential Type	Medium Residential (56%)
Selectivity	S-3 Selectivity
Financial Aid	Some Aid 46 ($1,208,204)
Prestige	No Prestige Rating
Designations	Religious; Theater; Business; College Town

Franklin and Marshall College
Lancaster, Pennsylvania

Category	Characteristics
School Type	College
School Funding	Private
Campus Structure	Integrated
Surrounding Area	Small City
Region	Mid-Atlantic
Size	Small Size (2,365)
Curriculum Type	Distribution Requirements
Residential Type	High Residential (97%)
Selectivity	S-3 Selectivity
Financial Aid	Best Aid 159 ($5,951,714)
Prestige	No Prestige Rating
Designations	Athletic; Pre-Med; Greek Life

Furman University
Greenville, South Carolina

Category	Characteristics
School Type	College
School Funding	Private
Campus Structure	Island
Surrounding Area	Suburb
Region	South
Size	Small Size (2,753)
Curriculum Type	Loose Core
Residential Type	High Residential (96%)
Selectivity	S-4 Selectivity
Financial Aid	Good Aid 51 ($1,607,743)
Prestige	No Prestige Rating
Designations	Athletic; Greek Life

George Washington University
Washington DC

Category	Characteristics
School Type	University
School Funding	Private
Campus Structure	Street-Side
Surrounding Area	City
Region	Mid-Atlantic
Size	Large Size (10,464)
Curriculum Type	Loose Core
Residential Type	Medium Residential (68%)
Selectivity	S-4 Selectivity
Financial Aid	Good Aid 190 ($3,742,943)
Prestige	No Prestige Rating
Designations	Government and Politics; Journalism; Pre-Med

Georgetown University
Washington DC

	Characteristics
School Type	University
School Funding	Private
Campus Structure	Island
Surrounding Area	City
Region	Mid-Atlantic
Size	Medium Size (7,552)
Curriculum Type	Loose Core
Residential Type	Medium Residential (67%)
Selectivity	S-2 Selectivity
Financial Aid	Good Aid 57 ($1,740,210)
Prestige	Most Prestigious
Designations	Sports; Government and Politics; Religious; Business; Pre-Med; International Student Body; College Town

Georgia Institute of Technology
Atlanta, Georgia

Category	Characteristics
School Type	University
School Funding	Public
Campus Structure	Island
Surrounding Area	City
Region	South
Size	Large Size (14,527)
Curriculum Type	Core
Residential Type	Medium Residential (56%)
Selectivity	S-3 Selectivity
Financial Aid	No Institutional Aid for International Students
Prestige	Prestigious
Designations	Techie; Engineering; Hard Sciences; Architecture; International Student Body

Gettysburg College
Gettysburg, Pennsylvania

Category	Characteristics
School Type	College
School Funding	Private
Campus Structure	Integrated
Surrounding Area	Town
Region	Mid-Atlantic
Size	Small Size (2,597)
Curriculum Type	Loose Core
Residential Type	High Residential (92%)
Selectivity	S-3 Selectivity
Financial Aid	Good Aid 35 ($1,297,308)
Prestige	No Prestige Rating
Designations	Athletic; Government and Politics; Greek Life; Housing

Goucher College
Baltimore, Maryland

Category	Characteristics
School Type	College
School Funding	Private
Campus Structure	Island
Surrounding Area	Suburb
Region	Mid-Atlantic
Size	Small Size (1,484)
Curriculum Type	Loose Core
Residential Type	High Residential (86%)
Selectivity	S-5 Selectivity
Financial Aid	Good Aid 26 ($653,317)
Prestige	No Prestige Rating
Designations	Athletic; Environmental Awareness and Activism

Grinnell College
Grinnell, Iowa

Category	Characteristics
School Type	College
School Funding	Private
Campus Structure	Island
Surrounding Area	Town
Region	Midwest
Size	Small Size (1,674)
Curriculum Type	Open
Residential Type	High Residential (82%)
Selectivity	S-2 Selectivity
Financial Aid	Best Aid 157 ($5,655,157)
Prestige	Prestigious
Designations	Social Activism and Community Service; Serious Academic; Quirky

Hamilton College
Clinton, New York

Category	Characteristics
School Type	College
School Funding	Private
Campus Structure	Island
Surrounding Area	Rural
Region	Mid-Atlantic
Size	Small Size (1,884)
Curriculum Type	Open
Residential Type	High Residential (98%)
Selectivity	S-2 Selectivity
Financial Aid	Best Aid 157 ($2,975,464)
Prestige	Prestigious
Designations	Athletic; Greek Life; Writing

Hampshire College
Amherst, Massachusetts

Category	Characteristics
School Type	College
School Funding	Private
Campus Structure	Island
Surrounding Area	Rural
Region	New England
Size	Small Size (1,464)
Curriculum Type	Open
Residential Type	High Residential (90%)
Selectivity	S-4 Selectivity
Financial Aid	Excellent Aid 87 ($1,924,573)
Prestige	Prestigious
Designations	Outdoors; Quirky; Humanities; Environmental Awareness and Activism

Harvard University
Cambridge, Massachusetts

Category	Characteristics
School Type	University
School Funding	Private
Campus Structure	Integrated
Surrounding Area	City
Region	New England
Size	Medium Size (6,658)
Curriculum Type	Loose Core
Residential Type	High Residential (97%)
Selectivity	S-1 Selectivity
Financial Aid	Best Aid 530 ($27,866,340)
Prestige	Most Prestigious
Designations	Social Activism and Community Service; Government and Politics; Serious Academic; Entrepreneurship; Journalism; Economics; Humanities; Hard Sciences; Pre-Med; International Student Body; College Town; Housing

Harvey Mudd
Claremont, California

Category	Characteristics
School Type	College
School Funding	Private
Campus Structure	Island
Surrounding Area	Town
Region	Pacific Coast
Size	Very Small Size (783)
Curriculum Type	Core
Residential Type	High Residential (99%)
Selectivity	S-1 Selectivity
Financial Aid	Good Aid 11 ($412,746)
Prestige	Prestigious
Designations	Serious Academic; Entrepreneurship; Techie; Quirky; Engineering; Hard Sciences

Haverford College
Lower Merion, Pennsylvania

Category	Characteristics
School Type	College
School Funding	Private
Campus Structure	Island
Surrounding Area	Suburb
Region	Mid-Atlantic
Size	Very Small Size (1205)
Curriculum Type	Distribution Requirements
Residential Type	High Residential (99%)
Selectivity	S-2 Selectivity
Financial Aid	Good Aid 12 ($548,575)
Prestige	Most Prestigious
Designations	Serious Academic

Hendrix College
Conway, Arkansas

Category	Characteristics
School Type	College
School Funding	Private
Campus Structure	Island
Surrounding Area	Suburb
Region	South
Size	Small Size (1,373)
Curriculum Type	Core
Residential Type	High Residential (88%)
Selectivity	S-4 Selectivity
Financial Aid	Excellent Aid ($1,687,347)
Prestige	No Prestige Rating
Designations	Religious, Theater, Humanities, Pre-Med

Hobart and William Smith Colleges
Geneva, New York

Category	Characteristics
School Type	College
School Funding	Private
Campus Structure	Island
Surrounding Area	Town
Region	Mid-Atlantic
Size	Small Size (2,292)
Curriculum Type	Open
Residential Type	High Residential (90%)
Selectivity	S-4 Selectivity
Financial Aid	Good Aid 89 ($2,210,772)
Prestige	No Prestige Rating
Designations	Athletic

Illinois Institute of Technology
Chicago, Illinois

Category	Characteristics
School Type	University
School Funding	Private
Campus Structure	Integrated
Surrounding Area	City
Region	Midwest
Size	Small Size (2,800)
Curriculum Type	Loose Core
Residential Type	Medium Residential (59%)
Selectivity	S-4 Selectivity
Financial Aid	Best Aid 592 ($10,703,818)
Prestige	No Prestige Rating
Designations	Serious Academic; Entrepreneurship; Techie; Journalism; Engineering; Hard Sciences; Environmental Awareness and Activism; Architecture; International Student Body; College Town

Indiana University – Bloomington
Bloomington, Indiana

Category	Characteristics
School Type	University
School Funding	Public
Campus Structure	Integrated
Surrounding Area	Small City
Region	Midwest
Size	Large Size (32,371)
Curriculum Type	Loose Core
Residential Type	Low Residential (38%)
Selectivity	S-5 Selectivity
Financial Aid	Some Aid 279 ($2,564,204)
Prestige	No Prestige Rating
Designations	Entrepreneurship; Music; Theater; Journalism; Business; International Student Body

Ithaca College
Ithaca, New York

Category	Characteristics
School Type	University
School Funding	Private
Campus Structure	Island
Surrounding Area	Small City
Region	Mid-Atlantic
Size	Medium Size (6,281)
Curriculum Type	Loose Core
Residential Type	Medium Residential (69%)
Selectivity	S-4 Selectivity
Financial Aid	Some Aid 98 ($2,499,092)
Prestige	No Prestige Rating
Designations	Music; Theater; Journalism

Johns Hopkins University
Baltimore, Maryland

Category	Characteristics
School Type	University
School Funding	Private
Campus Structure	Island
Surrounding Area	City
Region	Mid-Atlantic
Size	Medium Size (6,153)
Curriculum Type	Distribution Requirements
Residential Type	Medium Residential (69%)
Selectivity	S-2 Selectivity
Financial Aid	Some Aid 32 ($1,069,309)
Prestige	Most Prestigious
Designations	Government and Politics; Serious Academic; Economics; Engineering; Hard Sciences; Pre-Med; International Student Body

Kalamazoo College
Kalamazoo, Michigan

Category	Characteristics
School Type	College
School Funding	Private
Campus Structure	Island
Surrounding Area	Small City
Region	Midwest
Size	Small Size (1,379)
Curriculum Type	Distribution Requirements
Residential Type	Medium Residential (75%)
Selectivity	S-5 Selectivity
Financial Aid	Some Aid (unreported)
Prestige	No Prestige Rating
Designations	Government and Politics; Quirky

Kenyon College
Gambier, Ohio

Category	Characteristics
School Type	College
School Funding	Private
Campus Structure	Island
Surrounding Area	Rural
Region	Midwest
Size	Small Size (1,667)
Curriculum Type	Distribution Requirements
Residential Type	High Residential (98%)
Selectivity	S-2 Selectivity
Financial Aid	Excellent Aid 58 ($2,304,722)
Prestige	No Prestige Rating
Designations	Theater; Humanities; Writing

Knox College
Galesburg, Illinois

Category	Characteristics
School Type	College
School Funding	Private
Campus Structure	Island
Surrounding Area	Small City
Region	Midwest
Size	Small Size (1,430)
Curriculum Type	Loose Core
Residential Type	High Residential (85%)
Selectivity	S-4 Selectivity
Financial Aid	Best Aid ($2,976,408)
Prestige	No Prestige Rating
Designations	Quirky; Writing

Lafayette College
Easton, Pennsylvania

Category	Characteristics
School Type	College
School Funding	Private
Campus Structure	Island
Surrounding Area	Small City
Region	Mid-Atlantic
Size	Small Size (2,488)
Curriculum Type	Loose Core
Residential Type	High Residential (92%)
Selectivity	S-3 Selectivity
Financial Aid	Excellent Aid 103 ($3,859,836)
Prestige	Prestigious
Designations	Athletic; Government and Politics; Engineering; Greek Life

Lawrence University
Appleton, Wisconsin

Category	Characteristics
School Type	College
School Funding	Private
Campus Structure	Integrated
Surrounding Area	Small City
Region	Midwest
Size	Small Size (1,525)
Curriculum Type	Core
Residential Type	High Residential (98%)
Selectivity	S-4 Selectivity
Financial Aid	Excellent Aid 103 ($2,222,784)
Prestige	No Prestige Rating
Designations	Athletic; Music

Lehigh University
Bethlehem, Pennsylvania

Category	Characteristics
School Type	University
School Funding	Private
Campus Structure	Island
Surrounding Area	City
Region	Mid-Atlantic
Size	Medium Size (4,883)
Curriculum Type	Open (some departments have requirements but there are no university-wide requirements)
Residential Type	Medium Residential (69%)
Selectivity	S-3 Selectivity
Financial Aid	Good Aid 63 ($2,548,772)
Prestige	No Prestige Rating
Designations	Sports; Business; Engineering; Greek Life

Loyola University Chicago
Chicago, Illinois

Category	Characteristics
School Type	University
School Funding	Private
Campus Structure	Integrated
Surrounding Area	City
Region	Midwest
Size	Medium Size (9,723)
Curriculum Type	Loose Core
Residential Type	Low Residential (41%)
Selectivity	S-5 Selectivity
Financial Aid	No Institutional Aid for International Students
Prestige	No Prestige Rating
Designations	Social Activism and Community Service; Religious; Entrepreneurship; Journalism; Pre-Med; College Town

Macalester College
Saint Paul, Minnesota

Category	Characteristics
School Type	College
School Funding	Private
Campus Structure	Island
Surrounding Area	City
Region	Midwest
Size	Small Size (2,070)
Curriculum Type	Loose Core
Residential Type	Medium Residential (62%)
Selectivity	S-2 Selectivity
Financial Aid	Best Aid 222 ($7,647,111)
Prestige	Prestigious
Designations	Government and Politics; International Student Body

Marquette University
Milwaukee, Wisconsin

Category	Characteristics
School Type	University
School Funding	Private
Campus Structure	Integrated
Surrounding Area	City
Region	Midwest
Size	Medium Size (8,293)
Curriculum Type	Loose Core
Residential Type	Medium Residential (54%)
Selectivity	S-4 Selectivity
Financial Aid	Best Aid 222 ($7,647,111)
Prestige	No Prestige Rating
Designations	School Spirit; Religious; Journalism; Business

Massachusetts Institute of Technology (MIT)
Cambridge, Massachusetts

Category	Characteristics
School Type	University
School Funding	Private
Campus Structure	Integrated
Surrounding Area	City
Region	New England
Size	Medium Size (8,293)
Curriculum Type	Core
Residential Type	High Residential (90%)
Selectivity	S-1 Selectivity
Financial Aid	Best Aid 129 (6,313,628)
Prestige	High Prestige Rating
Designations	Entrepreneurship; Quirky; Techie; Business; Economics; Engineering; Hard Sciences; International Student Body; College Town; Housing; Writing

Michigan State University
East Lansing, Michigan

Category	Characteristics
School Type	University
School Funding	Public
Campus Structure	Island
Surrounding Area	Suburb
Region	Midwest
Size	Large Size (37,454)
Curriculum Type	Distribution Requirements
Residential Type	Low Residential (42%)
Selectivity	S-5 Selectivity
Financial Aid	Some Aid 169 ($1,193,653)
Prestige	No Prestige Rating
Designations	Journalism; International Student Body

Middlebury College
Middlebury, Vermont

Category	Characteristics
School Type	College
School Funding	Private
Campus Structure	Island
Surrounding Area	Town
Region	New England
Size	Small Size (2,516)
Curriculum Type	Distribution Requirements
Residential Type	High Residential (97%)
Selectivity	S-2 Selectivity
Financial Aid	Best Aid 129 ($6,313,628)
Prestige	Most Prestigious
Designations	Humanities; Environmental Awareness and Activism; International Student Body; Housing

Mount Holyoke College
South Hadley, Massachusetts

Category	Characteristics
School Type	College
School Funding	Private
Campus Structure	Integrated
Surrounding Area	Town
Region	New England
Size	Small Size (2,322)
Curriculum Type	Distribution Requirements
Residential Type	High Residential (95%)
Selectivity	S-2 Selectivity
Financial Aid	Best Aid 129 ($6,313,628)
Prestige	No Prestige Rating
Designations	Serious Academic; Humanities; Pre-Med; International Student Body; Housing; Single Sex (all-female)

New College of Florida
Sarasota, Florida

Category	Characteristics
School Type	College
School Funding	Public
Campus Structure	Island
Surrounding Area	Suburb
Region	South
Size	Very Small Size (832)
Curriculum Type	Open
Residential Type	Medium Residential (75%)
Selectivity	S-4 Selectivity
Financial Aid	Some Aid 2 ($19,000)
Prestige	No Prestige Rating
Designations	Social Activism and Community Service; Quirky; Humanities

New York University (NYU)
New York, Illinois

Category	Characteristics
School Type	University
School Funding	Private
Campus Structure	Street-Side
Surrounding Area	City
Region	Mid-Atlantic
Size	Large Size (22,948)
Curriculum Type	Loose Core
Residential Type	Medium Residential (50%)
Selectivity	S-2 Selectivity
Financial Aid	No Institutional Aid for International Students
Prestige	Prestigious
Designations	Artistic; Music; Theater; Journalism; Economics; Business; International Student Body; College Town; Writing

Northeastern University
Boston, Massachusetts

Category	Characteristics
School Type	University
School Funding	Private
Campus Structure	Integrated
Surrounding Area	City
Region	New England
Size	Large Size (13,107)
Curriculum Type	Loose Core
Residential Type	Medium Residential (55%)
Selectivity	S-3 Selectivity
Financial Aid	Good Aid 365 ($5,145,175)
Prestige	Prestigious
Designations	International Student Body; College Town

Northwestern University
Evanston, Illinois

Category	Characteristics
School Type	University
School Funding	Private
Campus Structure	Integrated
Surrounding Area	City
Region	Midwest
Size	Medium Size (8,600)
Curriculum Type	Distribution Requirements
Residential Type	Medium Residential (65%)
Selectivity	S-1 Selectivity
Financial Aid	Some Aid 38 ($1,580,078)
Prestige	Most Prestigious
Designations	Entrepreneurship; Music; Theater; Journalism; Economics; Business; Engineering; Pre-Med; Greek Life; College Town

Oberlin College
Oberlin, Ohio

Category	Characteristics
School Type	College
School Funding	Private
Campus Structure	Integrated
Surrounding Area	Town
Region	Midwest
Size	Small Size (2,930)
Curriculum Type	Distribution Requirements
Residential Type	High Residential (89%)
Selectivity	S-2 Selectivity
Financial Aid	Excellent Aid 146 ($4,343,742)
Prestige	Prestigious
Designations	Social Activism and Community Service; Music; Theater; Quirky; Pre-Med

Occidental College
Los Angeles, California

Category	Characteristics
School Type	College
School Funding	Private
Campus Structure	Island
Surrounding Area	City
Region	Pacific Coast
Size	Small Size (2,176)
Curriculum Type	Distribution Requirements
Residential Type	High Residential (80%)
Selectivity	S-3 Selectivity
Financial Aid	Good Aid 14 ($614,157)
Prestige	No Prestige Rating
Designations	Economics

Ohio State University
Columbus, Ohio

Category	Characteristics
School Type	University
School Funding	Public
Campus Structure	Integrated
Surrounding Area	City
Region	Midwest
Size	Large Size (43,058)
Curriculum Type	Loose Core
Residential Type	Low Residential (25%)
Selectivity	S-4 Selectivity
Financial Aid	Some Aid 426 ($2,499,338)
Prestige	No Prestige Rating
Designations	Sports; School Spirit; Business; Hard Sciences

Ohio Wesleyan University
Delaware, Ohio

Category	Characteristics
School Type	University
School Funding	Private
Campus Structure	Integrated
Surrounding Area	Suburb
Region	Midwest
Size	Small Size (1,821)
Curriculum Type	Loose Core
Residential Type	High Residential (90%)
Selectivity	S-5 Selectivity
Financial Aid	Excellent Aid 149 ($3,368,998)
Prestige	No Prestige Rating
Designations	Social Activism and Community Service; Government and Politics; Religious; Music; Pre-Med; Greek Life

Olin College
Needham, Massachusetts

Category	Characteristics
School Type	College
School Funding	Private
Campus Structure	Island
Surrounding Area	Suburb
Region	New England Region
Size	Very Small Size (355)
Curriculum Type	Core
Residential Type	High Residential (100%)
Selectivity	S-1 Selectivity
Financial Aid	Best Aid 20 ($560,000) Half scholarship guaranteed to all students
Prestige	No Prestige Rating
Designations	Entrepreneurship; Techie; Engineering

Penn State University
State College, Pennsylvania

Category	Characteristics
School Type	University
School Funding	Public
Campus Structure	Island
Surrounding Area	Small City
Region	Mid-Atlantic
Size	Large Size (39,192)
Curriculum Type	Core
Residential Type	Low Residential (36%)
Selectivity	S-4 Selectivity
Financial Aid	No Institutional Aid Available to International Students
Prestige	Prestigious
Designations	Sports; School Spirit; Journalism; Business; Engineering; Hard Sciences; Greek Life; College Town

Pepperdine University
Malibu, California

Category	Characteristics
School Type	University
School Funding	Private
Campus Structure	Island
Surrounding Area	Suburb
Region	Pacific Coast
Size	Small Size (3,488)
Curriculum Type	Core
Residential Type	Medium Residential (58%)
Selectivity	S-4 Selectivity
Financial Aid	Good Aid 68 ($1,447,933)
Prestige	No Prestige Rating
Designations	Religious; Journalism; Business; Housing

Pitzer College
Claremont, California

Category	Characteristics
School Type	College
School Funding	Private
Campus Structure	Island
Surrounding Area	Town
Region	Pacific Coast
Size	Very Small Size (1,084)
Curriculum Type	Distribution Requirements
Residential Type	Medium Residential (74%)
Selectivity	S-3 Selectivity
Financial Aid	Some Aid 3 ($182,217)
Prestige	No Prestige Rating
Designations	Social Activism and Community Service; Humanities; Environmental Awareness and Activism

Pomona College
Claremont, California

Category	Characteristics
School Type	College
School Funding	Private
Campus Structure	Island
Surrounding Area	Town
Region	Pacific Coast
Size	Small Size (1,607)
Curriculum Type	Distribution Requirements
Residential Type	High Residential (98%)
Selectivity	S-1 Selectivity
Financial Aid	Good Aid 37 ($1,457,826)
Prestige	Most Prestigious
Designations	Outdoors; Pre-Med; Housing

Pratt Institute
New York, New York

Category	Characteristics
School Type	University
School Funding	Private
Campus Structure	Integrated
Surrounding Area	City
Region	Mid-Atlantic
Size	Medium Size (3,076)
Curriculum Type	Core
Residential Type	Medium Residential (52%)
Selectivity	S-4 Selectivity
Financial Aid	Good Aid 160 ($1,175,000)
Prestige	No Prestige Rating
Designations	Artistic; Architecture; College Town

Princeton University
Princeton, New Jersey

Category	Characteristics
School Type	University
School Funding	Private
Campus Structure	Island
Surrounding Area	Town
Region	Mid-Atlantic
Size	Medium Size (5,336)
Curriculum Type	Distribution Requirements
Residential Type	High Residential (97%)
Selectivity	S-1 Selectivity
Financial Aid	Best Aid 409 ($16,397,219)
Prestige	Most Prestigious
Designations	Social Activism and Community Service; Government and Politics; Serious Academic; Entrepreneurship; Techie; Economics; Engineering; Hard Sciences; International Student Body; Housing

Purdue University – West Lafayette
West Lafayette, Indiana

Category	Characteristics
School Type	University
School Funding	Public
Campus Structure	Island
Surrounding Area	Small City
Region	Midwest
Size	Large Size (20,147)
Curriculum Type	Loose Core
Residential Type	Low Residential (35%)
Selectivity	S-5 Selectivity
Financial Aid	Some Aid 224 ($369,665)
Prestige	No Prestige Rating
Designations	Sports; School Spirit; Techie; Engineering; Hard Sciences; International Student Body

Reed College
Portland, Oregon

Category	Characteristics
School Type	College
School Funding	Private
Campus Structure	Island
Surrounding Area	City
Region	Pacific Coast
Size	Small Size (1,492)
Curriculum Type	Core
Residential Type	Medium Residential (67%)
Selectivity	S-2 Selectivity
Financial Aid	Excellent Aid 45 ($2,080,424)
Prestige	No Prestige Rating
Designations	Government and Politics; Humanities

Rensselaer Polytechnic Institute
Troy, New York

Category	Characteristics
School Type	University
School Funding	Private
Campus Structure	Island
Surrounding Area	Small City
Region	Mid-Atlantic
Size	Medium Size (5,394)
Curriculum Type	Core
Residential Type	Medium Residential (57%)
Selectivity	S-3 Selectivity
Financial Aid	No Institutional Aid for International Students
Prestige	Prestigious
Designations	Techie; Engineering; Hard Sciences; Architecture; International Student Body

Rhodes College
Memphis, Tennessee

Category	Characteristics
School Type	College
School Funding	Private
Campus Structure	Island
Surrounding Area	City
Region	South
Size	Small Size (1,915)
Curriculum Type	Loose Core
Residential Type	Medium Residential (71%)
Selectivity	S-4 Selectivity
Financial Aid	Good Aid 59 ($1,075,991)
Prestige	No Prestige Rating
Designations	Social Activism and Community Service; Religious; Pre-Med; Greek Life

Rice University
Houston, Texas

Category	Characteristics
School Type	University
School Funding	Private
Campus Structure	Island
Surrounding Area	City
Region	South
Size	Small Size (3,848)
Curriculum Type	Distribution Requirements
Residential Type	Medium Residential (72%)
Selectivity	S-1 Selectivity
Financial Aid	Good Aid 75 ($1,828,575)
Prestige	Most Prestigious
Designations	Government and Politics; Serious Academic; Techie; Music; Economics; Engineering; Hard Sciences; Pre-Med; Architecture; International Student Body; Housing

Rutgers University – New Brunswick
New Brunswick, New Jersey

Category	Characteristics
School Type	University
School Funding	Public
Campus Structure	Integrated
Surrounding Area	Small City
Region	Mid-Atlantic
Size	Large Size (31,499)
Curriculum Type	Loose Core
Residential Type	Medium Residential (53%)
Selectivity	S-4 Selectivity
Financial Aid	Some Aid 4 ($3,750)
Prestige	No Prestige Rating
Designations	Social Activism and Community Service; School Spirit

Sarah Lawrence College
Bronxville, New York

Category	Characteristics
School Type	College
School Funding	Private
Campus Structure	Island
Surrounding Area	Suburb
Region	Mid-Atlantic
Size	Very Small Size (1,235)
Curriculum Type	Open
Residential Type	High Residential (85%)
Selectivity	S-3 Selectivity
Financial Aid	Best Aid 73 ($2,592,487)
Prestige	No Prestige Rating
Designations	Artistic; Serious Academic; Theater; Quirky; Humanities; Writing

Scripps College
Claremont, California

Category	Characteristics
School Type	College
School Funding	Private
Campus Structure	Island
Surrounding Area	Town
Region	Pacific Coast
Size	Very Small Size (945)
Curriculum Type	Core
Residential Type	High Residential (95%)
Selectivity	S-2 Selectivity
Financial Aid	Good Aid 18 ($580,522)
Prestige	Prestigious
Designations	Humanities, Housing, Single Sex (all-female)

Sewanee: The University of the South
Sewanee, Tennessee

Category	Characteristics
School Type	College
School Funding	Private
Campus Structure	Island
Surrounding Area	Rural
Region	South
Size	Small Size (1,478)
Curriculum Type	Distribution Requirements
Residential Type	High Residential (96%)
Selectivity	S-4 Selectivity
Financial Aid	Some Aid 7 ($289,789)
Prestige	No Prestige Rating
Designations	Athletic; Outdoors; Religious; Greek Life

Shimer College
Chicago, Illinois

Category	Characteristics
School Type	College
School Funding	Private
Campus Structure	Street-Side
Surrounding Area	City
Region	Midwest
Size	Very Small Size (140)
Curriculum Type	Core
Residential Type	Low Residential (42%)
Selectivity	S-4 Selectivity
Financial Aid	Some Aid 1 ($10,000)
Prestige	No Prestige Rating
Designations	Quirky; Humanities; College Town

Skidmore College
Saratoga Springs, New York

Category	Characteristics
School Type	College
School Funding	Private
Campus Structure	Island
Surrounding Area	Small City
Region	Mid-Atlantic
Size	Small Size (2,660)
Curriculum Type	Distribution Requirements
Residential Type	High Residential (86%)
Selectivity	S-4 Selectivity
Financial Aid	Excellent Aid 80 ($4,281,849)
Prestige	No Prestige Rating
Designations	Artistic; Theater

Smith College
Northampton, Massachusetts

Category	Characteristics
School Type	College
School Funding	Private
Campus Structure	Island
Surrounding Area	Town
Region	New England
Size	Small Size (2,664)
Curriculum Type	Open
Residential Type	High Residential (86%)
Selectivity	S-2 Selectivity
Financial Aid	Best Aid 168 ($7,338,206)
Prestige	Prestige Rating
Designations	Serious Academic; Humanities; Engineering; Pre-Med; College Town; Housing; Single Sex (all-female)

Soka University of America
Aliso Viejo, California

Category	Characteristics
School Type	College
School Funding	Private
Campus Structure	Island
Surrounding Area	Town
Region	Pacific Coast
Size	Very Small Size (436)
Curriculum Type	Core
Residential Type	High Residential (100%)
Selectivity	S-4 Selectivity
Financial Aid	155 ($5,308,880)
Prestige	No Prestige Rating
Designations	Outdoors; Social Activism and Community Service; Environmental Activism and Awareness; International Student Body

Southern Methodist University
Dallas, Texas

Category	Characteristics
School Type	University
School Funding	Private
Campus Structure	Integrated
Surrounding Area	City
Region	South
Size	Medium Size (6,249)
Curriculum Type	Loose Core
Residential Type	Low Residential (32%)
Selectivity	S-4 Selectivity
Financial Aid	Good Aid 189 ($5,068,739)
Prestige	No Prestige Rating
Designations	Sports; School Spirit; Religious; Business; Greek Life

St. John's College - Annapolis
Annapolis, Maryland

Category	Characteristics
School Type	College
School Funding	Private
Campus Structure	Island
Surrounding Area	Small City
Region	Mid-Atlantic
Size	Very Small Size (475)
Curriculum Type	Core
Residential Type	Medium Residential (70%)
Selectivity	S-3 Selectivity
Financial Aid	Best Aid 39 ($1,229,271)
Prestige	No Prestige Rating
Designations	Serious Academic; Quirky; Humanities

St. John's College – Santa Fe
Santa Fe, New Mexico

Category	Characteristics
School Type	College
School Funding	Private
Campus Structure	Island
Surrounding Area	Small City
Region	West
Size	Very Small Size (375)
Curriculum Type	Core
Residential Type	High Residential (82%)
Selectivity	S-3 Selectivity
Financial Aid	Some Aid (unreported)
Prestige	No Prestige Rating
Designations	Outdoors; Serious Academic; Quirky; Humanities

St. Lawrence University
Canton, New York

Category	Characteristics
School Type	College
School Funding	Private
Campus Structure	Island
Surrounding Area	Rural
Region	Mid-Atlantic
Size	Small Size (2,398)
Curriculum Type	Distribution Requirements
Residential Type	High Residential (97%)
Selectivity	S-4 Selectivity
Financial Aid	Best Aid 155 ($5,939,516)
Prestige	No Prestige Rating
Designations	Athletic, Outdoors

St. Mary's College of Maryland
St. Mary's City, Maryland

Category	Characteristics
School Type	College
School Funding	Public
Campus Structure	Island
Surrounding Area	Rural
Region	Mid-Atlantic
Size	Small Size (1,901)
Curriculum Type	Loose Core
Residential Type	High Residential (86%)
Selectivity	S-5 Selectivity
Financial Aid	Some Aid 21 ($115,000)
Prestige	No Prestige Rating
Designations	Athletic; Outdoors; Environmental Awareness and Activism

St. Olaf College
Northfield, Minnesota

Category	Characteristics
School Type	College
School Funding	Private
Campus Structure	Island
Surrounding Area	Town
Region	Midwest
Size	Small Size (3,176)
Curriculum Type	Loose Core
Residential Type	High Residential (91%)
Selectivity	S-3 Selectivity
Financial Aid	Excellent Aid ($5,309,947)
Prestige	No Prestige Rating
Designations	Religious; Humanities; Music

Stanford University
Palo Alto, California

Category	Characteristics
School Type	University
School Funding	Private
Campus Structure	Island
Surrounding Area	Suburb
Region	Pacific Coast
Size	Medium Size (6,999)
Curriculum Type	Loose Core
Residential Type	High Residential (91%)
Selectivity	S-1 Selectivity
Financial Aid	Excellent Aid 187 ($9,088,919)
Prestige	Most Prestigious
Designations	Athletic; Serious Academic; Entrepreneurship; Techie; Economics; Engineering; Hard Sciences; Environmental Awareness and Activism; Pre-Med

Stony Brook University
Stony Brook, New York

Category	Characteristics
School Type	University
School Funding	Public
Campus Structure	Island
Surrounding Area	Suburb
Region	Mid-Atlantic
Size	Large Size (16,003)
Curriculum Type	Loose Core
Residential Type	Medium Residential (53%)
Selectivity	S-4 Selectivity
Financial Aid	Some Aid 108 ($1,323,350)
Prestige	No Prestige Rating
Designations	Journalism; Engineering; Hard Sciences; Pre-Med; International Student Body

Swarthmore College
Swarthmore, Pennsylvania

Category	Characteristics
School Type	College
School Funding	Private
Campus Structure	Island
Surrounding Area	Suburb
Region	Mid-Atlantic
Size	Small Size (1,552)
Curriculum Type	Distribution Requirements
Residential Type	High Residential (93%)
Selectivity	S-1 Selectivity
Financial Aid	Excellent Aid 56 ($2,604,476)
Prestige	Most Prestigious
Designations	Artistic; Social Activism and Community Awareness; Serious Academic; Humanities; Engineering

Texas A&M University
College Station, Texas

Category	Characteristics
School Type	University
School Funding	Public
Campus Structure	Island
Surrounding Area	Small City
Region	South
Size	Large Size (40,103)
Curriculum Type	Loose Core
Residential Type	Low Residential (22%)
Selectivity	S-5 Selectivity
Financial Aid	Good Aid 239 ($4,597,643)
Prestige	No Prestige Rating
Designations	Sports; Business; Engineering; Hard Sciences

Thomas Aquinas College
Santa Paula, California

Category	Characteristics
School Type	College
School Funding	Private
Campus Structure	Island
Surrounding Area	Rural
Region	Pacific Coast
Size	Very Small Size (370)
Curriculum Type	Core
Residential Type	High Residential (99%)
Selectivity	S-3 Selectivity
Financial Aid	Good Aid 10 ($195,716)
Prestige	No Prestige Rating
Designations	Religious; Humanities

Trinity College
Hartford, Connecticut

Category	Characteristics
School Type	College
School Funding	Private
Campus Structure	Island
Surrounding Area	City
Region	New England
Size	Small Size (2,301)
Curriculum Type	Loose Core
Residential Type	High Residential (89%)
Selectivity	S-3 Selectivity
Financial Aid	Best Aid 146 ($7,446,464)
Prestige	No Prestige Rating
Designations	Greek Life

Tufts University
Medford, Massachusetts

Category	Characteristics
School Type	University
School Funding	Private
Campus Structure	Island
Surrounding Area	Suburb
Region	New England
Size	Medium Size (5,255)
Curriculum Type	Distribution Requirements
Residential Type	Medium Residential (64%)
Selectivity	S-2 Selectivity
Financial Aid	Good Aid 134 ($2,521,166)
Prestige	Most Prestigious
Designations	Government and Politics; Entrepreneurship; Engineering

Tulane University
New Orleans, Louisiana

Category	Characteristics
School Type	University
School Funding	Private
Campus Structure	Island
Surrounding Area	City
Region	South
Size	Medium Size (8,423)
Curriculum Type	Loose Core
Residential Type	Medium Residential (64%)
Selectivity	S-3 Selectivity
Financial Aid	Good Aid 134 ($2,521,166)
Prestige	Most Prestigious
Designations	School Spirit; College Town

Union College
Schenectady, New York

Category	Characteristics
School Type	College
School Funding	Private
Campus Structure	Island
Surrounding Area	Small City
Region	Mid-Atlantic
Size	Small Size (2,241)
Curriculum Type	Loose Core
Residential Type	High Residential (89%)
Selectivity	S-3 Selectivity
Financial Aid	Excellent Aid 82 ($2,706,410)
Prestige	No Prestige Rating
Designations	Engineering; Hard Sciences; Pre-Med; Greek Life

University of California - Berkeley
Berkeley, California

Category	Characteristics
School Type	University
School Funding	Public
Campus Structure	Integrated
Surrounding Area	City
Region	Pacific Coast
Size	Large Size (25,774)
Curriculum Type	Loose Core
Residential Type	Low Residential (26%)
Selectivity	S-2 Selectivity
Financial Aid	No Institutional Aid Available for International Students
Prestige	Most Prestigious
Designations	Social Activism and Community Service; Serious Academic; Entrepreneurship; Techie; Economics; Business; Engineering; Hard Sciences; Architecture; International Student Body; College Town

University of California – San Diego (UCSD)
La Jolla, California

Category	Characteristics
School Type	University
School Funding	Public
Campus Structure	Island
Surrounding Area	City
Region	Pacific Coast
Size	Large Size (22,676)
Curriculum Type	Loose Core
Residential Type	Low Residential (43%)
Selectivity	S-3 Selectivity
Financial Aid	Good Aid 109 ($2,990,851)
Prestige	Prestigious
Designations	Techie; Economics; Hard Sciences; Pre-Med; International Student Body

University of California – Davis (UCD)
Davis, California

Category	Characteristics
School Type	University
School Funding	Public
Campus Structure	Island
Surrounding Area	Small City
Region	Pacific Coast
Size	Large Size (25,759)
Curriculum Type	Loose Core
Residential Type	Low Residential (25%)
Selectivity	S-4 Selectivity
Financial Aid	Good Aid 140 ($2,157,642)
Prestige	Prestigious
Designations	School Spirit; Environmental Awareness and Activism

University of California – Irvine (UCI)
Irvine, California

Category	Characteristics
School Type	University
School Funding	Public
Campus Structure	Island
Surrounding Area	Suburb
Region	Pacific Coast
Size	Large Size (22,216)
Curriculum Type	Loose Core
Residential Type	Low Residential (38%)
Selectivity	S-5 Selectivity
Financial Aid	Good Aid 117 ($1,623,896)
Prestige	Prestigious
Designations	Hard Sciences; Pre-Med

University of California – Santa Barbara (UCSB)
Santa Barbara, California

Category	Characteristics
School Type	University
School Funding	Public
Campus Structure	Integrated
Surrounding Area	Suburb
Region	Pacific Coast
Size	Large Size (18,977)
Curriculum Type	Loose Core
Residential Type	Low Residential (37%)
Selectivity	S-4 Selectivity
Financial Aid	Some Aid 33 ($972,015))
Prestige	Prestigious
Designations	Athletic; Hard Sciences, Pre-Med; Greek Life

University of California – Santa Cruz (UCSC)
Santa Cruz, California

Category	Characteristics
School Type	University
School Funding	Public
Campus Structure	Island
Surrounding Area	City
Region	Pacific Coast
Size	Large Size (15,978)
Curriculum Type	Loose Core
Residential Type	Low Residential (48%)
Selectivity	S-5 Selectivity
Financial Aid	Some Aid 6 ($112,104)
Prestige	No Prestige Rating
Designations	Outdoors; College Town

University of California – Los Angeles (UCLA
Los Angeles, California

Category	Characteristics
School Type	University
School Funding	Public
Campus Structure	Integrated
Surrounding Area	City
Region	Pacific Coast
Size	Large Size (25,774)
Curriculum Type	Distribution Requirements
Residential Type	Low Residential (35%)
Selectivity	S-3 Selectivity
Financial Aid	Good Aid 69 ($2,100,705)
Prestige	Most Prestigious
Designations	Sports; School Spirit; Entrepreneurship; Economics; Engineering; Hard Sciences; Pre-Med; International Student Body

University of Chicago
Chicago, Illinois

Category	Characteristics
School Type	University
School Funding	Private
Campus Structure	Integrated
Surrounding Area	City
Region	Midwest
Size	Medium Size (5,590)
Curriculum Type	Core
Residential Type	Medium Residential (60%)
Selectivity	S-1 Selectivity
Financial Aid	Good Aid 57 ($3,215,600)
Prestige	Most Prestigious
Designations	Serious Academic; Entrepreneurship; Theater; Quirky; Economics; Humanities; Hard Sciences; International Student Body; Housing

University of Colorado – Boulder
Boulder, Colorado

Category	Characteristics
School Type	University
School Funding	Public
Campus Structure	Integrated
Surrounding Area	City
Region	West
Size	Large Size (25,805)
Curriculum Type	Loose Core
Residential Type	Low Residential (28%)
Selectivity	S-5 Selectivity
Financial Aid	Some Aid 51 ($587,927)
Prestige	No Prestige Rating
Designations	Sports; Outdoors; Entrepreneurship; Hard Sciences; Environmental Awareness and Activism; International Student Body; College Town

University of Connecticut
Storrs, Connecticut

Category	Characteristics
School Type	University
School Funding	Public
Campus Structure	Island
Surrounding Area	Rural
Region	New England
Size	Large Size (17,528)
Curriculum Type	Loose Core
Residential Type	Medium Residential (72%)
Selectivity	S-5 Selectivity
Financial Aid	No Institutional Aid for International Students
Prestige	No Prestige Rating
Designations	Sports; Athletic; Greek Life

University of Delaware
Newark, Delaware

Category	Characteristics
School Type	University
School Funding	Public
Campus Structure	Integrated
Surrounding Area	Small City
Region	Mid-Atlantic
Size	Large Size (17,427)
Curriculum Type	Loose Core
Residential Type	Low Residential (44%)
Selectivity	S-4 Selectivity
Financial Aid	No Institutional Aid for International Students
Prestige	No Prestige Rating
Designations	Sports; Greek Life

University of Florida
Gainesville, Florida

Category	Characteristics
School Type	University
School Funding	Public
Campus Structure	Island
Surrounding Area	Small City
Region	South
Size	Large Size (32,776)
Curriculum Type	Distribution Requirements
Residential Type	Low Residential (24%)
Selectivity	S-3 Selectivity
Financial Aid	No Institutional Aid for International Students
Prestige	Prestigious
Designations	Sports; Athletic; School Spirit; Journalism; Engineering; Pre-Med; Greek Life

GES

University of Georgia
Athens, Georgia

Category	Characteristics
School Type	University
School Funding	Public
Campus Structure	Island
Surrounding Area	Small City
Region	South
Size	Large Size (26,259)
Curriculum Type	Loose Core
Residential Type	Low Residential (28%)
Selectivity	S-4 Selectivity
Financial Aid	No Institutional Aid for International Students
Prestige	No Prestige Rating
Designations	Sports; Athletic; Journalism; Pre-Med: Greek Life; College Town

University of Illinois
Champaign, Illinois

Category	Characteristics
School Type	University
School Funding	Public
Campus Structure	Integrated
Surrounding Area	Small City
Region	Midwest
Size	Large Size (32,281)
Curriculum Type	Loose Core
Residential Type	Low Residential (37%)
Selectivity	S-3 Selectivity
Financial Aid	Good Aid ($7,127,097)
Prestige	Most Prestigious
Designations	Sports; Athletic; Techie; Journalism; Business; Engineering; Hard Sciences; Pre-Med; International Student Body; Greek Life

University of Iowa
Iowa City, Iowa

Category	Characteristics
School Type	University
School Funding	Public
Campus Structure	Integrated
Surrounding Area	Small City
Region	Midwest
Size	Large Size (21,999)
Curriculum Type	Loose Core
Residential Type	Low Residential (31%)
Selectivity	S-5 Selectivity
Financial Aid	No Institutional Aid for International Students
Prestige	No Prestige Rating
Designations	Sports; School Spirit; Journalism; Business; Environmental Awareness and Activism; International Student Body; Writing

University of Maine
Orono, Maine

Category	Characteristics
School Type	University
School Funding	Public
Campus Structure	Island
Surrounding Area	Rural
Region	New England
Size	Medium Size (8,778)
Curriculum Type	Loose Core
Residential Type	Low Residential (40%)
Selectivity	S-5 Selectivity
Financial Aid	Good Aid 517 ($2,787,664)
Prestige	No Prestige Rating
Designations	Sports; Outdoors

University of Maryland – Baltimore County (UMBC)
Baltimore, Maryland

Category	Characteristics
School Type	University
School Funding	Public
Campus Structure	Island
Surrounding Area	Suburb
Region	Mid-Atlantic
Size	Large Size (10,953)
Curriculum Type	Loose Core
Residential Type	Low Residential (34%)
Selectivity	S-5 Selectivity
Financial Aid	No Institutional Aid Available for International Students
Prestige	No Prestige Rating
Designations	Artistic; Music; Hard Sciences; Pre-Med

University of Maryland – College Park
College Park, Maryland

Category	Characteristics
School Type	University
School Funding	Public
Campus Structure	Island
Surrounding Area	Suburb
Region	Mid-Atlantic
Size	Large Size (26,487)
Curriculum Type	Loose Core
Residential Type	Low Residential (47%)
Selectivity	S-3 Selectivity
Financial Aid	No Institutional Aid Available for International Students
Prestige	No Prestige Rating
Designations	Sports; Government and Politics; School Spirit; Entrepreneurship; Journalism; Economics; Hard Sciences; Greek Life

University of Massachusetts – Amherst
Amherst, Massachusetts

Category	Characteristics
School Type	University
School Funding	Public
Campus Structure	Island
Surrounding Area	Town
Region	New England
Size	Large Size (21,928)
Curriculum Type	Distribution Requirements
Residential Type	Medium Residential (61%)
Selectivity	S-4 Selectivity
Financial Aid	No Institutional Aid Available for International Students
Prestige	Prestigious
Designations	Economics; Engineering; Hard Sciences

University of Miami
Coral Gables, Florida

Category	Characteristics
School Type	University
School Funding	Private
Campus Structure	Island
Surrounding Area	Suburb
Region	South
Size	Large Size (10,590)
Curriculum Type	Loose Core
Residential Type	Low Residential (39%)
Selectivity	S-3 Selectivity
Financial Aid	Good Aid 118 ($3,318,202)
Prestige	Prestigious
Designations	Sports; Athletic; School Spirit; Music; Pre-Med; International Student Body

University of Michigan
Ann Arbor, Michigan

Category	Characteristics
School Type	University
School Funding	Public
Campus Structure	Integrated
Surrounding Area	Small City
Region	Midwest
Size	Large Size (27,979)
Curriculum Type	Open (individual departments may have requirements but no university-wide requirements)
Residential Type	Low Residential (34%)
Selectivity	S-3 Selectivity
Financial Aid	No Institutional Aid for International Students
Prestige	Most Prestigious
Designations	Sports; School Spirit; Techie; Music; Business; Economics; Engineering; Hard Sciences; Pre-Med; Greek Life; College Town; Writing

University of Minnesota – Twin Cities
Minneapolis, Minnesota

Category	Characteristics
School Type	University
School Funding	Public
Campus Structure	Integrated
Surrounding Area	City
Region	Midwest
Size	Large Size (34,469)
Curriculum Type	Loose Core
Residential Type	Low Residential (21%)
Selectivity	S-3 Selectivity
Financial Aid	Some Aid (unreported)
Prestige	No Prestige Rating
Designations	Sports; Journalism; Economics; Business; Engineering; Hard Sciences; Pre-Med

University of New Hampshire
Durham, New Hampshire

Category	Characteristics
School Type	University
School Funding	Public
Campus Structure	Island
Surrounding Area	Town
Region	New England
Size	Large Size (12,811)
Curriculum Type	Loose Core
Residential Type	Medium Residential (57%)
Selectivity	S-5 Selectivity
Financial Aid	Good Aid 52 ($1,569,516)
Prestige	No Prestige Rating
Designations	Athletic; Outdoors; Greek Life

University of New Mexico
Albuquerque, New Mexico

Category	Characteristics
School Type	University
School Funding	Public
Campus Structure	Island
Surrounding Area	City
Region	West
Size	Large Size (22,773)
Curriculum Type	Loose Core
Residential Type	Low Residential (8%)
Selectivity	S-5 Selectivity
Financial Aid	Some Aid (unreported)
Prestige	No Prestige Rating
Designations	Sports; Business; Engineering; Pre-Med

Jniversity of North Carolina – Chapel Hill
Chapel Hill, North Carolina

Category	Characteristics
School Type	University
School Funding	Public
Campus Structure	Integrated
Surrounding Area	Suburb
Region	South
Size	Large Size (18,503)
Curriculum Type	Loose Core
Residential Type	Low Residential (46%)
Selectivity	S-3 Selectivity
Financial Aid	No Institutional Aid for International Students
Prestige	Prestigious
Designations	Sports; School Spirit; Entrepreneurship; Journalism; Business; Hard Sciences; Pre-Med

University of Notre Dame
Notre Dame, Indiana

Category	Characteristics
School Type	University
School Funding	Private
Campus Structure	Island
Surrounding Area	Small City
Region	Midwest
Size	Medium Size (8,475)
Curriculum Type	Loose Core
Residential Type	High Residential (80%)
Selectivity	S-2 Selectivity
Financial Aid	Good Aid 89 ($2,770,314)
Prestige	Most Prestigious
Designations	Sports; Athletic; School Spirit; Religious; Business

University of Pennsylvania
Philadelphia, Pennsylvania

Category	Characteristics
School Type	University
School Funding	Private
Campus Structure	Integrated
Surrounding Area	City
Region	Mid-Atlantic
Size	Medium Size (9,682)
Curriculum Type	Loose Core
Residential Type	Medium Residential (66%)
Selectivity	S-1 Selectivity
Financial Aid	Excellent Aid 332 ($14,245,353)
Prestige	Most Prestigious
Designations	Entrepreneurship; Economics; Business; Engineering; Hard Sciences; Pre-Med; International Student Body

University of Pittsburgh
Pittsburgh, Pennsylvania

Category	Characteristics
School Type	University
School Funding	Public
Campus Structure	Integrated
Surrounding Area	City
Region	Mid-Atlantic
Size	Large Size (18,429)
Curriculum Type	Loose Core
Residential Type	Low Residential (44%)
Selectivity	S-4 Selectivity
Financial Aid	No Institutional Aid for International Students
Prestige	No Prestige Rating
Designations	Sports; Engineering; Environmental Awareness and Activism

University of Richmond
Richmond, Virginia

Category	Characteristics
School Type	College
School Funding	Private
Campus Structure	Island
Surrounding Area	Suburb
Region	South
Size	Small Size (3,074)
Curriculum Type	Distribution Requirements
Residential Type	High Residential (89%)
Selectivity	S-3 Selectivity
Financial Aid	Excellent Aid 128 ($5,628,674)
Prestige	Prestigious
Designations	Business; Greek Life

University of Rochester
Rochester, New York

Category	Characteristics
School Type	College
School Funding	Private
Campus Structure	Island
Surrounding Area	Suburb
Region	Mid-Atlantic
Size	Medium Size (5,785)
Curriculum Type	Open
Residential Type	High Residential (86%)
Selectivity	S-3 Selectivity
Financial Aid	Excellent Aid 328 ($6,538,139)
Prestige	Prestigious
Designations	Music; Business; Economics; Hard Sciences; Pre-Med

University of Southern California
Los Angeles, California

Category	Characteristics
School Type	University
School Funding	Private
Campus Structure	Integrated
Surrounding Area	City
Region	Pacific Coast
Size	Large Size (18,316)
Curriculum Type	Loose Core
Residential Type	Low Residential (38%)
Selectivity	S-2 Selectivity
Financial Aid	Good Aid 221 ($4,254,635)
Prestige	Most Prestigious
Designations	Sports; Entrepreneurship; Techie; Music; Journalism; Business; Architecture; International Student Body; Greek Life

University of Texas - Austin
Austin, Texas

Category	Characteristics
School Type	University
School Funding	Public
Campus Structure	Integrated
Surrounding Area	City
Region	South
Size	Large Size (39,955)
Curriculum Type	Loose Core
Residential Type	Low Residential (19%)
Selectivity	S-3 Selectivity
Financial Aid	Some Aid (unreported)
Prestige	Prestigious
Designations	Sports; School Spirit; Entrepreneurship; Techie; Journalism; Business; Engineering; Hard Sciences; Pre-Med; Architecture; College Town

University of Vermont
Burlington, Vermont

Category	Characteristics
School Type	University
School Funding	Public
Campus Structure	Integrated
Surrounding Area	Small City
Region	New England
Size	Large Size (11,211)
Curriculum Type	Loose Core
Residential Type	Medium Residential (50%)
Selectivity	S-5 Selectivity
Financial Aid	Good Aid 93 ($1,516,467)
Prestige	No Prestige Rating
Designations	Outdoors; Environmental Awareness and Activism; College Town

University of Virginia
Charlottesville, Virginia

Category	Characteristics
School Type	University
School Funding	Public
Campus Structure	Integrated
Surrounding Area	Small City
Region	South
Size	Large Size (15,822)
Curriculum Type	Distribution Requirements
Residential Type	Low Residential (42%)
Selectivity	S-2 Selectivity
Financial Aid	No Institutional Aid for International Students
Prestige	High Prestige Rating
Designations	Sports; Government and Politics; Business; Pre-Med; Architecture; Greek Life

University of Washington
Seattle, Washington

Category	Characteristics
School Type	University
School Funding	Public
Campus Structure	Integrated
Surrounding Area	City
Region	Pacific Coast
Size	Large Size (28,933)
Curriculum Type	Distribution Requirements
Residential Type	Low Residential (13%)
Selectivity	S-5 Selectivity
Financial Aid	No Institutional Aid for International Students
Prestige	Prestigious
Designations	Sports; Entrepreneurship; Techie; Hard Sciences; Pre-Med; International Student Body; College Town

University of Wisconsin
Madison, Wisconsin

Category	Characteristics
School Type	University
School Funding	Public
Campus Structure	Integrated
Surrounding Area	Small City
Region	Midwest
Size	Large Size (30,863)
Curriculum Type	Distribution Requirements
Residential Type	Low Residential (25%)
Selectivity	S-3 Selectivity
Financial Aid	No Institutional Aid for International Students
Prestige	Prestigious
Designations	Sports; School Spirit; Entrepreneurship; Techie; Journalism; Economics; Business; Engineering; Hard Sciences; Pre-Med; College Town

Vanderbilt University
Nashville, Tennessee

Category	Characteristics
School Type	University
School Funding	Private
Campus Structure	Integrated
Surrounding Area	City
Region	South
Size	Medium Size (6,756)
Curriculum Type	Loose Core
Residential Type	High Residential (83%)
Selectivity	S-1 Selectivity
Financial Aid	Good Aid 62 ($2,869,569)
Prestige	Most Prestigious
Designations	Theater; Pre-Med; Greek Life

Vassar College
Poughkeepsie, New York

Category	Characteristics
School Type	College
School Funding	Private
Campus Structure	Island
Surrounding Area	Small City
Region	Mid-Atlantic
Size	Small Size (2,406)
Curriculum Type	Open
Residential Type	High Residential (94%)
Selectivity	S-2 Selectivity
Financial Aid	Excellent Aid 92 ($4,445,049)
Prestige	Prestigious
Designations	Artistic; Social Awareness and Activism; Theater

Virginia Polytechnic Institute (Virginia Tech)
Blacksburg, Virginia

Category	Characteristics
School Type	University
School Funding	Public
Campus Structure	Island
Surrounding Area	Town
Region	South
Size	Large Size (23,859)
Curriculum Type	Loose Core
Residential Type	Medium Residential (51%)
Selectivity	S-4 Selectivity
Financial Aid	No Institutional Aid for International Students
Prestige	No Prestige Rating
Designations	Sports; School Spirit; Techie; Engineering; Architecture; Greek Life

Wabash College
Crawfordsville, Indiana

Category	Characteristics
School Type	College
School Funding	Private
Campus Structure	Island
Surrounding Area	Town
Region	Midwest
Size	Very Small Size (906)
Curriculum Type	Core
Residential Type	High Residential (87%)
Selectivity	S-5 Selectivity
Financial Aid	Excellent Aid 53 ($936,950)
Prestige	No Prestige Rating
Designations	Sports; Athletic; Humanities; Hard Sciences; Greek Life; Single Sex (all-male)

Wake Forest University
Winston-Salem, North Carolina

Category	Characteristics
School Type	University
School Funding	Private
Campus Structure	Island
Surrounding Area	Town
Region	South
Size	Medium Size (4,815)
Curriculum Type	Loose Core
Residential Type	Medium Residential (68%)
Selectivity	S-3 Selectivity
Financial Aid	Some Aid (unreported)
Prestige	High Prestige Rating
Designations	Athletic; School Spirit; Greek Life

Washington and Lee University
Lexington, Virginia

Category	Characteristics
School Type	College
School Funding	Private
Campus Structure	Island
Surrounding Area	Town
Region	South
Size	Small Size (1,838)
Curriculum Type	Loose Core
Residential Type	Medium Residential (59%)
Selectivity	S-2 Selectivity
Financial Aid	Excellent Aid 73 ($3,640,194)
Prestige	Most Prestigious
Designations	Business; Greek Life

Washington University – St. Louis
St. Louis, Missouri

Category	Characteristics
School Type	University
School Funding	Private
Campus Structure	Island
Surrounding Area	Suburb
Region	Midwest
Size	Medium Size (7,259)
Curriculum Type	Loose Core (plus one mandatory writing class)
Residential Type	Medium Residential (79%)
Selectivity	S-1 Selectivity
Financial Aid	Good Aid ($4,308,928)
Prestige	Most Prestigious
Designations	Entrepreneurship; Business; Pre-Med; Greek Life

Wellesley College
Wellesley, Massachusetts

Category	Characteristics
School Type	College
School Funding	Private
Campus Structure	Island
Surrounding Area	Suburb
Region	New England
Size	Small Size (2,481)
Curriculum Type	Distribution Requirements
Residential Type	High Residential (93%)
Selectivity	S-2 Selectivity
Financial Aid	Best Aid 114 ($5,417,075)
Prestige	Most Prestigious
Designations	Government and Politics; Serious Academic; Theater; Humanities; Hard Sciences; Pre-Med; Housing; Single Sex (all-female)

Wesleyan University
Middletown, Connecticut

Category	Characteristics
School Type	College
School Funding	Private
Campus Structure	Integrated
Surrounding Area	Small City
Region	New England
Size	Small Size (2,940)
Curriculum Type	Open
Residential Type	High Residential (99%)
Selectivity	S-2 Selectivity
Financial Aid	Best Excellent Aid 83 ($4,270,370)
Prestige	Prestigious
Designations	Artistic; Social Activism and Community Service; Quirky; Humanities

Wheaton College (IL)
Wheaton, Illinois

Category	Characteristics
School Type	College
School Funding	Private
Campus Structure	Island
Surrounding Area	Small City
Region	Midwest
Size	Small Size (2,508)
Curriculum Type	Loose Core
Residential Type	High Residential (90%)
Selectivity	S-3 Selectivity
Financial Aid	Some Aid 14 ($195,752)
Prestige	No Prestige Rating
Designations	Athletic; Religious; Music

Wheaton College (MA)
Norton, Massachusetts

Category	Characteristics
School Type	College
School Funding	Private
Campus Structure	Island
Surrounding Area	Suburb
Region	New England
Size	Small Size (1,616)
Curriculum Type	Loose Core
Residential Type	High Residential (95%)
Selectivity	S-4 Selectivity
Financial Aid	Excellent Aid 103 ($2,344,486)
Prestige	No Prestige Rating
Designations	Athletic; Artistic

Whitman College
Walla Walla, Washington

Category	Characteristics
School Type	College
School Funding	Private
Campus Structure	Island
Surrounding Area	Small City
Region	Pacific Coast
Size	Small Size (1,539)
Curriculum Type	Core
Residential Type	Medium Residential (67%)
Selectivity	S-3 Selectivity
Financial Aid	Good Aid 31 ($1,117,916)
Prestige	No Prestige Rating
Designations	Athletic; Outdoors; Serious Academic; Greek Life

Willamette University
Salem, Oregon

Category	Characteristics
School Type	College
School Funding	Private
Campus Structure	Integrated
Surrounding Area	City
Region	Pacific Coast
Size	Small Size (2,103)
Curriculum Type	Loose Core
Residential Type	Medium Residential (68%)
Selectivity	S-4 Selectivity
Financial Aid	Some Aid 9 ($104,000)
Prestige	No Prestige Rating
Designations	Sports; Athletic; Religious

Williams College
Williamstown, Massachusetts

Category	Characteristics
School Type	College
School Funding	Private
Campus Structure	Integrated
Surrounding Area	Town
Region	New England
Size	Small Size (2,052)
Curriculum Type	Distribution Requirements
Residential Type	High Residential (94%)
Selectivity	S-1 Selectivity
Financial Aid	Best Aid 80 ($4,373,650)
Prestige	Most Prestigious
Designations	Athletic; Outdoors; Serious Academic; Humanities; Housing

Worcester Polytechnic Institute
Worcester, Massachusetts

Category	Characteristics
School Type	University
School Funding	Private
Campus Structure	Integrated
Surrounding Area	City
Region	New England
Size	Small Size (3,952)
Curriculum Type	Distribution Requirements
Residential Type	Medium Residential (50%)
Selectivity	S-3 Selectivity
Financial Aid	Best Aid 375 ($8,148,755)
Prestige	No Prestige Rating
Designations	Entrepreneurship; Techie; Engineering; International Student Body; Greek Life

Yale University
New Haven, Connecticut

Category	Characteristics
School Type	University
School Funding	Private
Campus Structure	Integrated
Surrounding Area	City
Region	New England
Size	Medium Size (5,405)
Curriculum Type	Distribution Requirements
Residential Type	High Residential (87%)
Selectivity	S-1 Selectivity
Financial Aid	Best Aid 350 ($18,639,436)
Prestige	Most Prestigious
Designations	Artistic; Social Activism and Awareness; Serious Academic; Entrepreneurship; Music; Theater; Journalism; Economics; Humanities; Hard Sciences; Pre-Med; International Student Body; Housing; Writing

Yeshiva University
New York, New York

Category	Characteristics
School Type	University
School Funding	Private
Campus Structure	Street-Side
Surrounding Area	City
Region	Mid-Atlantic
Size	Small Size (2,869)
Curriculum Type	Core
Residential Type	Medium Residential (69%)
Selectivity	S-5 Selectivity
Financial Aid	Excellent Aid 133 ($3,209,689)
Prestige	Prestigious
Designations	Religious; Music; Pre-Med

Chapter 18
Resources

Congratulations! You now have a college list. Now is the time when you will need to do some additional research. Even if you don't decide to narrow down your list further, I still recommend doing some additional research about each school you've selected so you can learn more about each school and possibly tweak the list if necessary. Additional research will also help you rank the schools on your college list (perhaps you'll have a clear first choice and may want to consider applying early), and of course, thorough knowledge of a school will help you ace your application.

The best way to do this (other than visiting each school in-person) is to visit the websites for all of the schools on your list, taking the virtual tour, looking at their academic programs and offerings, looking up their application requirements and financial aid policies, and reading about student life. In this chapter, you'll find additional resources that will help you find out even more useful information such as college reviews directly from current students, detailed admissions statistics, and other useful information that may or may not be provided directly by the school. After doing a little research, you will want to make sure you feel confident that you could have a great experience at any of the schools on your list.

Once you've done that, take a moment to celebrate. You did it! You should have a definitive college list you feel good about. Put the names of these schools in an Excel or Word file, and fill in any information that will help you stay organized about early admissions programs, application deadlines, special requirements, and scholarships. This document will guide you through the complex admissions process and help you stay on track.

To get you started, I have also included a list of financial aid resources and some other useful information on testing optional schools at the end of the chapter.

If you've made it this far in this book – through the introspection required to figure out your College Match Profile, past the (likely) scary admissions section, and through the tedium of identifying your top choice schools – you clearly have what it takes to make it at an American college despite the obstacles you may need to overcome to make it here.

I hope that in the midst of facing the challenges that may lie before you that you find some enjoyment in the process of imagining what life might be like once you arrive at the school of your dreams. I can assure you that when you choose the right school, your four years in college can be some of the most fun, enjoyable, and meaningful years of your life.

Whatever stress the application process will bring, when you eventually make it here, and things calm down, I would love to hear from you about the school you chose and your experience there. The students I work with on the other side of the world who are trying to navigate the complex American college admissions process always love to hear stories from the students that have made it here and have found their happiness. I would love to hear from you. I invite you to email me anytime at <u>Pallas@thecollegematchmaker.com</u>. I look forward to hearing from each and every one of you!

Other Admissions and College Search Resources

A is for Admission – Michele Hernandez

This is one of the most comprehensive guides out there on how elite colleges evaluate college applications. Michele Hernandez is an elite college counselor in New York City and a former admissions officer at Dartmouth. She gives some great advice on each of the components of the application.

The Gatekeepers – Jacques Steinberg

This book was written by a *New York Times* reporter who observed the inside of the admissions office at Wesleyan University for a year. He reveals details about the students who got in that year, didn't get in, and the exact process the admissions committee went through to build a class. This is the best book out there if you want to know what really goes on inside an admissions office.

College Confidential – www.collegeconfidential.com

This website has the most active college forum on the web. You will find message boards for just about every American college, and you'll see many threads where prospective students discuss the unique features of each school. You can also find "stats" threads where students post their profiles and say whether or not they were accepted. These can be a bit intimidating to look through (and some posts seem to be placed to intimidate and are not necessarily accurate), but will help you get a better sense of what types of students are getting in to the colleges on your list.

US News & World Report's College Compass – www.usnews.com/usnews/store/college_compass.htm

US News & World Report puts together an annual list of college rankings using a huge database gathered from schools all around the country. For $30 a year, you can gain access to their College Compass service, which is a database that includes the data they used to create these rankings. Much of the data I used in this book came from College Compass, but their database of information is much more extensive than what I've included here, covering everything from most popular majors at each school, percentage of students involved in Greek life, male/female ratios, details on financial aid, and more. They also have detailed admissions statistics available including average GPAs, SAT scores, and class ranks among admitted students. Finally, they also have a collection of photographs of different colleges so you can get a sense of what the campus looks like.

The Princeton Review – www.princetonreview.com

The Princeton Review publishes an online database of college information. It is free to access, and you can look up basic statistics about each college regarding the campus, location, size, popular majors, selectivity, etc. They also publish top 20 lists each year in a number of categories like Most Beautiful Campus, Best Campus Food, Best College Theater, Best College Food, etc., which are based on student surveys.

50 Successful Harvard Application Essays – Staff of The Harvard Crimson

This book is a collection of personal essays written by students who were accepted to Harvard. It is a useful resource to look through to get a sense of what types of essays are effective.

The Insider's Guide to Colleges – Yale Daily News Staff

I recommend this book to every student I work with, and many have told me it played a huge role in helping them rank the colleges on their college lists. The book is written by Yale students who conducted interviews with students at different colleges around the country. In 2-3 page profiles, 330 schools are reviewed using direct quotes from students giving their honest opinions about their college's strengths, weaknesses, and student culture.

Colleges That Change Lives: 40 Schools That Will Change the Way You Think About Colleges – Loren Pope

This book contains 40 detailed profiles of colleges around the country that are particularly distinctive. Each school is profiled thoroughly, and you get a strong sense of the culture at each school. Even if you are not interested in the specific schools in this book, getting a nuanced sense of the different cultures at each of these schools may influence your own college search.

Unigo - www.unigo.com

Unigo is a collection of college students' reviews of their own colleges. You can find reviews about academics, safety, dorms, food, and many other relevant topics for each school on your list.

The College Matchmaker – www.thecollegematchmaker.com

This is my blog where I continue to post short pieces on college admissions, college search, and profiles (with pictures) of the colleges I tour and visit.

College Websites

There is no better resource for getting basic information about specific colleges than each college's own website. Most colleges have an "admissions" section where you can learn about academics, student life, and extracurricular activities. And don't forget to look for photo galleries, videos, and the virtual tour. There is nothing quite like visiting a school in-person, but if you can't do it, most colleges will give you the closest experience possible virtually.

Financial Aid Resources and Outside Scholarships for International Students

There are literally thousands of outside scholarships open to international students. There are also many resources and directories online you can use to search for these scholarships. Some of them also provide general information about the financial aid process as well.

I've included some of the best of these websites on the list below as a place to start. Some of these websites are exclusively devoted to scholarships for international students, and others allow you to filter their search results to display only options available for international students studying in the United States.

International Education Financial Aid Website - iefa.org

Big Future by The College Board - bigfuture.collegeboard.org/scholarship-search

Scholarship Experts – scholarshipexperts.com

International Scholarships - internationalscholarships.com

Fastweb - fastweb.com

Mach 25 - collegenet.com/mach25/app

Schools that do not require SAT/ACT

Some of the colleges below have gone completely "testing optional." This decision means that you do not have to submit any standardized test scores with your application for admission. Others on this list offer alternative testing options such as submitting AP, IB, or other test scores instead of the traditional SAT/ACT options. Check each college's website for the details on their policy.

Testing Optional Schools

American University
Bard College
Bates College
Bennington College
Bowdoin College
Bryn Mawr College
College of the Holy Cross
Colorado College
Connecticut College
Denison University
Franklin and Marshall College
Gettysburg College
Goucher College
Hamilton College
Hampshire College

Hobart and William Smith Colleges
Ithaca College
Knox College
Lawrence University
Mount Holyoke College
New York University (NYU)
St. Johns College-Annapolis
St. Johns College-Santa Fe
University of Rochester
Sarah Lawrence College
Sewanee University of the South
Smith College
Union College
Wake Forest University
Worcester Polytechnic Institute

Glossary

ACT – An admissions examination accepted by most US colleges. The ACT is the SAT's biggest competitor and is administered nationally and worldwide. The test is graded on a 36-point scale and is divided into four sections – English, Mathematics, Reading, and Science. There is also an optional writing test, which some colleges require.

Admissions Rate – The percentage of students admitted to a college from the pool of total applicants in a given year.

Alumni – The graduates of a college or university. Once you graduate from a college, you will become an alumnus (male) or alumna (female) of a school. Alumni networks are a valuable source of internships and jobs for college students.

Best Fit Schools – Schools that are grouped in the same selectivity category that best matches your credentials but that are also aligned with your other preferences on your College Match Profile. In other words, these are schools that fit your preferences but where you also have a good shot at getting in.

Binding Decision – An admissions offer that requires you to enroll in the school provided you have the financial means to do so or are offered an adequate financial aid package. Admissions are binding if you apply and are accepted through a college early decision. If you are not accepted, you have no commitment to the school. This is not a system every college uses, but if they do, it is called a binding admissions process.

Class – The grouping of students who will graduate in the same year. For instance, all of the students who will graduate in 2020 are referred to as "The Class of 2020".

College – A school that focuses on undergraduate education or the undergraduate division of a university.

College List – The set of colleges to which you decide to apply. Usually, a college list would include somewhere between eight and twelve colleges that you believe best meet your preferences and requirements.

College Rankings – Lists of colleges published by various publications ranked by varying types of criteria. The most recognized rankings include *US News & World Report* and *Forbes* college rankings.

Common Application – An application used by the majority of colleges featured in this book. It is accessible online (www.commonapp.org) and can be submitted to multiple colleges at one time.

Co-ops – A type of housing offered at some schools. Co-ops are usually dorms or houses devoted to collaborative living where residents take on chores, cook together, and usually develop their own governing policies.

Core Curriculum – A curricular model based on the philosophy that every student at a college should take a common set of classes.

Curriculum – How a college organizes the distribution of classes students must take in order to graduate.

Deferred – When you apply during an early round of admissions at many schools, you will either be accepted, rejected, or deferred. If you are deferred, your application will be put in the regular pool, and you will be given a decision on the date that the regular round decisions are released.

Distribution Requirements – A curricular system that divides the course catalogue into 3-6 broad categories and requires students to take some number of courses from each category in order to graduate.

Early Action – One type of early admissions program where schools allow students to apply in the fall and receive their admissions decision in December or January instead of on the regular decision date (usually February or March).

Early Decision – A type of early admissions program that is usually binding. Students who apply to schools early decision (or "ED") can usually only apply to one school during the early cycle, and if they are accepted, must enroll in the college. If they are not accepted, they can apply to other colleges during the regular round.

Endowment – The total value of an institution's investments (an indication of a college or university's wealth).

Freshmen – Students in their first year of high school or in their first year of college.

Fraternities – See **Greek Life**

Grade Point Average (GPA) – The average value of all of your grades earned during 9th, 10th, 11th, and 12th grade. Most American schools calculate this number by converting A grades into a 4.0, B grades into 3.0, C grades into a 2.0, etc., and then calculating the value of all classes taken over four years. If you were graded with a different grading system, colleges may convert your grades into a grade point average using their own system.

Greek Life – A system of social organizations, also called fraternities (usually all-male but in some cases co-ed) and sororities (all-female), popular at many American colleges. Fraternities and sororities are known for hosting parties in houses they own either on or near college campuses, doing community service, and are sometimes residential.

Holistic Admissions Process – The type of admissions evaluation that is based on qualitative as well as quantitative aspects of the application. This is the most common system of evaluation at American colleges.

Integrated Campus – A type of campus that has grassy enclosed areas as well as areas that are entwined in the surrounding neighborhood.

Island Campus – A type of campus that is physically enclosed or separated from the surrounding communities.

Juniors – Students in their third year of high school or third year of college.

Liberal Arts – Broad subjects such as philosophy, mathematics, social sciences, natural sciences, etc. that are not specifically oriented towards a technical application or career.

Loose Core – A type of curriculum where students take courses from a set of specific categories in order to graduate but not requiring any specific courses of all students.

Major – The area of focus in most undergraduate degree programs (e.g. biology, chemistry, civil engineering, economics, philosophy, etc.). At most colleges between one third and one half of a student's courses are related to their major. Many colleges do not require students to "declare" a major until their second or third year in the university although some programs may require students to list their expected major at the time they apply.

Matriculate – To commit to a college after being accepted. For the regular admissions round, accepted students typically must decide whether or not to matriculate by May 1st before enrolling in August or September.

Merit-Based Aid – The type of financial assistance offered by some colleges that is based on personal characteristics, accomplishments, or essays rather than financial need.

Minor – A secondary field of focus students choose to pursue in addition to their major (e.g. you can major in biology but minor in history). Not all schools offer students the opportunity to earn a minor, but usually at the schools that do, the requirements for earning this distinction are substantially less extensive than those to earn a major in an equivalent field.

Need-Aware – An admissions decision or deliberation made by taking into account the applicant's financial need.

Need-Based Aid – Financial aid administered based on one's ability to pay. Merit has no bearing on the amount of the package offered.

Need-Blind – An admission decision or deliberation made without taking into account the applicant's financial need.

Off-Campus Housing – Housing that is not affiliated with the university (typically apartments or homes located within close proximity to college campuses).

On-Campus Apartments – Housing that is affiliated with a university (typically dorms, college-owned houses or apartments, etc.).

Open Curriculum – A type of curriculum where colleges do not require students to take any specific classes outside of the requirements for their major.

Pre-Professional Approach – An approach to education prevalent in many other countries and at some American colleges that sets students on disciplinary tracks that will feed directly into post-graduate degree programs or into a career. An example of a pre-professional educational program would be a pre-med or pre-law major. Many top US colleges do not have a strong pre-professional orientations compared to in other countries (instead adopting a liberal arts philosophy).

Private College/University – Colleges or universities that do not receive the majority of their funding from the government and are administered independently.

Public College/University – Colleges or universities that are predominately funded by the government.

Reach School – Schools that are at least one selectivity category higher (or more competitive) than a student's overall profile would suggest. The term is also used to refer to the country's most competitive schools where even the most impressive candidates can't necessarily count on being admitted.

Rolling Admissions – A system of admissions that some schools have adopted where applicants receive an admissions decision several weeks after applying instead of on a fixed decision date shared by all applicants.

Rushing – The process of trying to gain admission to a fraternity or sorority (usually by participating in a number of social events over the course of several weeks or months).

Safety School – Schools that are at least one selectivity category lower (or less competitive) than a student's overall profile would suggest.

SAT – The most common entrance exam used by American colleges to evaluate applicants. Administered by The College Board across the United States and the world, the exam is comprised of three sections – critical reading, mathematics, and writing. The maximum score for each section is 800 points meaning the best composite score possible is 2400 points.

Seniors – Students in their fourth (and usually final) year of high school or college.

Single Choice Early Action – A type of early admissions program offered by several schools where students can apply to *one* school early without having to make a binding commitment (they can still apply to other schools during the regular round regardless of the outcome of this first application).

Sophomores – Students in their second year of high school or their second year of college.

Sororities – See **Greek Life**

Specialty Housing – A living option adopted by some schools where dorms or floors of dorms house students with particular interests such as sustainability, Spanish, freedom from "substances," and so on.

Street-Side Campus – A type of campus where college buildings are located right on city streets (i.e.. there is no significant enclosed portion of the campus).

Superscoring – A practice adopted by some colleges where the admissions committee only considers the highest SAT test score in each subject category rather than an applicant's overall composite scores from each sitting. This is a favorable system if you scored better on the math section of the SAT the first time you took the test but then dropped to a lower score the next time you took it, despite the fact that your verbal score improved.

TOEFL – The most commonly accepted English exam most colleges require of non-native English speakers (especially if their high school education was taught in a language besides English).

Traditional Dorm – College-owned student residences.

Upperclassmen – Students in their third and fourth year of college (also known as "juniors" and "seniors" respectively).

Universal Application – A competitor to the Common Application that is accepted by some of the colleges featured in this book. You can find more information and access the application online at www.universalcollegeapp.com.

University – An institution of higher learning that includes undergraduates, graduate students, and research faculty members.

Unweighted Grades – The traditional American grading system, based on a scale of 4.0 possible points (A=4.0, B=3.0, etc.).

Waitlisted – One of three possible outcomes when you receive your final admissions decision. You can be accepted, rejected, or waitlisted. Waitlisted students may receive an offer of admission if additional spots open up after the matriculation deadline of May 1st. Waitlisted students typically receive their final decision between May and August but should matriculate at another college or university in the meantime.

Weighted Grades – A variation on the traditional American grading system where most courses are graded on a 4.0 scale (A=4.0, B=3.0, etc.), but some courses are deemed more difficult are given an additional .5 or 1 point and carry more weight in the final average. Thus, an "A" in an honors course may be given 4.5 rather than the traditional 4 points, or a B in an Advanced Placement course may be given 4 rather than the 3 points it would receive in an unweighted system.

Want more college tips?

Sign up for FREE college guides at
www.thecollegematchmaker.com

About the Author

' Pallas Snider is a college counselor, writer, and speaker specializing in college search and selection, admissions to elite colleges, and applying to American universities from abroad. She is a graduate of Harvard College where, as a student, she worked at the Harvard College Undergraduate Admissions Office. She currently lives in Cambridge, Massachusetts. Visit her blog and website at <u>www.thecollegematchmaker.com</u>.

Printed in Great Britain
by Amazon.co.uk, Ltd.,
Marston Gate.